Cities on the Shore

The Urban Littoral Frontier

Cities on the Shore

The Urban Littoral Frontier

Brian J. Hudson

PINTER

First published in 1996 by
Pinter, *A Cassell Imprint*
Wellington House, 125 Strand, London WC2R 0BB
215 Park Avenue South, New York 10003

First published 1996

British Library Cataloguing-in-Publication Data

Hudson, Brian James
 Cities on the shore : the urban littoral frontier.
 1. Cities and towns – Growth 2. City planning 3. Urbanization
 4. Reclamation of land I. Title
 711.4'09
 ISBN 1–85567–381–9

Library of Congress Cataloging-in-Publication Data

Hudson, Brian J. (Brian James)
 Cities on the shore : the urban littoral frontier/Brian J. Hudson.
   p. cm.
 Includes bibliographical references and index.
 ISBN 1–85567–381–9
 1. City planning. 2. Waterfronts. 3. Reclamation of land.
 4. Land use, Urban. 5. Urban renewal. I. Title.
 HT166.H83   1996
 307.1'216—dc20   95–38758
                                                                      CIP

Typeset by York House Typographic Ltd, London
Printed and bound in Great Britain by Redwood Books, Trowbridge, Wiltshire

Contents

To my parents who were at the beginning, to Anne who joined me along the way, and to Dominic and Alexis who were with us at the finish.

Preface

The origins of this book may be traced back to 1959 when, as a final-year undergraduate in the Department of Geography at the University of Liverpool, I made a study of industrial development on Teesside. Having learned that reclamation from the Tees estuary had played a significant role in the development of that urban area, I made this topic the focus of another study which I undertook as part of the requirements for the degree of Master of Civic Design at Liverpool. Later, after working as a planner in England and as a university lecturer in Ghana, I was awarded a Commonwealth Scholarship which enabled me to undertake research at the University of Hong Kong from 1965 to 1967. During this time I made a comprehensive study of reclamation from the sea for urban development with particular reference to Hong Kong itself. There followed a few years of work as a town planner in England and Jamaica before I returned to academic life as a lecturer in the Department of Geography at the University of the West Indies (UWI). I left UWI in 1985 to take up an appointment in Brisbane, Australia, where I now lecture in Urban and Regional Planning at the Queensland University of Technology (QUT).

During all this time, while working in Britain, West Africa, Hong Kong, the West Indies and Australia, I maintained my interest in land reclamation and urban development, writing papers on the subject which were published in various journals. It had long been my intention to write a book on the subject and, at last, the ideal opportunity arose when the QUT granted me a year's leave and financial support enabling me to undertake research and field studies in Hong Kong, Japan, Britain, Jamaica, the USA and New Zealand, and to work on the book on my return to Brisbane.

I am very grateful to QUT, and I also wish to acknowledge the other universities and the many organizations and individuals whose kind assistance made it possible for me to obtain the information I required to write this book. Some of the people who have helped me in my researches over the past thirty-odd years have already been acknowledged in published and unpublished works of mine, but here, without repeating their names, I wish to pay tribute to the invaluable contribution which they have made to the present book. Even in acknowledging those who kindly helped me during the recent year which I spent researching and writing the book, I will name only some people and organizations whose assistance was particularly valuable, otherwise the list would be tediously long.

In Japan, the Tokyo Geographical Society responded generously to my request for assistance, and Professor Yoshio Yoshida gave invaluable help, putting me in touch with various organizations and arranging meetings and site visits. Among those who provided me with important information in Tokyo were senior technical staff of the Tokyo Metropolitan Government, including Takaadi Massuda and Kunihisa Watanabe of the Bureau of Port and Harbour, and Y. Karibe, K. Matsuzawa and T. Takeuchi of the Land Readjustment Division, Bureau of Construction. In Hiroshima, members of the University of Hiroshima's Geography Department conducted me on site visits and provided me with a wealth of information, and I am particularly grateful to Professor Kenzo Fujiwara and his colleagues, Takasha Nakata, Kozo Yamamoto and Hideaki Maemoku for giving up so much of their time to assist me. Among those who provided me with invaluable information and assistance in Hong Kong were Dr Peter Hills of the Centre of Urban Planning and Environmental Management, University of Hong Kong, Dr Ted Pryor, Principal Government Town Planner, Michael Stokoe, Assistant Director, Environmental Protection Department, and Peter Whiteside, Secretary of the Fill Management Committee. In England, staff of the University of Teesside and the Tees and Hartlepool Port Authority (THPA) were particularly helpful. Special thanks are due to the university's Professor Les Hobson, Dean of Science and Technology, and Dr Ken Tomlinson, co-ordinator of the Environmental Technology programme, and to the THPA's David Palmer, Engineering Director, and J. Auty, Estates Officer. Also on Teesside, Oliver Sherratt and Malcolm Steele, both of Cleveland County Council's Department of Environment, Development and Transportation, were most helpful in providing useful information. John Bentley, Head of Social and Environmental Studies at King Alfred's College, Winchester, was helpful, as always, during my visit to the Southampton area.

At the University of California, Berkeley, I was privileged to be attached to the Geography Department as Research Associate for which I am very grateful to Professor David Stoddart, Chair. Much of my time at Berkeley was spent in its various libraries, but I was also able to hold valuable discussions with people from several different organizations. These included Berkeley's Emeritus Professor James Vance Jnr who kindly conducted me on a tour of Oakland and the adjacent bayshore areas, and Roger Crawford of the Geography Department, San Francisco State University who gave me useful advice on reading and other sources of information about the Bay area. Marcia Brockbank and Ron Sokolov of the San Francisco Bay Estuary Project, and Bob Batha, Environmental Planner with the Bay Conservation and Development Commission, were both extremely helpful in providing information on the work of their respective organizations. In Australia, I have received useful information from Dr John R.C. Hsu, Environmental and Civil Engineering Department, University of Western Australia, and Dr Iraphne Childs, School of the Humanities, QUT, helped me in matters relating to Japanese language and culture.

Some of the people named above helped me not only by providing information, arranging meetings and the like, but also by offering generous hospitality. Among many people who showed me such kindness around the world were my good friends Fred and Angela Castro in Hong Kong, David and Caroline Bulmer and Robert Girling and Sherry Keith in the USA, and family and friends in England and Jamaica to all of whom I am eternally grateful.

I am fortunate in having received strong support and encouragement from Phil Heywood, who was Head of QUT's School of Planning, Landscape Architecture and Surveying when I applied for leave to write this book, and to his successor, Chung-Tong Wu who arranged for assistance in the preparation of the maps and diagrams. The excellent quality of these illustrations is testimony to the cartographic skills of Bruce Chapman and Ian Pagan. I also owe a great debt of gratitude to my QUT Planning and Landscape Architecture colleagues who willingly shouldered the additional burdens of work caused by my year's absence. Thanks, too, to Vivienne Walsh and Paula O'Shea for their wordprocessing skills which enabled me to submit a well-presented manuscript to the publisher. To Pinter: I am grateful for their confidence in my project and for the ongoing support and encouragement which I received from three commissioning editors – Feona Hamilton, Jane Greenwood and Lara Burns.

Finally, I wish to acknowledge with thanks the Centre of Asian Studies at the University of Hong Kong for granting me permission to reproduce part of my article, 'Paul Chater and the Praya Reclamations: Wetland Development in Hong Kong 1887–1930' which was published in 1978 in the *Journal of Oriental Studies*, (**16** (1 & 2): 79–86).

Excerpt from *Midnight's Children* by Salman Rushdie, © Salman Rushdie 1981. Reprinted by kind permission.

... at the dawn of time, when Bombay was a dumbbell-shaped island tapering, at the centre, to a narrow shining strand beyond which could be seen the finest and largest harbour in Asia, when Mazagoan and Worli, Matunga and Mahim, Salsette and Colaba were islands, too – in short, before reclamation ...

Salman Rushdie, *Midnight's Children* (1981)

There was water to a point just west of the site of Faneuil Hall; Post Office Square was largely tidal, and the tide ran a little west of south right up to the corner of Franklin and Federal streets. Where the South Station stands there was once no land; and where Atlantic Avenue turns into Kneeland Street, for several blocks a fish was more at home than a human being.

David McCord, *About Boston: Sight, Sound, Flavour and Inflection* (1948)

Introduction

Many studies of individual cities, mainly coastal centres, make reference to the reclamation of land from the sea or other large water bodies for urban expansion. Writers usually relate this process to the special circumstances of a particular location, especially in places where development pressures are great and there are severe topographical constraints. This book, however, is written in the belief that the reclamation of land for urban development is much more common than is generally realized and that, far from being a phenomenon which occurs only in special circumstances, is a normal process of city expansion.

Human settlements are normally established beside some kind of water body and, almost inevitably, their development involves some advance of the waterfront, often extending the built-up area over the former shore, nearby wetlands, adjacent shallows and even into deeper water further out. While the importance of land reclamation as a concomitant of urban development varies considerably, in relatively few cities, essentially those without a waterside location, has this process not occurred to some extent. Even where the scale of reclamation has been small, the significance of this development is often disproportionately great, in terms of the value of the additional land and of the environmental consequences, for example. Hence a comprehensive study of this ancient and widespread urban phenomenon appears well overdue.

Half of the world's people live by the sea or along rivers and estuaries, many of them in highly urbanized areas. Most of the world's cities with populations exceeding half a million are located along the coast. Of the world's fifty most populous cities, those with some four million or more inhabitants, half are on coastal or estuarine sites and several more are built on deltas or beside great lakes. Most of the others lie on major rivers. Among the exceptions, Mexico City is notable for having practically obliterated the lake on which it originally stood, urban development now occupying most of the old bed of the former Lake Texcoco. Other lakeside cities, which have expanded into the water, include several on the Great Lakes system of North America, notably Chicago and Toronto. Riverside cities, too, have commonly extended their built-up areas across floodplains which were periodically inundated and even into the watercourses themselves, the channels becoming narrower and generally straighter in the process. It is in the estuaries and on the sea coast itself, however, that 'cities on the shore' have made their most spectacular advances into the water.

The advance of the urban littoral frontier by the reclamation of land from the sea and other water bodies is the subject of this book; it is the first, I believe, to attempt to treat the topic from a global perspective as a normal process of urban development. *Cities on the Shore* is the result of research undertaken in many different parts of the world over a period of more than thirty years. It is an attempt to fill a perceived gap in the literature on urban geography and planning, treating the subject of reclamation for urban development as a global process, but drawing on individual case studies, largely of places which I have studied on the spot. For this reason, throughout the book, frequent reference is made to a limited number of cities and regions with which I am most familiar and which exemplify particularly well various aspects of reclamation for urban development. Among the places most frequently cited are Hong Kong, San Francisco Bay and Teesside, but many other examples and case studies are used, usually places which I have been fortunate enough to visit. The reader is asked to forgive me if I am seen to favour especially examples from Britain, West Africa, the Caribbean, Hong Kong and Australia, places in which I have lived for periods ranging from a year to over two decades, and I hope that my extensive travels in all continents except Antarctica have ensured that my book is well-balanced geographically. I am, nevertheless, conscious of some important gaps in my personal acquaintance with cities on the shore, among them the excellent examples of Cape Town and Rio de Janeiro.

Rather than writing the book as a collection of city by city case studies, I treat the subject thematically, drawing on appropriate examples to illustrate various aspects of the topic. While global and interdisciplinary in approach, the book is by no means intended to be exhaustive, and I hope that it will stimulate further work on individual urban areas and on specific aspects of reclamation. I hope, too, that it will encourage other writers on urban topics to recognize in their work the important, but often neglected, role that reclamation has played, and continues to play, in city development.

In this book, the terms 'reclamation' and 'land reclamation' always refer to the winning of dry land from large water bodies such as the sea, lakes, rivers, estuaries and wetlands of different kinds. This needs to be emphasized because the word 'reclamation' has several meanings and is often used in connection with work on degraded farmland, desert margins and derelict industrial sites. In the sense in which I use the word here, reclamation may be regarded as a geomorphological process, comparable, perhaps, with 'natural' processes such as delta-formation. Indeed, although, like other writers I sometimes find it useful to distinguish between artificial or anthropogenic landforms and processes on the one hand and 'natural' ones on the other, I prefer to consider the human species as part of the natural environment. I share Arnold Bennett's (1924:451) view that 'a town is just as much a product of Nature as the most remote countryside'.

Another way in which one can consider reclamation is as the advance of the urban littoral frontier, the expansion of development into areas formerly permanently or periodically under water. Many books on urban geography discuss the growth of cities in terms of the expansion of the built-up area into the surrounding rural or undeveloped region, but most writers appear to overlook the extension of the urban area into adjacent water bodies. The term 'urban frontier' is commonly used by writers on cities who apply it to several different concepts. Some, including Vance (1964) and Downs (1970), recognize two urban frontiers: one in the decaying central districts, the other on the expanding outer fringe. The urban littoral frontier of cities which have developed beside water may be considered as a special case of the latter, but it may also represent a combination of both. It lies at the waterside edge of development, but is also often very close to the heart of the city and frequently includes a decaying waterfront district. Peter Hall (1991) recognizes this in his paper *Waterfronts: a new urban frontier*, but this title is rather misleading because what the study discusses is only the latest phase of a process of growth and renewal which dates back to the remote origins of cities on the shore.

This book, then, is concerned with the physical growth of human settlements, focusing on the urban development of aquatic areas on the margins of oceans and inland water bodies. Cities on the shore form the urban littoral frontier which has been advancing, sometimes retreating, all over the habitable world since prehistoric times, and the first chapters of the book examine the history of this process, starting with the legacy which past reclamation has left in the townscape of today. There follows an analysis of the motivation for reclaiming land from water bodies and an examination of the role of the real estate business, then a brief account of the reclamation process, its techniques and problems. Next, the influence of reclamation on urban morphology is examined, after which there is a discussion of the environmental impacts of this form of development and recent responses by littoral zone policy makers and managers. The final chapter draws together the main themes explored in the book, summarizing these by reference to a model which attempts to demonstrate the pattern and sequence of city development involving reclamation. It concludes with a brief consideration of alternatives to reclamation and some present trends which are likely to influence the future development of cities on the shore.

1

The Tidemarks of Time

Place names

To a city visitor seeking visual clues to the changing position of the urban waterfront, some may be as obvious as the historical markers which indicate the original shoreline in downtown San Francisco and Wellington, others as subtle as the gradual change in the architectural style of buildings erected on an advancing reclamation front, so admirably displayed in Boston's Back Bay.

A glance at the street map of many a coastal or waterfront city will reveal helpful clues to the reclamation history of the place. Reclamation Road in Gibraltar and Reclamation Street in Lagos, Nigeria and Kowloon, Hong Kong, clearly bespeak their origins. London's famous Strand and Strands and Strand Streets from Liverpool to Cape Town, Auckland to Montego Bay, all mark the original waterfront. Hong Kong's Bonham Strand was formerly the seaward edge of a nineteenth century reclamation undertaken during the governorship of Sir George Bonham. Similarly, of the many Beach Roads in Auckland, the one in the heart of the city is separated from the sea by a strip of developed land indicating the extent of reclamation since the former seafront road was named. Also in New Zealand, Wellington's Lambton Quay, seemingly an odd name for a city street so far from the waterfront, reminds us that much of the capital city's downtown area is built on land reclaimed since 1840, a fact recorded in commemorative brass plaques placed there. Like Lambton Quay, Boston's Dock Square is deeply embedded in the city centre and long since deprived of its former waterfront position by reclamation.

Changing circumstances, both physical and political, have prompted name changes which may now deny us clues such as those previously mentioned. Port of Spain's Marine Square, formerly on the waterfront and now cut off from the sea, has been renamed Independence Square, and in Kingston, Jamaica, Foreshore Road, separated from the harbour by land reclaimed in the 1960s, is now known as Marcus Garvey Drive. A more subtle name change is found in Fort Street, Auckland. Originally Fore Street when it stood on the foreshore of Waitemata Harbour, its name was changed after reclamation had separated it from the waterfront and Fort Britomart constructed nearby (Davenport, 1990).

Auckland's Britomart Place commemorates the site of the fort and of Point Britomart, the rocky headland on which it stood, and which was completely quarried away to provide fill for nearby reclamation works (Johnson, 1988; Reed, 1955). Similarly, Possession Street in Hong Kong marks the site of the former Possession Point, the place where the British put ashore to raise the flag and annex the colony in 1841. Not only headlands but bays now swallowed up by reclamation, survive only as place names as in Causeway Bay, Hong Kong, and Back Bay in Boston. For similar reasons, islands such as Boston's Castle Island, Sydney's Garden Island, and Bay Farm Island on San Francisco Bay, remain islands only in name. In London, too, there are several island place names dating back to the earliest times when people chose these sites for their settlements in the marshes beside the Thames. For those familiar with the etymology of English place names, the insular origins of the London districts of Bermondsey, Hackney, and Battersea are denoted by the suffix 'ey' or 'ea' which is derived from an Old English word for island. In the north of England, the Cleveland coastal towns of Marske (marsh) and Redcar (reedy swamp) are reminders of the extensive wetlands which their Anglo-Saxon and Scandinavian founders encountered near the mouth of the River Tees over a thousand years ago.

Of course, it is not only place names in the English-speaking world that refer to water bodies now vanished and to the process of reclamation which contributed to urban development. Not surprisingly, such names abound in The Netherlands where 'dijk' and 'dam' are among the most common place name elements (Burke, 1956). Two well-known examples in Amsterdam are the shopping street of Nieuwendijk, a 'new dike' many centuries ago, and Zeedijk, now no longer holding back the arm of the sea it formerly fronted. Old dikes, now well inland, are found in the cities of many other countries, including Japan where several urban districts have names incorporating the word 'tsutsumi', meaning 'dike'. The widely occurring suffix 'shima' or 'jima' means 'island', and Hiroshima, built on a largely reclaimed deltaic site, means 'wide island'. Hibya, a district in central Tokyo, was the name of an inlet of Tokyo Bay, its name apparently derived from 'hibi', rows of bamboo stakes and nets set out in mudflats to trap oysters and seaweed (Waley, 1991).

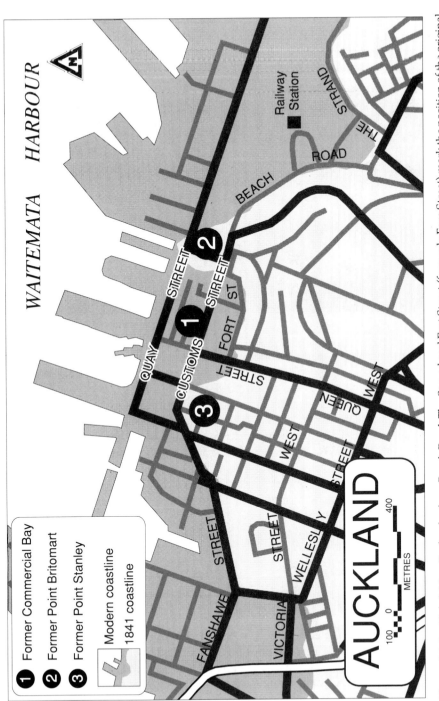

Figure 1.1 Auckland, New Zealand, where Beach Road, The Strand and Fort Street (formerly Fore Street) mark the position of the original shoreline. *Source:* Bloomfield (1967) and recent maps of Auckland

Figure 1.2 Auckland, New Zealand, 4 October 1859, from Point Britomart, showing the reclamation of Commercial Bay in progress. At the head of the bay (left) Fort Street (formerly Fore Street), marks the original waterfront.

Nearby, close to the present waterfront, Tsukiji, meaning 'built' or 'reclaimed land', is part of the city reclaimed in the seventeenth century.

Street names in several cities hint at a sequence of reclamations, stages of the advance into the water being recorded in surviving references to former waterfronts. In the West Indies, Port of Spain's Marine (now Independence) Square and South Quay, and Montego Bay's Strand Street and Harbour Street, now all inland, tell this story, as do Toronto's Front Street and Esplanade which mark former positions of the Lake Ontario waterfront. Auckland's Fort (Fore) Street, mentioned earlier, was succeeded by Customs Street (named after the old quayside Custom House), and Quay Street as the waterfront roads; and today much of Quay Street is cut off from the sea by further reclamation (Figures 1.1 and 1.2).

Street patterns and landforms

While the street names themselves do not always refer to reclamation or waterfront features, it is sometimes possible to distinguish the former coast road by its usually sinuous path, skirting former bays and promontories, in contrast with the generally straight streets on the level reclaimed land on the

Beside Queen Street Wharf, projecting into Waitemata Harbour (right), Smailes Point (alternatively known as Stanley Point) is being demolished to provide fill.
Source: Auckland City Libraries (reproduced with permission)

seaward side. This is particularly well seen in Hong Kong where Queens Road follows quite closely the former southern shore of the harbour (Figure 8.6). Along much of Queens Road, the land on the seaward side slopes fairly steeply towards the flat reclaimed strip beside the harbour, a sharp break of slope sometimes indicating the original shoreline. This is most clearly seen in the streets which descend from Queens Road and in the occasional flights of steps which connect it with the lower levels.

In many cities, such as Hong Kong, where extensive reclamation has contributed to urban expansion, relict features of the area's previous natural and cultural landscape commonly survive. Parts of Queens Road were literally on the strand or foreshore of the harbour, and in places sea cliffs rose steeply behind. Though much modified, these survive at Battery Path Steps in Central District, and other remnants of old clifflines can be seen embedded in the city on both sides of the harbour. Here, as commonly elsewhere, the steeper cliff faces are artificial, sites of former excavations from which material was taken to use as fill in reclamation schemes. This is well seen behind Britomart Place in Auckland where the former headland of Point Britomart is sharply truncated. In several cities, such as Bombay (Figure 1.3) and Hiroshima (Figure 1.4), former islands rise above the artificial coastal plain created by

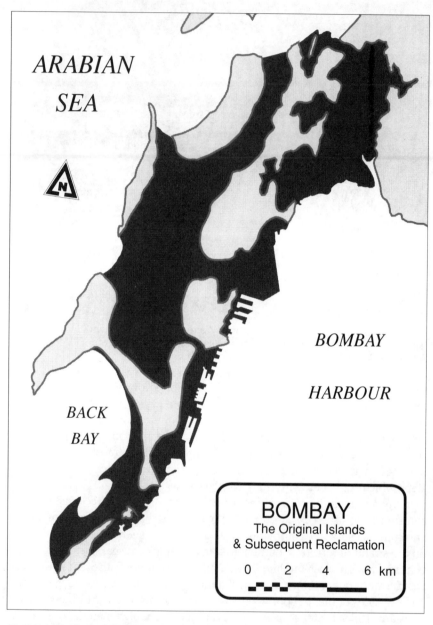

Figure 1.3 In the early seventeenth century the site of Bombay was a group of offshore islands. Reclamation joined these together to form the peninsula on which the modern city now stands.
Source: Morgan (1958) and recent maps of Bombay

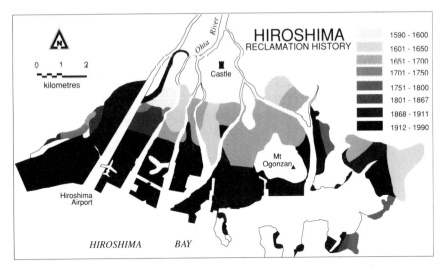

Figure 1.4 Hiroshima has developed on a river delta which has been modified and enlarged by four centuries of reclamation.
Source: Hori (1984)

reclamation, some of them preserved as open space. One remarkable example, in a suburb of Hiroshima, is a picturesque rocky islet or stack, preserved, even now encircled by water, in a small public park within an urban development on reclaimed land at Seibu-Kaihatsu. Long revered as a fertility symbol and site of a religious shrine, this rock stood at the entrance to a small fishing harbour, now vanished, and a masonry pier on breakwater still projects from the islet oddly marooned in its artificial lake.

Buildings and structures

Old buildings and other structures associated with former shorelines and quaysides commonly provide visual clues to the history of reclamation in urban areas. Religious shrines, many associated with water-related deities, were traditionally built on waterside sites in various parts of the world. In areas where reclamation has subsequently occurred, these may now be separated from the water which gave the sites their original significance. Hong Kong provides numerous examples, particularly the Tin Hau temples dedicated to a sea goddess, many of which have been stranded far inland by reclamation. Best known, perhaps, is the Tin Hau Temple at Causeway Bay, standing on the former shoreline of that vanished coastal inlet, now reclaimed from the sea and densely built up.

Relict features associated with former waterfronts also include buildings and structures which performed functions related to transport by or across the water, such as lighthouses, watergates and bridges. London's seventeenth-century York Gate, formerly giving access from York House to the Thames, and Queen's Steps which used to descend to the river edge, both survive to remind us of the time when the River Thames was the city's major highway. Now separated from the water by the Embankment, these structures also provide visible evidence of the process of reclamation by which the city has encroached upon the river. Such encroachment has led to the total disappearance of some rivers and streams as surface features, sometimes leaving bridges which formerly spanned them standing incongruously among streets and buildings no longer divided by water. For example, Tokyo's now vanished Takabashi (Tall Bridge) was made redundant when the river which it spanned was cut off by the construction of an artificial new channel. Hiroshima's Takanobashi (Hawk Bridge) was similarly deprived of the channel it formerly spanned but, although the structure itself has gone, there is a commemorative monument on the site in the form of a bridge which stands, appropriately, at a pedestrian crossing on a busy city street. In England, Crowland's medieval Trinity Bridge still stands in the centre of the town, its arches no longer reflected in the watercourse which formerly flowed beneath.

A surviving stone pier within an urban reclamation area has already been mentioned, and many old quay walls, or their remains, lie under the fill of later reclamations, as in Hong Kong. Here they have made difficulties for the construction of foundations in subsequent development projects (*PLA Monthly*, 1960; Styles and Hansen, 1989). Even sunken boats may survive, buried beneath the fill, to be excavated by archaeologists possibly centuries after the vessels had foundered. A modern sunken wreck was left only partly buried beneath the rubble fill of a 1970s' reclamation at Plymouth, Montserrat in the West Indies. After hurricane-lashed seas eroded twenty metres of this reclaimed land in 1979, the presence of the sunken vessel with its cargo of molasses presented engineers with a particularly sticky problem when excavating the sea-bed during work on the new reclamation and sea-wall (Slater *et al.*, 1987).

Among the buildings which normally stand on the quayside, and which may survive as relict features when reclamation separates them from the waterfront, are warehouses and customs houses. A well-known example of the latter, Boston's Custom House, was built in neo-classical style between 1837 and 1847, its once controversial sixteen-storey tower added in 1913–15, still a prominent landmark indicating the position of the former waterfront. In New Zealand, Auckland's old Custom House was built overlooking the harbour in 1889 but, in the following decade, this building was separated from the waterfront by a block of reclaimed land (Johnson, 1988). Today, it is conserved as part of Auckland's heritage, now serving as a cultural and entertainment centre with a theatre, night-club, bar, restaurant and book-shop. Similar new uses have been found for former waterfront buildings across the Tasman Sea in Hobart. Here, Salamanca Place boasts a splendid row of early nineteenth century stone-built warehouses which originally stood beside a quay where whalers moored their ships. Here, too, the old quay has been separated from the harbour by reclamation, the whalers now replaced by tourists, the warehouses housing art and craft galleries, restaurants, bookshops and a puppet theatre.

Heritage conservation, gentrification and tourist development in former docklands and old waterfront areas are modern topics related to the most recent phase in the long history of the urban littoral frontier. The two chapters which follow attempt to summarize the history of urban land reclamation, illustrating the mainly chronological account with examples from many different parts of the world. As will be seen, reclamation for urban development is a widespread as well as a very ancient practice, and it has been necessary to be very selective in the choice of examples for discussion. The following historical account uses many examples which may be regarded as typical of the urban land reclamation process at various times, but it also notes several of the more exceptional cases of cities that have been built out into the water.

2
Waterside Camp to Littoral Metropolis

The marked concentration of human settlement beside or near the sea and other water bodies is not a recent phenomenon. There is abundant evidence to indicate that, from the earliest times, hominids usually lived close to water. With increasing population and developing technology, primitive people began to modify their environment, and the beginnings of littoral reclamation can be traced back at least to the end of the last ice age some 10,000 years ago.

In his essay, 'Seashore: Primitive Home of Man', Carl Sauer (1963:303) suggested that 'A riparian location is indicated for his earliest living', but it was 'the sea, in particular the tidal shore [that] presented the best opportunity to eat, settle, increase and learn' (1963:309). Compared with many creatures, humans are particularly dependent on water and, like most animals, the early hominids probably needed to be near enough to fresh water to be able to drink at least once a day (Leakey and Lewin, 1979). Early humans were attracted to the littoral zone for other reasons, too. The margins of water bodies are where the terrestial and aquatic environments meet and often merge at the interface of the lithosphere, hydrosphere and atmosphere. Consequently, these areas are normally endowed with particularly rich and diverse ecosystems supporting a variety of plant and animal life including fish and birds. These can be exploited by the hunter–gatherer who has long found ecologically rich wetlands particularly attractive. Water can also provide a useful defence against attack, and islands, peninsulas and marshes have very commonly been chosen as settlement sites for the security they afford (Coles, 1990; Coles and Coles, 1989).

It is thus not surprising that archaeological evidence of early hominids is especially abundant near the shores of ancient lakes and large rivers. Leakey and Lewin (1979:53), however, warn that 'the archaeological record is bound to be biased ... because in places where there are no gently lapping lakeside waters or silt-laden streams or rivers, there is virtually no chance of hominid skeletons being fossilized, no chance of our finding them eons later'. On the other hand, the erosive action of rivers and seas together with the rise in sea-level since the last ice age must have removed, destroyed or obliterated much of the archaeological record, including evidence of ancient human habitations on or near former shores and riverbanks. This is sometimes dramatically illustrated by the occasional recovery of prehistoric artefacts from the sea-bed by dredging operations or fishing activity, or by the discovery of submerged or partly submerged ancient structures.

The structures with which this book is mainly concerned are those associated with land reclamation such as dikes and drainage canals, landfill and revetments. In tracing the history of reclamation for urban development, we commence with what may for convenience be termed 'primitive', then 'ancient' and, later, 'maritime' settlements. The chapter which follows this deals with 'industrial' and 'modern' developments. While the approach is generally chronological, it must be remembered that social and technological developments have taken place at different rates in different parts of the world and, in the discussion, there are considerable overlaps and some forward and backward leaps in time.

Even today there are many waterside and wetland settlements where construction techniques, including reclamation methods, have scarcely changed since prehistoric times. Modern tourists in South America go by boat to see the floating villages of Lake Titicaca where simple dwellings constructed of tortora reeds stand on thick layers of the same plant deposited in the shallow water. In the lagoons of the South Pacific many villages are built on artificial islands of coral rubble, some centuries old, some recently constructed. In the wetlands near the confluence of the Tigris and Euphrates rivers at the head of the Persian Gulf, the 'Marsh Arabs' live on artificial islands in an aquatic environment which probably resembles that of ancient Mesopotamia before the development of agriculture and the rise of cities. Some places have long histories in which several different phases of reclamation can be identified, the settlements of the Venetian Lagoon, for example; in others the reclamation history is much simpler. On many shores the story of reclamation starts and ends with accumulated deposits of domestic refuse.

Primitive settlements

All over the world middens, some of them thousands of years old, others quite recent, testify to the long and widespread human occupation of foreshore areas. Some, like several in the San Francisco Bay area (Dreisbach,

1969), are now partly under water and we cannot tell how many others have been lost to the encroaching sea. These middens usually comprise mainly seashells, but often include bones of fish and other animals, ash, charcoal, rock and other materials, even human burials. They are probably among the oldest surviving forms of human modification of the landscape and may, perhaps, be regarded as a precursor of littoral land reclamation associated with human settlement.

Middens are artificial mounds which resulted from the disposal of refuse, but there is evidence that some pre-historic people deposited material in littoral areas in order to provide a more or less solid foundation or platform for their settlements, particularly in wetlands such as the marshy edges of lakes. Two examples are the sites at Star Carr near Scarborough, England, and Bergschenhoek north of Rotterdam in The Netherlands. Star Carr, occupied about 10,000 years ago, was the waterside edge of a Mesolithic settlement, possibly hunters, beside the now vanished glacial Lake Pickering. Here, archaeologists found the remains of a platform created by dumping birch brushwood, stones and lumps of clay in the reed swamp bordering the lake. While it is probable that stone tools were used to cut down trees for this waterside structure, there is evidence that beavers had felled some of the trunks found on the site (Coles, 1990; Hawkes and Hawkes, 1958). The much later Bergschenhoek site (*c.* 3450 BC) was also adjacent to a freshwater lake and, like Star Carr, was probably a temporary camp or the outpost of a more permanent settlement. In a fashion similar to that we can observe on Lake Titicaca today, this prehistoric European settlement site was made passable by laying down several layers of bundled reeds on the wet surface (Te Brake, 1985).

The large amount of archaeological material, including remarkably well preserved human remains, discovered in the peat bogs of Europe suggest that, in that region, as elsewhere, prehistoric peoples tended to settle in or near to wetlands. Again, it is necessary to be cautious in our interpretation because the environmental conditions of these areas are particularly favourable for the preservation of organic matter and thus could easily distort the evidence on the distribution of prehistoric settlement. Nevertheless, there can be little doubt that the littoral zones were important areas for human occupation in Europe after the ice age. Lakeshore and, later, coastal sites were favoured by the Mesolithic inhabitants who increasingly exploited the resources of the seashore, including shellfish, crustacea, stranded sea mammals and inshore fish (Clark, 1967).

This was also the period of lakeside pile dwellings in what is now Switzerland and northern Italy. These structures can be regarded as very early examples of what today is sometimes referred to as 'pile–supported fill', and which, even in the more primitive form, can still be found in many coastal areas of the world where dwellings, even substantial settlements, are built over the water on pile supports.

Ancient civilizations

The transition from a hunter – gatherer economy to one based increasingly on livestock rearing and agriculture by no means lessened human dependence on water and, while the home of the nomadic herdsman was the temporary camp, that of the farmer was typically a more permanent dwelling, often in a village. While much farming relied on rainfall, many agricultural societies depended on irrigation, drawing water by artificial means from rivers and streams. Wittfogel (1956; 1957) differentiates between what he terms *hydro–agriculture* (small-scale irrigation farming) and *hydraulic farming* involving large-scale waterworks. During the past several thousand years, 'hydraulic societies' based on the manipulation of water for irrigation and flood control have arisen (and declined) in many parts of the world including Egypt, Mesopotamia, India, parts of Southeast Asia, Hawaii, the Andean zone of South America, Meso-America (notably Mexico), and Arizona.

The control of rivers commonly enabled people to advance their settlement frontiers from *terra firma* (or dry land) areas into what had formerly been flood plains subject to periodic, even permanent inundation. Now, there are many parts of the world where few rivers remain in their natural state, at least in their middle and lower reaches. Formerly flowing in meandering or braided courses which shifted across wide, seasonally inundated corridors, many rivers have been artificially confined to permanent, relatively narrow single channels. This process which began thousands of years ago with the development of hydro–agriculture and, especially, hydraulic farming, has continued to recent times, particularly dramatic changes having occurred in mid-latitude regimes such as Western Europe and the USA since the late sixteenth century (Cosgrove, 1990; Petts, 1990).

The rapid and often spectacular achievements in hydraulic engineering which have taken place over the past two or three centuries reflect important technological advances and the emergence of centralized state capitalism in the modern era. In the more distant past, too, progress in wetland reclamation may be largely attributed to significant advances in technology and developments in social organization. It is not necessary to agree with all of Witfogel's theory to recognize that the civilizations of the Nile Valley and Mesopotamia developed in circumstances strongly influenced by the innovation of metal tools, first of copper and bronze, later iron, and the evolution of agricultural societies organized to control and exploit water resources and on a large scale.

In Mesopotamia, the region of the Tigris and Euphrates rivers, the Sumerian civilization arose five thousand years ago on former alluvial marshland which was converted into agricultural polders by the construction of dikes, canals and drainage ditches (Wagret, 1968). Flooding remained a serious threat, as is suggested by the Gilgamesh legend, possibly the origin of the story of the biblical Noah Flood story. Consequently, where possible, settlements were located on more elevated sites which rose above the general level of the flood plain. The city of Ur, for example, was built on an island in the middle of the marshes.

Today, the sites of ancient cities of Mesopotamia may be identified by the tells or mounds, now often deserted, which were created over time as successive phases of redevelopment took place on top of the layers of remains of earlier buildings. This gradual elevation of levels is common among cities where demolition and reconstruction have recurred over many centuries. In addition to the debris of demolished buildings, domestic refuse and other waste contributed to the accumulation of material over which towns commonly developed. Archaeological evidence suggests that, in ancient Sumeria, village and town extensions were often made on land formed by the dumping of rubbish (Kramer, 1956; Woolley, 1954), and in Iraq, modern Mesopotamia, the practice of constructing dryland village sites in wetland areas, including the creation of artificial islands, has continued in the Marsh Arab settlements near the confluence of the Tigris and Euphrates rivers (Mitsch and Gosselink, 1986). Indeed, the raising of settlement site levels and the creation of refuge mounds have long been common practices in inhabited flood plains and low-lying coastal areas throughout the world. Among the best known examples are the terpen settlements of the North Sea coast of Europe.

Probably the most famous ancient city in Mesopotamia is Babylon, on the Euphrates River. This became Hammurabi's capital some 4,200 years ago and was rebuilt and enlarged by Nebuchadnezzar 1,600 years later. Described as 'the mother city of the manufactured landscape' (Jellicoe and Jellicoe, 1987:27), Babylon well illustrates the way in which from ancient times urban development often involved control of, and extension into, water bodies. Today, the Euphrates at Babylon follows a distinctly angular course, strongly suggesting human interference, and air photos clearly show the former river bed within the boundaries of the old city site. According to Herodotus (cited in Jellicoe and Jellicoe, 1987:27) 2,600 years ago, three artificial bends and a lake upstream were excavated for military reasons. The city defences were further strengthened by the excavation of a system of moats and canals which no doubt also served to drain the site. Herodotus (quoted at length in Mumford, 1966:95–6) describes how mud excavated from the moat was baked into bricks which were used with bitumen to provide a strong facing along the water's edge and to construct on top a high brick wall.

Herodotus reported a similar waterfront development from the Nile at Memphis, possibly dating back to the beginning of pharaonic Egypt some 5,000 years ago:

> The priests informed me, that Menes, who first ruled Egypt, in the first place protected Memphis by a mound; for the whole river formerly ran close to the sandy mountain on the side of Libya; but Menes, beginning about a hundred stades above Memphis, filled in the elbow towards the south, dried up the old channel and conducted the river into a canal . . . this bend of the Nile, which flows excluded from its ancient course, is still carefully upheld by the Persians, being made secure every year; for, if the river should break through and overflow in this part there would be danger lest all Memphis should be flooded. When the part cut off had been made firm land by this Menes, who was first king, he in the first place built on it the city that is now called Memphis . . . (Herodotus, translated by Henry Cary, 1882:130)

The 'mound' built by Menes to protect Memphis was obviously a dike, and is so described in some translations.

From early times until quite recently, defence considerations often greatly influenced the location and development of settlement sites. Islands, pen-insulas and hilltops were particularly suitable for this purpose, especially where there was easy and safe access to a reliable source of fresh water such as a spring or a well within the defence perimeter. As we have seen, landscape features such as rivers, which could be used to provide natural defences, were commonly modified to enhance the security of settlements. In marshes on the shallow margins of lakes and rivers, and even in sheltered sea inlets, artificial islands were often constructed to provide dry sites, firm foundations and good defensive positions for human settlements.

A British Iron Age example is the La Tène culture lake village about 1.5 km north of Glastonbury, Somerset. Here iron billhooks were used to cut down alder and willow on the marshy site which was then built up to create an artificial island some 10,000 square metres in area. On the island stood some sixty circular huts with wattle walls, reed-thatched roofs and trodden clay floors, each with a stone or clay hearth, cobbled alleyways winding between the dwellings. The construction of the settlement must have required labour on an immense scale, and without iron tools the task might not have been feasible. The main bulk of the island was a bed of closely packed horizontal logs, up to a metre or more thick, but made even more substantial by deposits of clay, stones, brushwood and bracken, much of which had to be transported from a distance. A stout palisade of vertical timbers, driven well into the marsh, was erected around the island to retain the fill material and to enclose the settlement with a protective fence. Agriculture, hunting, fishing and craft industry were the main occupations of the inhabitants who also traded with other communities, but relationships with outsiders may not always have been friendly; hence the defensive site and the enclosing fence (Hawkes and Hawkes, 1958).

The Glastonbury lake village, which flourished before the Roman colonization of Britain, was on the outer fringe of the then civilized world which
centred on the Mediterranean. For millennia cities had grown up in the lands
that bordered the Mediterranean Sea from which trading ships had sailed
even as far as the British Isles. Among the most successful of these seafarers
were the Phoenicians whose major cities were ports which served as the bases
for their trading voyages. Notable among these port cities was Tyre which
provides a very early example of reclamation from the sea for urban development. Like many Phoenician cities, Tyre was a maritime settlement whose
existence and prosperity depended mainly of shipping; but, as one of the
major centres of the ancient world and one which anticipated several forms of
urban development which characterized much coastal city growth in later
periods, it is discussed here rather than in the later section entitled 'Maritime
settlements'.

Three thousand years ago Hiram, king of Tyre, decided to transfer his town
on the eastern Mediterranean coast to a site about 600 metres offshore where
two flat, partly submerged rocky ledges provided the unpromising natural
foundations of one of the great cities of the ancient world. To make sufficient
space for development and to create the two harbours, rubble and boulders
were transported from the mainland to infill the channel which separated the
two natural rocky islets, a reclamation work which must have taken thousands of men, years to complete. The defensive advantages of Tyre's insular
site with its excellent harbours appealed to the seafaring Phoenicians despite
water supply problems. Significantly, Tyre fell to the siege by Alexander the
Great in 332 BC only after the attacking army deprived the city of its insularity
by constructing a causeway linking it to the mainland. As in many cases,
where security considerations encouraged the foundation of settlements in
naturally defensible locations, the pressures of Tyre's urban growth caused
serious development problems on the confined insular site. The Phoenician
city's response to this was much like that of modern New York or Hong Kong:
it built upwards in the form of high density multi-storey buildings, it expanded into the sea by reclamation, and it probably overspilled onto the
mainland (Fleming, 1915; Harden, 1962; Herm, 1975).

Very far from the ancient Mediterranean world, and at a considerable
distance from the nearest sea coast, the centre of the Aztec civilization of pre-
Columbian America, Tenochtitlan, developed on a lake island site which was
eventually to grow into one of the world's most populous cities, Mexico City.
Security was the main reason why the Tenochas sought refuge on the
lowlying islands of Lake Texcoco, and by the mid-fourteenth century there
were two island communities established there, Tenochtitlan and Tlalteloco.
Over the next two centuries, the whole area had been converted into a
geometrical network of canals and raised earthworks. These 'havens of
malcontents from the mainland' (Vaillant, 1950:100) had developed into the

magnificent capital of the Aztec Empire, over 1,000 hectares in area, with an estimated population of over 500,000. Together with the suburbs which stretched along the shores of the lake this pre-Columbian Meso-American conurbation housed a population of over a million (Soustelle, 1964). Hardoy (1968) has challenged the estimates of Soustelle and others, suggesting a total area of 750 hectares, about 25 per cent of which was solid ground, housing a population of some 65,000 inhabitants. Nevertheless, the Aztec capital was an exceptionally large and important urban centre of Pre-Columbian America, and Mexico City, which succeeded it on that lacustrine site has grown to become one of the world's most populous urban agglomerations.

Under the pressure of growth, the people of the island city of Tenochtitlan expanded their land area by reclaiming the shallow margins of the lake, a practice which appears to have been followed by other communities on the shores of Lake Texcoco. Often misleadingly called 'floating gardens', the chinampas were agricultural plots on artificial islands built of mud excavated from the marshy lake edge. They were first held in place by reed or wicker-work structures and were later stabilized by the roots of trees which were established on the chinampas. The fertility of the plots was maintained and their levels raised by the continual application of fresh mud, and the ex-cavated areas between the islands developed into a network of canals which served as the main streets of the city, bordered by footpaths and crossed by frequent bridges. Access to the city was gained by raised roads, as much dikes as causeways, which extended from the lakeshore to the island metropolis. These were constructed by sinking two parallel lines of piles into the shallow lake bed and filling the space between them with stones and beaten earth. Here and there gaps, spanned by bridges, were provided to allow for lake currents (Soustelle, 1964).

As the city grew, land reclaimed for agriculture was built over, the buildings constructed on raised platforms faced with stone. New chinampas were created on the fringes of the expanding island city, and this urban develop-ment process is vividly described by Vaillant (1950:218) who imaginatively evokes the impressions of a contemporary observer: 'Now the visitor could realize how the city expanded through the successive creation of artificial islands which bore first a crop, then a modest hut and finally became integral with the masonry of the city proper.' Today little remains of Lake Texcoco, most of which has disappeared beneath modern urban development; but the vegetable gardens and canals of the Xochimilco and Chalco districts survive to remind us of the lacustrine origins of Mexico City.

Maritime settlements

The development of Tenochtitlan in many ways resembled that of Venice, formerly one of the world's great centres of commerce and a major maritime power. Both cities were at the zenith of their power in the fifteenth century, but Venice was founded much earlier, at the end of the western Roman Empire. Like Tenochtitlan, Venice started as a collection of scattered island communities, the great difference being Venice's location, not on an inland lake but in a coastal lagoon subject to the tides. The original Venetians were hunters, fishermen, farmers and salt makers who turned increasingly to trade using vessels capable of navigating the shallow lagoon channels. With rising prosperity, they artificially stabilized and enlarged their small muddy islands, eventually developing them into a magnificent city intersected by canals, the heart of a powerful empire. Like Tenochtitlan, too, though considerably earlier, the development of Venice was boosted by the arrival of refugees from the mainland. Many fled to the comparative security of the Venetian Lagoon islands during times of violent unrest following the collapse of the Roman Empire.

A description of the way of life of the lagoon dwellers in the early sixth century, before the main influx of refugees, is found in a letter from the high-ranking Roman official, Cassiodorus, who wrote:

> For you live like sea birds, with your homes dispersed, like the Cyclades, across the surface of the water. The solidarity of the earth on which they rest is secured only by osier and wattle; yet you do not hesitate to oppose so frail a bulwark to the wildness of the sea. (Variarum, Book XII, Letter 24, quoted in Norwich, 1982:6)

This observation suggests that the method by which the early Venetians consolidated and enlarged their land was similar to that used by the in-habitants of Lake Texcoco. Hazlitt (1900:11) uses a somewhat different translation of Cassiodorus which is more suggestive of the reclamation process: 'To the waves of the ocean you do not hesitate to oppose a frail barrier of dykes, flanked by fascines of interlaced vine stems.'

Great changes occurred with the immigration of refugees which began with the Lombard invasion of Italy in AD 568. By the ninth century peaceful conditions returned allowing the foundations to be laid for the Venice we know today. To build a capital worthy of the emerging Venetian Republic, it was necessary to stabilize, drain and enlarge by reclamation the low-lying muddy islands of the Rialto and to improve the sea defences of the Lagoon. A commission of three men was appointed by the Doge to undertake these works which involved the excavation of canals, the shoring up of islands, the preparation of building sites, and the construction of sea and military de-fences on the coastal sandbar islands which separate the Lagoon from the Adriatic.

Material excavated from the canals was used to raise ground levels but, because of the poor foundations provided by the lagoon mud, most of the early buildings were light structures. Later, with more massive construction and the increasing use of stone and brick, it became necessary to sink thousands of timber piles into the oozy ground, often so close together that their sawn-off tops made a practically continuous solid surface (Norwich, 1982). This practice continued into the twentieth century and, indeed, many houses in Venice are still supported on piles driven into the waterlogged ground almost a thousand years ago. With the later maritime and industrial development of Venice and other towns of the Lagoon, more modern reclamation techniques were introduced.

Before leaving nascent Venice, however, it is worth noting how the city's aquatic site encouraged the early emergence of city planning, a development which has its parallels in other parts of the world where urban growth has necessitated comprehensive water management and site formation work on a large scale. Lane (1973:16) asserts that 'it was because they were building a city on the water that Venetians realized from an early date the need for city planning of some kind'. Regulations were introduced to control the activities of private citizens which might be detrimental to the public, such as the location of stoneyards and the dumping of ballast and other materials which could cause the blockage of waterways. The control of the canals was a major responsibility of the Doge and his highest councils, and among the official bodies which emerged to regulate urban development was the *Magistrato del Piovego*, a kind of zoning board one of whose responsibilities was to grant or refuse permits to build on mud flats.

The rise of Venice as a maritime power was largely due to the city's strategic coastal location at the head of the Adriatic Sea on the main trade route between Europe and the Orient. The Venetian Empire began to decline in the late fifteenth century as European voyages of exploration discovered new lands to exploit and mapped out new sea routes for trade. While this global expansion of European influence greatly stimulated maritime trade and port development, in many parts of the world, vessels driven by sail and oar had been engaged in coastal and overseas trade since prehistoric times. For ages, boats and ships were beached on the shore or moored offshore to load and unload cargo, a practice which in some places continued into the twentieth century. With the evolution of shipping and the expansion of maritime trade, however, improved accommodation for ships was provided in the form of structures designed for better protection of vessels and to facilitate port operations, including jetties, breakwaters and marginal quays. These early port engineering works commonly involved landfill which began a process of reclamation that often continued for centuries, advancing the port further and further into the water.

Archaeological excavations in many European coastal and riverside cities have revealed evidence of port-related reclamations dating back to medieval and, in some cases, much earlier times (Milne and Hobley, 1981). In London, archaeologists have found a sequence of waterfront structures including old walls, revetments and landfills, tracing these Thameside developments back to the Roman origins of the city (Figure 2.1). Between the first and third

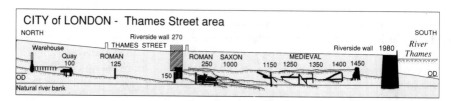

Figure 2.1 This diagramatic cross-section of the City of London illustrates the historical evolution of the north bank of the River Thames from Roman times to the late twentieth century. Approximate dates are indicated.
Source: Redrawn from *Discoveries*, compiled by Hugh Chapman, Museum of London (1986:6)

centuries, the Romans built a series of riverside quays, gradually advancing the land on the north bank into the Thames. This process continued on both banks in Saxon and Medieval times and later, reducing the width of the river and increasing the city's land area even as the sea-level rose and the tide extended further upstream (Hobley, 1981; Milne 1981; Milne and Milne, 1982).

Founded as a colonial city of the Roman Empire, London itself eventually became the hub of a vast overseas empire and the major focus of a world-wide system of maritime trade. Like the Romans, the British, together with other European nations, developed colonial towns and cities, typically ports, to serve their sea-borne trade and provide bases for the control of their territories and trade routes. As they extended their contacts with other parts of the world, the Europeans encountered many peoples with their own long histories of maritime trade and urban development, sailing for the first time into flourishing ports which were sometimes superior to those with which they were familiar at home.

Between AD 1100 and AD 1450, it was the Chinese who had the greatest sea-going navy in the world and China has a history of coastal land reclamation and sea-wall construction which goes back over a thousand years (Needham, 1964; 1971). Japan, too, has a long history of coastal land reclamation, and many Japanese towns and cities expanded into the sea in this way, often in association with port development. When in 1603 Edo, later Tokyo, became Japan's chief political and economic centre, there followed a spate of building involving considerable reclamation on the shores of Tokyo Bay, much of it for purposes related to the port. As in Venice, excavated canals yielded material for fill, on which a waterfront area developed with warehouses and other uses, including residences of the provincial lords who owned them (Mogi, 1966).

Nevertheless, in both Japan and China, as in other parts of the world, European commercial penetration led to an enormous expansion of port development, often involving extensive coastal reclamation. In some Chinese and Japanese port cities, during the nineteenth century, European settlements were established on artificial islands of reclaimed land separated by canals from the 'native quarters', as in Canton (Kwangchou), and Yokohama. The European quarter in the former city was known as the Shameen, meaning 'sand bank', a reminder of its origin as a shoal in the Pearl River. Much older is fan-shaped Dejima Island, Nagasaki, constructed in 1634, first a Portuguese and then a Dutch trading settlement (Matsutaro *et al.*, 1973).

Shanghai, now China's largest city, like Calcutta in India, was essentially a European creation where a modern commercial and industrial metropolis grew up in an area that had been little more than a tract of deltaic wetlands. On a very different kind of site, the mountainous island of Hong Kong, the British founded a city whose development from the very beginning required the reclamation of land from the harbour and where subsequent urban growth has involved large-scale extensions into the sea (Hudson, 1978; 1979). Similar developments, but on a smaller scale, have taken place in the nearby much older Portuguese colony of Macau, and another Portuguese colonial settlement in many ways comparable with Hong Kong is Rio de Janeiro. This Brazilian city, too, developed on a magnificent harbour tightly enclosed by precipitous, rugged terrain, making coastal land reclamation a normal concomitant of urban expansion (Stamp, 1957).

The earliest European cities to be established in the Americas were founded by the Spaniards in the Caribbean from the end of the fifteenth century onwards. Other European nations, including the French, Dutch, and English, soon followed, they, too, founding colonial towns and cities in the West Indies. Most of the major urban centres developed on coastal sites on the leeward sides of the islands, and the reclamation of land from the sea and swamps was commonly undertaken, normally with slave labour, for port development and urban expansion. Port Royal, Kingston, Port of Spain and Castries are but a few of the many West Indian examples of towns and cities where much of the waterfront area occupies land won from the sea and coastal wetlands (Hudson, 1983, 1989b).

In North America, as elsewhere, colonial towns on the sea coast and on major lakes, too, resorted to land reclamation from the earliest days of European settlement. Probably in few places has reclamation played as great a role in urban development as in Boston, Massachusetts (Figures 2.2 and 2.3). Here, between 1630 and 1852, the area of the town was practically doubled by infilling the coves and shallows which surrounded the Shawmut peninsula on which Boston was built. Subsequent reclamations have made further large additions for urban development, this process having as much as tripled the area of the peninsula which probably covered between 250 and 350 hectares at the time of the original European settlement (Drake, 1971; Whitehill, 1975).

In common with many maritime settlements, at first, Boston reclaimed
land largely for port and port-related developments; but soon the restrictions
imposed by the hilly peninsular site, chosen partly for security against hostile
Indians, also encouraged grading and landfill for residential and other urban
uses. In the nineteenth century, Boston's economic shift from commerce to
manufacturing put greater pressures on land for industry and related uses,

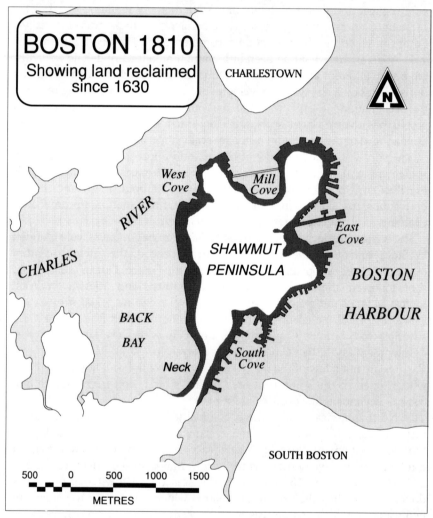

Figure 2.2 The peninsular site of Boston was enlarged considerably by foreshore
reclamation in the two centuries following the establishment of the colonial settlement but, in 1810, much of the area now occupied by the modern city remained under
water.
Source: Kennedy (1992)

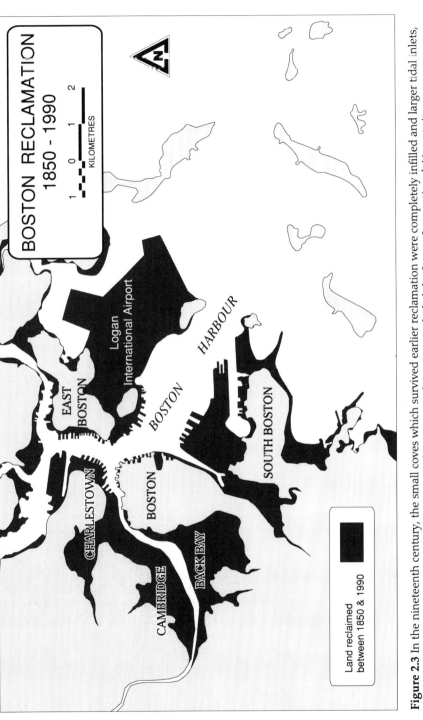

Figure 2.3 In the nineteenth century, the small coves which survived earlier reclamation were completely infilled and larger tidal inlets, notably Back Bay, were reclaimed. Major twentieth-century reclamations included the Logan International Airport site. *Sources*: Kennedy (1992), Conzen and Lewis (1976) and recent maps of Boston.

many requiring waterfront locations which further encouraged reclamation. Indeed, the start of the Industrial Age, which began in eighteenth-century Europe and from there spread far around the globe, heralded a new era of urban development and urban land reclamation.

3

Industrial Waterfront to Littoral Ecumenopolis

The Industrial Revolution both encouraged and facilitated large-scale littoral reclamation. This activity was boosted by important technological innovations including the steam engine, the railway, reinforced concrete and powerful pumps, and by increased demand for sites suitable for industry.

Among the old industries traditionally sited on navigable waterways, shipbuilding and repairing was one of those revolutionized by the new technology of the industrial age; the great expansion of this waterfront activity further encouraged reclamation in cities such as Boston, Belfast and Yokohama. Many other industrial and associated activities found it necessary, or at least advantageous, to be located on or near large water bodies. These were commonly navigable inlets or channels which allowed the transport of bulky raw materials, manufactured products and fuel by water.

In the past, sites on rivers and tidal inlets had often been chosen for industrial uses because of the attraction of water power. Now, with the adoption of the steam engine to operate machinery, large quantities of water were required for the boilers. Increasingly, too, enormous supplies of water were needed for cooling purposes in various industrial processes, including electric power generation. As steam power was replaced by electricity in an expanding and increasingly diverse range of industries, the growing need for thermal power stations helped to maintain the demand for large industrial sites in waterfront areas. These often fronted navigable waterways along which were transported the coal and, later, oil used as fuel in the generation of electricity.

Power generation and shipbuilding are two of the activities discussed in the section on 'Industrial Ports' in F.W. Morgan's (1958) now dated but still useful little book, *Ports and Harbours*. In the following discussion of land reclaimed for industry, it is convenient to use Morgan's three-fold classification of ports with significant industrial functions, a system based partly on the work of Amphoux (1949). It should be remembered, however, that there are many areas of reclaimed land put to industrial uses which have no connection with port development. These include various industrial developments in the flood plains of rivers and in some reclaimed sea- and lake-shore areas where proximity to the waterfront may be quite irrelevant to the local industrial activities.

The three classes of port industry distinguished by Morgan (1958:132) are:

1. those carried on at what may be called 'industrial ports';
2. general port industries; and
3. industries attracted to a port as a large centre of population.

Industries which are typically found in 'industrial ports' usually require special port installations ranging from a private wharf within a port to a purpose-built facility. The latter may involve the construction of an entirely new harbour and associated port works. In Morgan's (1958:132) words: 'Such industry necessitates a good deal of ground for works, storage dumps or tanks and, in this connection, it should be noted that estuarine ports often have tracts of relatively cheap land near them, suitable for these purposes.' Morgan might have added that usually much of this cheap land is low-lying marsh, swamp or tidal mudflats which require reclamation before they can be developed for industrial on other use.

Two industrial ports: Teesside and Gladstone

Part of the solution to this problem, however, can come from the industrial activity itself and from the associated port works. Industrial waste, such as slag from steel works or pulverized fuel ash from coal-fired power stations, may be usefully dumped on foreshore areas thus reclaiming land for future development. One typical example is that of Teesside, England; in the heyday of Middlesbrough's iron and steel industry large quantities of slag were dumped on the foreshore of the tidal River Tees and also used in the construction of retaining walls behind which harbour dredgings were deposited. In this way, Teesside, like many other estuarine industrial areas, solved a waste disposal problem by relatively economical means which created new land for development (Hudson, 1962; Le Guillou, 1978).

Beginning modestly as a coal-exporting port, Middlesbrough was transformed into a booming iron and steel town by the exploitation of iron ore from the nearby Cleveland Hills from the 1850s to the 1950s. Middlesbrough began to import ore as local sources declined in both quality and quantity; hence much of the industrial waste material which forms part of the made land beside the Tees must have originated as far away as the ore-fields of Sweden, Spain and North Africa. Among the industries which have developed on land reclaimed from the Tees estuary, are chemical manufacture and oil-refining. One of the major terminals for the North Sea oil-field is built on the reclaimed Seal Sands industrial site where, as in many parts of the world, oil-refining plant and extensive tank farms occupy large areas of level waterfront land which has been won from coastal wetlands and shallows. Of the many examples which could be cited, Porta Marghera, one of Italy's largest oil-refining and storage complexes, is worth special mention because of its proximity to a famous historic example of littoral reclamation for urban development. Here, the refinery and storage tanks stand in stark contrast with the ancient city across the water, Venice, arguably the most beautiful of all cities on the shore, which, like its modern industrial neighbour, rose on land won from the lagoon marshes.

Like the oil industry, the extraction and processing of bauxite have expanded greatly since World War II, and while coastal reclamation associated with this industry is not as widespread as that for oil, the shipping and refining of bauxite have made demands for land which have sometimes been met by winning land from the sea. In Gladstone, beside mangrove-fringed Port Curtis on the east coast of Australia, reclamation had already been undertaken for port-related purposes when, in the 1960s, the large-scale exploitation of Queensland's coal and bauxite transformed the small town into a major industrial port handling more shipping tonnage per annum than Sydney.

Gladstone's rapid development followed the decision to locate a huge alumina plant there exploiting Queensland's large reserves of bauxite and coal, the latter already being shipped through the port to Japan. Built on the southern shore of Port Curtis, the alumina plant was to expand to become the 'largest in the world, and its development involved the reclamation of coastal wetlands, some of it using red mud waste from the refining process as fill material' (Harris and Stehbens, 1981). In 1982, a smelter was opened on nearby Boyne Island for processing the alumina into aluminium. The electricity for these huge energy-consuming industries is generated at the Gladstone Power Station which began operation in 1967. This project, too, involved coastal reclamation, and, indeed, '[t]he local authorities . . . saw the power station as a giant reclamation device' (McDonald, 1988:350). Part of the adjacent tidal foreshore has been enclosed with bunds for the disposal of ash from the power station and the creation of some 160 hectares for future industrial and harbour development.

Gladstone's industries are not confined to those related to the processing of bauxite, and a variety of industrial enterprises are found within the city, much of it on reclaimed land. Some of these activities fall within Morgan's (1958) 'general port industries' category. Industries in this group generally operate on smaller amounts of heavy material than those of the industrial port category, and they tend to locate at ports taking advantage of their role as break-of-bulk points. Economy in handling imports being less important as a locational factor, these industries do not often require a port of their own and thus are commonly found in ports which handle a wide range of cargoes. Processing and packaging imported produce for human consumption, such as wheat and sugar, and for feeding livestock, are typically found at such ports, as are sawmilling and tanning, as well as a range of engineering associated with port activities.

Metropolis on the shore: the case of Hong Kong

As attractive markets and sources of labour, the large concentrations of population and wealth found in and around metropolitan port cities such as New York, London, Tokyo and Sydney encourage a wide range of industrial and related activities which have no direct link with the port function. These industries belong to Morgan's (1958) third category. Even those industries which do not require waterfront sites or are not related to the port may contribute to pressures on land which encourage reclamation. This is particularly so where there is very limited space for development.

Nowhere better illustrates this than Hong Kong. Having developed as an important entrepôt and major centre of maritime trade, this British colony underwent a dramatic economic transformation in the 1950s when commerce was eclipsed by manufacturing industry as the mainstay of Hong Kong's economy (Szczepanik, 1960). Importing nearly all its raw materials and mainly relying on the export of its products, most of Hong Kong's manufacturing industry was as dependent on the port and shipping as was its entrepôt function. Further stimulus to manufacture was provided by Hong Kong's large industrious population. This increased from about 2,000,000 in 1950 to some 6,000,000 as the twentieth century comes to an end, endowing Hong Kong with a vast pool of labour and a useful home market which encourages industrial enterprise.

The 'Made in Hong Kong' label which became so common on goods sold throughout the world might have been attached with equal validity to the land on which most of these products were manufactured. While some of Hong Kong's industries had good reason to be sited on or near the waterfront, many, perhaps most, merely needed relatively level land for development with reasonable access to the port. In mountainous Hong Kong sites of this kind usually had to be created artificially, reclamation of land from the sea being the common means (Hudson, 1979).

Born of nineteenth-century imperialism, Hong Kong today is a modern industrial and commercial city, a major world business and financial centre, and an important tourist destination. The latest urban developments, including port expansion and a new airport, like those in the past, involve large-scale reclamation of land from the sea. Hong Kong Planning Department's (1991) *Metroplan* envisages a twenty-first-century city where continuing economic development is matched by an improved urban environment. While coastal land reclamation will continue to play an essential role in Hong Kong's development, for the first time in the territory 'a number of compensatory conservation measures' (Environmental Protection Department, 1992:39) are now being prescribed.

Hong Kong exemplifies many of the trends experienced world-wide in the latter part of the twentieth century. These include developments in port technology which greatly increased demand for large areas of level waterfront land, notably containerization and roll-on-roll-off facilities, and the expansion of high-technology industries. Airport construction which increased enormously with the growth of international air travel after World War II, also consumed vast areas, much of it created by reclamation from the sea or wetlands. This, in part, reflects the littoral location of many of the world's cities, but the need for huge areas of flat land, free from nearby obstructions and other hazards to aircraft landing and taking off, also encouraged airport and runway construction beside, and often projecting into, large water bodies. Notable among the airports to be completed in the 1990s is that at Hong Kong's Chek Lap Kok which, like Kai Tak Airport replaced by the new development, is built mostly on reclaimed land. Of the total area of over 900 hectares, 300 hectares were created by levelling two islands, the rest being won from the sea, here up to 10 metres deep (Wong *et al.*, 1987).

Leisure, recreation and tourism

The explosive world-wide post-war expansion in air travel was largely associated with increasing opportunities for leisure and demands for recreation which boosted the tourist industry. This development has had its greatest physical impact on littoral areas, especially the coast. From time immemorial, leisure pursuits have commonly involved water – fishing, fowling, swimming, skating, boating and surfing to mention some of the more obvious water-related recreational activities. Moreover, there is strong evidence to suggest that people generally have an aesthetic preference for landscapes which include water features, a taste clearly reflected in the popularity of places notable for their river, lake and coastal scenery (Bourassa, 1991).

The modern phenomenon of mass tourism can be said to have begun with the traditional British seaside holiday, a custom which has diffused and evolved throughout much of the world (Urry, 1990). The beach continues to attract millions of tourists as well as local recreation seekers in many different countries, often being a major factor in the growth of tourism in the tropical Third World.

While the littoral orientation of much of the development associated with recreation and tourism increases pressure on waterfront land, thus encouraging reclamation, there are generally good reasons to avoid encroachment on or damage to beaches, foreshores and water bodies which are among the main attractions for the visitor. Nevertheless, much reclamation has been directly associated with tourism and recreation, some of it having unfortunate environmental and social consequences, as at Gros Islet, St Lucia. Here at a swampy site beside the Caribbean Sea, dredge and fill operations were begun in 1969 to create dry land and an artificial lagoon for the development of the Rodney Bay resort. In addition to creating land for development, this wetland conversion scheme was intended to mitigate a sandfly nuisance which hoteliers believed was detrimental to their business. Among the unanticipated consequences of the scheme were the destruction of local fisheries and beach erosion. The sandflies remained, however (Towle, 1985).

Resort developments similar to Rodney Bay can be found in many parts of the world where beaches and coastal wetlands are juxtaposed. Sites of this kind also lend themselves to the creation of marina and canal developments. In the 'developed world' especially, these have proliferated on many coasts, often linked with tourism, but commonly associated with the hedonistic life style characteristic of places such as the Florida and California coasts of the USA and Australia's Gold Coast. Very often, too, these areas attract large numbers of retired people embarking on what might, perhaps, be regarded as their terminal vacation.

Inspired by its more famous Italian namesake, and dating from the early part of the twentieth century, the Los Angeles coastal suburb of Venice was a pioneer of the modern residential canal estate. More recently canal estates, typified by houses with cars parked at the front and boats moored at the back, have spread to other climatically favourable areas of the USA, and to Australia and elsewhere, destroying large areas of coastal wetland in the process. Marina development, another typical phenomenon of the leisure society, has also contributed to wetland destruction, as in the case of Marina del Rey, close to Venice, LA. One of the world's largest marinas, this huge development was built between 1957 and 1965 on former swampland behind the beach known as the Playa del Rey. Marina del Rey is a complex of apartments, condominiums, restaurants and shops overlooking a pleasure boat haven accommodating nearly 6,000 craft, all catering 'to a way of life geared to youth, the sun, and the sea' (Nelson, 1983:21).

Accommodation for that much larger leisure craft, the cruise ship, has also necessitated coastal reclamation in some tourist areas. Montego Freeport, reclaimed from mangrove swamps and coral shallows on Jamaica's north coast includes a cruise ship dock as well as berths for small leisure craft, together with a beach resort including a condominium hotel and tourist shopping facilities. Nearby, the demands of the tourist industry have encouraged reclamation of a different kind, the creation of three artificial beaches which extend into the waters of Montego Bay. Urban development pressures on the city of Montego Bay, Jamaica's major tourist centre, have also led to reclamation along the old waterfront, close to the Central Business District. This is a process which has become common throughout the world as waterfront redevelopment, often associated with gentrification, leisure and tourism, follows in the wake of the decline and decay of former port areas (Craig-Smith and Fagence, 1995; Hoyle *et al.*, 1988). Another Jamaican example of urban renewal is the Kingston Waterfront Scheme. Dating from the 1960s, this project, like the Montego Bay waterfront development, has been built partly on areas reclaimed over the past two hundred years or more, and partly on land newly won from the sea. With its prestige offices, hotel, luxury apartments, shopping mall and tree-lined boulevard, the Kingston Waterfront has much in common with many larger and better-known developments elsewhere (Hudson, 1983; 1989b; 1995).

Between Kingston's Ocean Boulevard and the famous Harbour is a narrow strip of parkland with a waterside promenade. Because of their attractive location, waterfront areas are often used for public and private open space and, particularly where land for development is scarce, reclamation is sometimes undertaken to create sites for this purpose. This is not a new practice. Boston's park system includes large areas of reclaimed wetland and former tidal estuary beside the Charles River and its tributary, the Muddy River, parts dating from the 1880s (Kennedy, 1992). The tradition of riverside gardens is an old one, of course, dating at least as far back as ancient Babylon.

Where space for development is scarce and urban pressures are severe, land for open space and recreational uses is now commonly created by reclamation. Open space is often the most suitable type of use for former refuse dumps and many disused coastal landfill sites have been turned into waterside parks, recreation grounds, sports fields and the like. Not all land reclaimed for recreational and open space uses is a by-product of waste disposal, however. The 23 hectare Victoria Park in central Hong Kong, for example, was reclaimed for that specific purpose using sand dredged especially for use as fill in the project.

As in Hong Kong, Japan's land shortage has encouraged coastal reclamation for the creation of open space, both public and private. A notable project on Tokyo Bay undertaken in the late 1980s and 1990s is the Kasaioki scheme, on a 380 hectare site, most of it reclaimed, where new urban development has been linked with the creation of Kasai Seaside Park. Part of this recreational area is devoted to the Tokyo Sea Life Park which stands within view of a more famous theme park, Tokyo's Disney World, itself built on former wetlands at the mouth of the Edo River. Elsewhere in the bay, the many other open space and recreational areas developed on reclaimed land include several 'seaside', 'marine' and 'wild bird' parks, as well as facilities catering for a wide variety of sports, including golf and tennis.

The future city on the shore

Generous provision of sporting and recreational facilities is one of the typical characteristics of the modern city image, and this is one of the many vaunted attractions of Tokyo Teleport Town now under construction on a 448-hectare reclaimed site in the heart of the Port of Tokyo. With major works scheduled for completion in 1999, Tokyo Teleport is planned as an urban sub-centre, a node in the international information transmission and reception network, and a venue for international conventions. In the twenty-first century, this 'futuristic city' is expected to have 60,000 residents, provide daily employment for 110,000 workers, and attract crowds of visitors to its shopping malls, plazas, amusement parks and hotels (Office of Tokyo Frontier Promotion, n.d.).

Another futuristic city 'based on the concept of marrying life style advantages to advanced technology' (Powell, 1992:51) is planned for a wetland site near Adelaide, South Australia. This so-called Multifunction Polis (MFP) was initiated by the Japanese Minister for International Trade and Industry as a co-operative venture between Japan and Australia. It was originally planned for a coastal site between Brisbane and the Gold Coast but, for reasons not clearly explained to the public, the scheme was rejected by the Queensland government and an alternative site in a mangrove swamp on the Port Adelaide estuary was selected.

Despite the construction difficulties, there are advantages in choosing a wild wetland site for the creation of a new city, notably the absence of existing development and the proximity to the water. The conversion of littoral swamps and shallows into a planned city of the future is by no means new. St Petersburg, built in the marshes at the head of the Gulf of Finland, was part of Peter the Great's vision of the future Russia and since then, especially in the 1950s and 1960s, there have been many proposals, often quite fantastic, for futuristic settlements, both on the shores and in the deeps. Some of these are described by Stewart (1970) who, influenced by Doxiadis, predicted littoral and marine ecumenopolis, parts of a global system of urban development spreading along and encroaching into the oceans, rivers and lakes.

While long stretches of coast and other littoral areas are being converted into modern urban developments designed for a hedonistic life style, and futuristic waterfront 'hi-tech' cities are already becoming a reality, there is plenty of evidence to indicate that any future littoral ecumenopolis would also include vast tracts of shanty town slums. On defiled shores from Kingston Harbour to Manila Bay, thousands of people live, or exist, quite literally, on garbage dumped in coastal swamps and shallows. Urban refuse provides both a livelihood of sorts and a place to dwell, much of the material used in the construction of the shanty towns themselves coming from the discarded waste of the nearby city. Jamaican sociologist and novelist, Orlando Patterson (1982:10) has described the notorious Dungle slum area on Kingston Harbour where men, women and children scavenged for a living on 'the mounds of filth [which] undulated towards the unseen shore'. The nearby shacks of these scavengers were 'dreadful, nasty little structures – a cluster of cardboard barrel sides, old cod-fish boxes, flattened tar-drums and timber scraps', some of the better habitations consisting of the carcasses of old cars (Patterson, 1982:7).

Less hideous, and more hopeful, is another, more recent, Caribbean shanty settlement, that at Four à Chaud, St Lucia, where squatters have illegally taken over land originally reclaimed from Castries Harbour for future legitimate urban development (Potter, 1985). Elsewhere, the urban poor do not wait for the creation of land on which to build before extending their settlements into the water. In some Third World countries, people construct their homes on piles sunk into tidal foreshore areas in advance of the land fill reclamation which the residents hope will soon be undertaken by the city authorities. Crooke (1971) has described this process in Guayaquil, Ecuador, where the first phase of development involves the erection of flimsy dwellings on piles connected by a network of light timber catwalks. During this early period of occupation of unreclaimed tidal mudflats health conditions are very bad and the mortality rate is high. Meanwhile, the new settlers press the city authorities to provide land fill for their streets and other amenities including water supplies and sewers. When the space under and between the dwellings has been turned into solid ground by landfill and the settlement is legalized, most of the shanties are rebuilt as more substantial houses which are then sometimes sold. This process is often repeated, continually pushing the urban frontier further into the sea, and in Guayaquil there has emerged a substantial number of 'professional settlers' who earn at least part of their livelihood by thus converting coastal swamps and shallows into residential areas.

Greening the city on the shore

Third World urbanization and housing are among the world's most pressing problems to which scholars and planners have given much attention in recent decades. Another serious concern, particularly since the 1960s, has been the environment, and wetlands, once widely ignored, have become a major focus of scientific research and a common topic in the classroom and the popular media. The history of littoral reclamation suggests that the conversion of wetlands into dry land was long generally regarded an entirely desirable, something which contributed to human well-being and progress. Opposition

sometimes came from people who made a living in or from such areas –
fishermen, fowlers, reed cutters and the like – as well those concerned with
navigation and shipping; and at times violent efforts have been made to
frustrate reclamation schemes (Cosgrove, 1990; Wagret, 1968). Nevertheless,
until recently at least, the commonly held view has been that marshes,
swamps and mudflats are, at worst, dangerous nuisances, unsightly sources
of unpleasant smells and disease, and, at best, convenient areas for dumping
waste or places which might be reclaimed to create useful dry land. The sea
itself was regarded with ambivalence. A source of wealth from fisheries and
maritime trade, the sea was also often an enemy from whose unceasing attack
the land had to be defended by all possible means. Sea defence and coastal
reclamation are activities which cannot always be easily distinguished, the
one usually combining with it some elements of the other.

Today, largely through the work of distinguished popular science writers
such as Rachel Carson (*Silent Spring*), Wesley Marx, (*The Frail Ocean*) and
Barry Commoner (*The Closing Circle*), it is widely acknowledged that the
seashore and even the oceans themselves are under threat from human
activity. The seas, lakes, rivers and wetlands are now recognized as valuable
resources which we need to conserve if human life is to be sustained on this
planet. Significantly, the term 'wetlands' came into common use only after
the 1960s. Since then around the world littoral societies and other environmental organizations have been formed to promote the understanding and
conservation of these previously neglected and misunderstood areas. Concern about the destruction of ecosystems, the loss of species and the dis-
figurement of landscape, as well as growing demands for outdoor leisure
amenities, including improved public access to the shore and waterfront,
soon led to an upsurge in opposition to littoral reclamation.

In the forefront of this movement was the San Francisco Bay area where, in
little more than a century after California's admission to the Union in 1850,
the Bay's water surface area at mean high tide had been reduced from about
1,760 to some 1,115 square kilometres. About 44 square kilometres of the
reclaimed area had been infilled for urban development, the rest having been
diked off mainly for agriculture and salt making. Much of the unreclaimed
tidal area remained at risk and, even as late as 1969, pending development
proposals alone threatened to infill another 150 square kilometres or more,
not counting schemes to fill and develop large areas of salt ponds (Figure 3.1).
It seemed likely that encroachment into the bay would continue, even
accelerate. Moreover, it was estimated that less than 16 kilometres of the 444
kilometre San Francisco Bay shoreline was open to the public, parks on the
shoreline having a total area of only some 2,000 hectares (Odell, 1972).

California in the 1960s was in a mood of rising environmental concern and
this, together with the much valued aesthetic qualities of the Bay, were
important factors which contributed to the public outcry that eventually led to

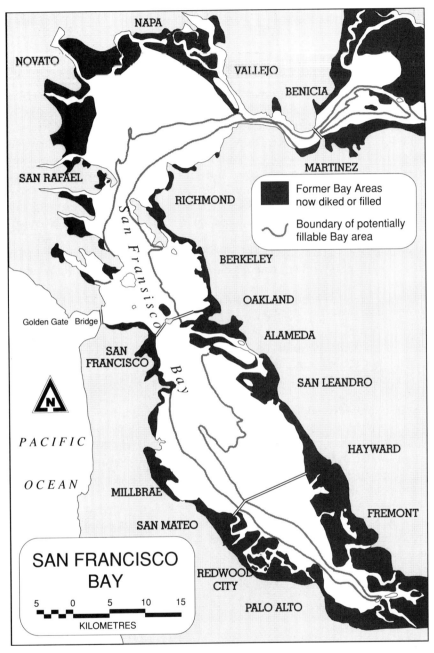

Figure 3.1 Between 1840 and 1965 the area of San Francisco Bay was reduced by about a third. The shallowness of the bay makes much of that which remains vulnerable to further reclamation.
Source: Gilliam (1969)

the publication of the San Francisco Bay Plan (San Francisco Bay Conservation and Development Commission, 1969). A particular advantage of the San Francisco Bay area was the presence of numerous environmental specialists and experts, many of them at academic institutions. Significantly, the Save San Francisco Bay Association was formed when three women, wives of Berkeley academics, called a meeting with some Bay Area conservationists to consider appropriate action (Gilliam, 1969; Odell, 1972).

The publication of the San Francisco Bay Plan in January, 1969 was a milestone, not only in the history of the Bay, but also in the world-wide movement to conserve wetlands and the oceans. The struggle to save San Francisco Bay is by no means over, and some reclamation is still permitted. Today there is much greater control, however, and wherever possible new extensions into the Bay are offset by mitigation measures including the restoration of former wetland areas to tidal influences. The San Francisco Bay experience, discussed in greater detail later in the book, was an inspiration to conservationists all over the world, and the Bay Plan has been seen as a model to be emulated by others responsible for harbours and estuaries in many countries.

Today, there are studies and management plans for marine inlets, rivers and lakes in many parts of the world, largely aimed at reducing pollution, but also concerned with halting and, where possible, reversing the ecological damage and other harmful consequences of reclamation. While this has not usually put a complete ban on future reclamation, it has often brought it under much stricter control. Despite growing environmental awareness and greater appreciation of the values of the littoral zone, landfill projects, some on an unprecedented scale, continue to advance the urban littoral frontier into the water in many parts of the world. The motives which have encouraged reclamation since prehistoric times are still very powerful, perhaps more so than in the past, and the technology is now available to undertake projects which could hardly be imagined centuries ago. It is, therefore, appropriate at this point to analyse the motivation for urban land reclamation. With reference to specific examples, the following two chapters discuss the various reasons why cities commonly expand by reclaiming land from the sea, rivers, lakes and wetlands, a normally expensive operation often undertaken even when dry land development sites may be readily available.

4

Urban Waste and Urban Space

There may seem a world of difference between the shoreline middens of primitive communities and the huge islands of urban refuse in Tokyo Bay, heart of one of the world's largest and most technologically advanced metropolitan regions, but both types of artificial landforms have their origins in essentially the same human activity – the disposal of waste. Waste disposal is one of the earliest and continues to be one of the most important reasons for the reclamation of land from the shore and adjacent waters. As F.M. Du-Plat-Taylor (1931:1) observed, the combination of waste disposal with any other object of reclamation 'may often suffice to render profitable a project which would otherwise not offer any prospects of success'.

Archaeologists have reason to be grateful for the primitive and often unwholesome waste disposal practices of our forebears. Middens, for example, yield large quantities of material which throw light on the lives of those who created them by depositing the remains of their meals, discarded tools, utensils and the like, even sometimes burying their dead in these mounds. In past centuries rivers, streams and foreshores in urban areas were commonly foul in consequence of their being used for the disposal of every kind of filth and refuse generated by the city. So great was the demand for refuse disposal sites in medieval London that this may well have been an important reason for reclaiming parts of the Thames foreshore. Scholars have even suggested that financial gain from the operation of garbage tips might have been an additional inducement for undertaking waterfront projects of this type, charges being made for permission to dump refuse on the reclamation sites behind timber revetments (Milne and Milne, 1982; Rhodes, 1982).

Urban waste: garbage

Until quite recently Hong Kong, like many other large cities, disposed of much of its urban refuse by dumping it on the foreshore and in shallow bays, a practice which gave rise to the place name Lap Sap Wan, translated as 'Garbage Bay', found on some older maps. In the nineteenth century, the name Lap Sap Wan was applied to Belcher Bay, a former inlet just beyond the western end of Victoria, the city on the southern shore of Hong Kong Harbour. To this place were brought street sweepings and other town refuse which were dumped on the beach. Eventually the bay was reclaimed and now forms the district known as Kennedy Town. In 1921, the inlet of Cheung Sha Wan, northwest of Kowloon, was opened as the main refuse dump for both Hong Kong Island and the Kowloon Peninsula. Part of the bay was reclaimed by covering the refuse with a layer of earth fill to bring it up to the required levels and, by 1932, nearly six hectares had been won from the sea in this way. Subsequent reclamation has completely infilled the bay which is now the site of the urban area still known as Cheung Sha Wan (Hudson, 1970).

Work stopped on the Cheung Sha Wan refuse dump reclamation in 1933, and it was followed by dumping behind a sea wall at Kwun Tong, east of Kowloon. By 1951 over 800 tonnes of domestic refuse were being carried by barge and lorry to this dump every day, but a more ambitious reclamation scheme for the creation of a new satellite industrial town here necessitated the closing of the Kwun Tong site as a refuse dump. A new site for Hong Kong's main refuse dump was chosen at Gin Drinker's Bay, also known by the alternative name of Lap Sap Wan, between Kowloon and Tsuen Wan. This dumping area was protected by a rubble retaining wall some 500 metres long, linking Tsing Chau, otherwise known as Pillar Island, to the mainland in order to prevent the removal of garbage by marine currents. A second bund had to be built in the other side of the dump when it was found that the original design was inadequate, allowing masses of rubbish to float off into the bay and thence into the harbour. The establishment of refuse incineration plants in Hong Kong in the 1960s made it possible to close the Gin Drinker's Bay dump which now forms part of the open space provision of Kwai Chung new town (Hudson, 1970; 1979).

In many parts of the world, foreshore areas, swamps and sheltered bays continue to be used for dumping refuse which, as we have seen in the case of Kingston, may provide both a meagre living and a squalid home for the urban poor. Even countries as wealthy and advanced as Japan use the sea as a garbage dump, and Tokyo's waste disposal problem has grown to such proportions as to attract considerable global media attention. *Time* magazine (11 January 1993:40) reported that 'Tokyo is overwhelmed by its own trash', warning that, at the present rate the city will run out of dump sites by 1995, and that its practice of building artificial islands to hold garbage cannot continue 'without threatening both the fishing and shipping industries'.

In the early 1980s, the Tokyo Metropolis produced about five million tonnes of waste annually, rising to six million tonnes by the end of the decade. Among the problems arising from this was increased pressure on dumping grounds. In response, a 'Waste Reduction Action Plan' was formulated at a conference of representatives of residents, business and government aimed at reducing waste by 23 per cent by the year 2000. Waste reduction and recycling together with the construction of ten new waste incineration plants are expected to ease the pressure on dumping grounds but, as the capacity of existing landfill sites approaches exhaustion, 'A new final dumping ground in Tokyo Bay is to be secured for use from 1996' (Bureau of City Planning, 1992:44).

Urban waste: industrial waste

To achieve Tokyo's waste reduction goal of 23 per cent by the year 2000, domestic refuse generation is to fall by 20 per cent, and industrial waste by 30 per cent. Industrial processes have generated waste by-products from ancient times, a fact clearly testified by the slag heaps produced by the iron works of Meroë, in modern Sudan, two thousand years ago. In Chapter 3, reference was made to the use of industrial waste for land reclamation, and the example of Gladstone, Australia, showed that the generation of industrial waste may even be seen as an advantage when the by-product, in this case ash from a power station, can be put to use as fill in a reclamation project. Only if the resultant land can be used by the industry or other responsible body such as a port authority, or sold at a profit, is this type of reclamation worthwhile other than as a ready means of waste disposal. In nineteenth century Teesside, large areas of land were reclaimed from the tidal river by the deposit of slag, and much of the made ground put to good use for industrial purposes. Nevertheless, slag heaps continued to grow in the vicinity of the iron works taking up land that might have been put to other use, and some companies shipped their slag down river to be deposited in the North Sea. A useful outlet for the waste was found in the construction of river training walls and breakwaters at the mouth of the Tees when the iron masters agreed to supply the slag free of charge and to pay for its removal and transport by rail and barges to the harbour improvement works (Le Guillou, 1978; Tees Conservancy Commissioners, 1952, 1954).

Urban waste: dredged spoil

Harbour works themselves normally yield vast quantities of waste, notably excavated and dredged materials produced during capital works and maintenance operations. In many ports, dredging must be continuous in order to combat the silting of channels and berths, and the vast quantities of dredgings produced by this activity can make spoil disposal a difficult problem. Port authorities, such as those of the Tees and Thames Rivers, have commonly disposed of dredged spoil out at sea, but this method has been criticized on the grounds that marine currents may return this material to the harbour from which it originally came (*PLA Monthly*, 1960). In the Tees estuary, there is no evidence that dredgings dumped at sea return to the river mouth, and, in any case, natural processes would continue to bring sand in from the North Sea as it has always done (Palmer, 1993). Nevertheless, there are other reasons for finding an alternative to the disposal of dredgings at sea, not least the cost of transporting the spoil which may involve round trips of over 200 kilometres (*PLA Monthly*, 1960). One reason why the practice of disposal at sea is continued by the Tees and Hartlepool Port Authority is that much of the dredged material contains too high a proportion of industrial pollutants, such as heavy metals, for it to be safely deposited on the foreshore as fill for land reclamation. This has the unfortunate consequence of contributing to marine pollution. Another reason is that some 95 per cent of Teesmouth's original intertidal area has already been reclaimed (Evans 1990a; Palmer, 1993)

The history of the Tees as a major port is largely concerned with the modification of its formerly shifting, shallow multiple channels by training, dredging and reclamation which have utterly transformed the estuary (Fallows 1878; Le Guillou, 1978; Pattenden, 1990). The importance of industrial waste disposal in Teesside's reclamation work, especially in the nineteenth and early twentieth centuries, has already been noted but, in later developments, harbour dredgings provided most of the fill. This is partly because the smelting of imported high-grade iron ore which eventually replaced the impure local Cleveland ironstone, yielded for less slag per tonne of metal produced, and new uses had been found for other industrial by-products formerly available as fill material for reclamation schemes. More important was the increased scale of port operations which required the dredging and maintenance of deeper navigation channels and berths. This yielded enormous quantities of silt, sand and soft clay which could be cheaply and, it was hoped, profitably disposed of in projects designed to utilize the spoil as fill for reclaiming land from estuarine mudflats and shallows. It was this kind of thinking which prompted the scheme to reclaim the 760 hectare Seal Sands, a project begun in 1928 using maintenance dredgings, mostly silt and sand, for 90 per cent of the fill (Figure 4.1). During the project some 40-50 per cent of the dredgings from the Tees were disposed of in this way (Hudson, 1962).

Reclamation as a useful means of dredged spoil disposal has been widely adopted, particularly where silting and shoaling are a constant problem. Most of Belfast's central district and dock area are built on land created in this way (Evans and Jones, 1955). Even where land thus reclaimed is of little or no practical value, this method of spoil disposal may be adopted on economic or other grounds, as long as there are suitable places available for use as dumping areas. In the 1970s, Baltimore was faced with such problems. Here there was an urgent need to find a suitable site for the disposal of mud dredged from the harbour as part of the channel and port development programmes. The dredging of the 15 metre channel and container port facilities was held up for over two years because of disagreements on where to dump the 1.76 million cubic metres of mud which this work would yield, in addition to which would be an annual yield of 1.5 million cubic metres from maintenance dredging. Older deepwater dumping grounds in the bay had already been filled and, being a fine silt containing 60 per cent water, the dredgings could not be easily compacted and drained, making the material unsuitable for use as fill on construction sites. Added to this was a pollution problem of a kind similar to that noted in the Tees estuary. The top layer of the mud, perhaps as much as a third, was contaminated by oil, lead, cadmium, molybdenum, nickel, manganese and cobalt, though unlike harbours elsewhere, little mercury was present. The US Environmmental Protection Agency was opposed to dumping the mud in the bay without dikes to retain it and, in a controversial decision, the port authority finally chose to dispose of

Figure 4.1 The formerly extensive tidal mud flats of the Tees Estuary have almost completely disappeared beneath made land which is used mainly for port and industrial purposes. The photograph shows the northern edge of the Seal Sands reclamation in 1965, before this industrial site was extended towards the mouth of the River Tees. (author's photo)

the dredgings behind enclosing dikes in the Hart and Miller Island area. Far from being a profit-generating means of waste disposal, this project was estimated to cost US$13 million, taking several years to build (Olson, 1976).

While fine silt is generally unsuitable for use as fill for construction sites, some harbour dredgings often can make ideal material for this purpose. Sand, in particular, is much used in site formation work, especially in reclamation schemes, and so valuable is it for this purpose that sea-bed sand is often dredged for this reason alone. In Hong Kong, where relatively little dredging has been required for port improvement and maintenance, sea-bed sand deposits have been deliberately sought out by systematic surveys and are exploited extensively for use in major reclamation works, especially the vast projects of recent years (Brand and Whiteside, 1990).

Urban waste: site formation spoil and demolition debris

Site formation work on dry land generally yields much excavated spoil material such as earth and rocks, which is often dumped on foreshore areas and has made a major contribution to land reclamation in many cities. For well over a century, this was the main source of fill for reclamation schemes in Hong Kong, being largely replaced by dredged sand only in recent decades. In Boston, the excavation of steep hillsides to create building sites began as early as the eighteenth century and there, too, spoil from this work was used to reclaim land from the sea. State House, built in 1795, stands on a terrace cut into the side of Beacon Hill which was much reduced by site formation work in the late eighteenth and early nineteenth centuries (Bunting 1967; Whitehill, 1975). Most of the site formation spoil produced in Boston and Hong Kong was highly suitable for use as fill for construction work, being mainly glacial gravel in the former and decomposed granite in the latter. In these and many other cities, excavation to create level ground on hillsides, even removing hills altogether, was widely undertaken in conjunction with reclamation schemes in order to create building sites at both the source and the destination of the spoil. With the increasing heights of buildings and the need for deeper foundations, development on level ground sites also contributed greatly to the production of excavated material.

Where, as is often the case, there is an immediate demand for the excavated earth and rock as fill for use in other site formation work, this material must be regarded as a valuable resource rather than waste to be disposed of. When there is no such demand, or the material is of an unsuitable type, such as large boulders, developers may seek to dispose of it as cheaply as possible, and illegal dumping on vacant land, in gullies and on foreshore areas is common. In order to deal with this problem, the Hong Kong government imposed strict regulations on site development while making available free public dumps on the coast. As more and more Crown Land was sold and Hong Kong's urban area expanded, it became increasingly difficult to dump site formation debris close to its source. Conditions of sale for hillside lots contained strict regulations governing the deposition of excavated earth so that it could not be dumped on the lot, or on adjoining Crown Land, in such a way as to allow the spoil to be washed down the slopes by the rain. This often necessitated turfing and the construction of expensive retaining walls; to avoid trouble and expense, some developers resorted to illegal roadside dumping even at times when there was great demand for fill for reclamation schemes. The shortage of convenient dumping grounds grew so acute that it became a normal practice for the government to open up coastal reclamation areas as public dumps and, in the past, much of the reclamation work in Hong Kong has been, in large measure, a response to this demand for spoil disposal areas (Hudson, 1970).

The redevelopment of an existing built-up site may also require further excavation yielding more spoil but, in addition there is the debris from the demolished buildings themselves which requires disposal. Again, this is often dumped on the foreshore, sometimes making a useful contribution to land reclamation. Disasters such as war, earthquakes and catastrophic fires all too frequently boost the supply of debris. In 1851, when Hong Kong's Lower Bazaar was destroyed by a conflagration, the businesspeople of the area proposed 'that the ruins from the late fire be thrown into the sea increasing the ground available for building, as far as the rubbish will go' (Colonial Office, 1852). Four years later, in the nearby Portuguese colony of Macau, another disastrous blaze provided large quantities of debris which also found use as fill in a reclamation project (*Friend of China and Hong Kong Gazette*, 1856). Debris from Boston's great fire of 1872 and the San Francisco earthquake and fire of 1906 was dumped on the adjacent foreshores, thus contributing to reclamations in those cities (Kay, 1980; Thomas and Witts, 1971), while at the end of World War II, Belfast's reclamations, which normally used dredged fill from the Lough, received a temporary supply of landfill in the form of debris from the demolition of bombed out buildings and disused air-raid shelters (Jones, 1960).

Urban space: character and location

Site formation works, both those on dry land and those involving reclamation from the sea and other water bodies, are undertaken to create usable space for development. Of all the reasons for reclaiming land, demand for useful space is the most obvious. In the words of the Hong Kong *Annual Report* for 1963 (Hong Kong Government, 1964:1), 'land is the base of all human activity and the source of all wealth', and, despite increasing human penetration of the oceans and of outer space, this statement remains essentially true. We are land-based creatures, and even the resources of the seas must be brought to land for them to contribute to wealth creation. In Hong Kong, a spatially confined and topographically difficult territory containing a major urban centre which is expanding economically, demographically and physically, the preoccupation with land and land development is certainly understandable. Yet, around the world in many large countries including China, the USA and Australia, despite the existence of vast tracts of little developed, often unused land, the reclamation of land for urban and other types of development is widespread. This is because much of the land in those countries possesses or lacks certain qualities which bear on its value or usefulness. Relief, soil fertility, climate, mineral wealth and relative location are among the important factors which influence and impose limitations on the way in which land is used. Because, as Cressey (1955:14) succinctly expressed it, 'good unused land does not exist in China', the Chinese have long practised land reclamation, including the drainage of extensive interior lakes and wetlands and the winning of large areas from the sea particularly in estuaries, deltas and shallow bays. From ancient times, similar reclamation work has been carried out in many parts of the world, mainly to expand the area under agriculture; hence, in those places, soil fertility is a major concern. This is usually a factor of little or no importance where land is reclaimed to provide sites for building.

For urban development, land should normally be relatively level to facilitate construction and allow for convenience of access and movement within the city. The ground should be sufficiently stable to support development, especially where it is in the form of dense and massive buildings, but preferably composed of material which permits easy drainage. Of overriding importance, however, is location. The reader must look elsewhere for an account of the considerable body of theory which economists and geographers have developed in their quest for explanation of the location and distribution of human settlements and of patterns of land use within cities themselves. Suffice it to say here that a variety of factors, including the localized occurrence of resources and the patterns of trade, have led to the location of specific cities often on sites which are far from ideal for urban development. In many coastal and other waterfront cities, this has commonly encouraged reclamation, sometimes from the earliest beginnings of the settlement.

Once a settlement is established, its scale, direction and form of growth usually indicate responses to several factors, commonly reflecting interaction between physical conditions and socio-economic forces. In waterfront cities, the major physical characteristic is the water frontier, commonly perceived, incorrectly as we have seen, as a limit to urban expansion. When concentric ring models of urban places are applied to cities on the sea coast or lake shore, the circular zones of land uses or values are shown as truncated, the rings coming to an abrupt end where they reach the water's edge. Discussion of such models normally emphasizes that the rings or zones may change,

usually by an annular process of outward expansion and zonal transformation. The normal sequence of development is that it occurs first in areas most
accessible, generally nearest, to the Central Business District (CBD), moving
out to the next sites as these become 'ripe' through increasing demand and
rising property values. It is generally recognized that topographic features,
such as hills and valleys, together with major transport routes strongly
influence this process of growth, distorting the rings into lobes and wedges,
but it is usually only at the water's edge that no possibility of further
expansion is perceived except on existing land parallel to the shore.

Development does, of course, normally take place in areas and in directions
of 'least resistance', and water bodies do pose serious obstacles; but when
there is a strong demand for space for development in waterfront cities, a
common response is to meet it by land reclamation. The influence of
reclamation on urban form is discussed in detail in Chapter 8, while Chapter
10 offers a model which seeks to describe the pattern and sequence of
reclamation in the context of overall urban expansion. Reclamation for urban
development often begins with the port.

Urban space: the port

Ports by their very nature and function need waterfront sites, and port
development inevitably requires the construction of docks and associated
facilities which normally involve at least some reclamation (Bird, 1971). Much
of this work may be to render stable swampy foreshore areas, much of it to
create deepwater berths for ships. As we are here concerned with reclamation
undertaken primarily to create usable space, discussion of deepwater frontage
requirements is deferred to the next chapter.

Ports require extensive areas of both water and land space, much of the
latter being occupied by functions such as the loading, unloading, storage and
movement of cargo, and port-related office and industrial activities. Developments in shipping technologies have stimulated reclamation not only by
requiring port facilities which can accommodate larger ships and handle their
huge cargoes, but 'not least because new and highly efficient plant could be
created adjacent to the modern harbour basins which enabled low-cost raw
materials to be imported. This factor undoubtedly encouraged activities such
as steel production, aluminium smelting, chemical production and oil refining
to flourish around the coastlines of industrial nations' (Pinder and Witherick,
1990: 240). Furthermore, in most ports, the scale and nature of cargoes carried
by the new generation of ships also stimulated increased and new demands
for storage space, including tank farms. In Rotterdam, for example, over 80
per cent of the land made available for industry following the construction of
Europoort was eventually used for commodity trans-shipment and storage
rather than for processing (Pinder and Witherick, 1990).

For reasons previously discussed, many industries, not necessarily just those directly linked with port activities, need to be sited on, or close to, large water bodies. Other urban uses for which waterside locations are often preferred include recreation, tourism and residence. Where waterfront sites are especially valuable and land space is at a premium, reclamation may be all the more attractive as a means of providing space for development. Both lack of space and the high value of waterfront sites in a flourishing sea port led to early land reclamation in Port Royal Jamaica, a town which, in the seventeenth century, at no time exceeded 25 hectares in area. Founded by the English in 1655 on a small cay at the end of a long, narrow spit, Port Royal developed rapidly on its extremely restricted site forcing up building densities and rents to London levels. After 1670, merchants whose land fronted the harbour began to request and receive grants of 'shoal water' to be reclaimed 'out of the sea' for private wharf and warehouse development (Pawson and Buisseret, 1975:81).

Urban space: city expansion

The maritime origin of many cities has meant that the commercial centre or central business district (CBD) developed close to the waterfront. As the city has grown and spread inland so, often, the old city centre or downtown district has become increasingly removed from the geographical centre of the urban area, sometimes experiencing relative decline as more accessible suburban or regional centres develop. Nevertheless, high land values close to the old city centre may help to offset the cost of land reclamation and make it economically feasible to expand the CBD into the adjacent river, lake or sea. It is mainly for this reason, not for any special need to be close to the water that, in many cities, much of the CBD is built on reclaimed land.

It is not only for CBD expansion that land is reclaimed for uses having little or no need for a waterfront location. Shortage of land has encouraged reclamation for almost every kind of urban development for commercial, industrial, residential, recreational and many other uses (Figures 1.2, 4.1, 7.1, 8.1 and 8.3). This is particularly so in large cities which are expanding on difficult sites, or where there is a severe shortage of space in relation to population and economic growth. The coastal cities of Japan, a country where a population of 120,000,000 lives on an area of 377,435 square kilometres, 85 per cent of which is mountainous, exemplify this well. Here, pressures on land have encouraged reclamation for urban development for at least 400 years.

The situation in Hong Kong is very similar. The selection of the site of the original colonial settlement of Victoria in 1841 was largely determined by the potential for land reclamation on the shores of the magnificent mountain-girt harbour which attracted the British to that part of the Chinese coast (*Canton*

Register, 1841:305). An English language South China newspaper suggested that the best site for the British settlement was that opposite the Kowloon peninsula because there by 'reducing the heights of the hills and filling up the small bay with their refuse' it was possible to obtain 'the largest level space for the site of a town that can be found along the whole range of the northern shore of the island of Hong Kong' (*Canton Register*, 1842:3). A century later, the British town planner, Sir Patrick Abercrombie (1948:5), recognized the continuing need for land reclamation to solve Hong Kong's two major planning problems: 'firstly the shortage of land for any sort of urban expansion or quarter; secondly an unlimited reservoir of possible immigration'. In the final decade of the twentieth century, as the era of British colonial government comes to an end, planners in Hong Kong envisage further land reclamation on an even greater scale than before, to make room for anticipated urban expansion at densities considerably lower than those which now characterize the overcrowded city (Hong Kong Planning Department, 1991).

Urban space: land for transport

Among the many different urban uses for which land is reclaimed, transport is one of the most important. A wide range of transport related facilities is accommodated on land which, in many cases, was reclaimed specifically for the purpose. Docks and related port facilities are obvious examples, but airports, roads, railways and railway terminals, too, are very often built on reclaimed land.

Like the sea ports already discussed, airports represent the terrestial terminals of a form of transport which uses land only at the start and end of each journey or stage; but air transport, nevertheless, consumes enormous areas of land in or close to urban areas. Normally, civilian airports and many military ones, too, need to be in or close to large concentrations of population and, as we have seen, these are commonly found in coastal areas or beside major lakes and rivers. Runways and manoeuvring areas require large expanses of level ground which can often be found in coastal or alluvial plains or which may be created relatively easily and economically by reclaiming littoral wetlands and shallows (Figures 2.3 and 8.5). In areas of difficult terrain, or where existing urban development has taken up all the most suitable sites, reclamation for airport development may involve very ambitious and costly reclamation work with runways extending into deep water. Notable examples include Hong Kong's Kai Tak Airport and that built to replace it at Chek Lap Kok. Another is Kansai International Airport on an artificial island 511 hectares in area about five kilometres off the Japanese coast near Osaka where sea-wall construction and landfill operations were undertaken in water 18 metres deep (Arai *et al.*, 1992). A common advantage of reclaimed airport sites such as these is that aircraft approaches and take-offs can usually be made over unobstructed water areas. In some mountainous regions, however, particularly where the land is heavily built up, this may not always be possible, as at Kai Tak Airport where the approach to the reclaimed runway projecting into Hong Kong Harbour is often over the mountain-girt high-rise buildings of Kowloon.

Not far from Kai Tak is the site of the old Kowloon–Canton Railway Terminal, the former station and its sidings having been demolished and redeveloped for a variety of cultural uses. Adjacent to the clock tower, which is all that remains of the old railway station, is a bus station which itself adjoins the Star Ferry terminal. All of this area at the tip of Kowloon Peninsula has been reclaimed from the harbour, and it well illustrates the important role that land reclamation has made in making provision for urban transport in Hong Kong.

Not only in Hong Kong, but in cities all over the world, land has been reclaimed for railways, including tracks, stations and marshalling yards, and for road transport, including bus stations and car parks as well as the roads, themselves. Similarly, where terrain presents difficulties or land is very costly, many waterfront cities have been tempted to route new railways and by-pass roads along the edge of the adjacent river, lake, or sea-front. Often these are built on narrow strips of land reclaimed from the relatively cheaply obtained foreshore or permanently submerged areas. Too frequently, this has had the effect of cutting off the city from its waterfront, as in Toronto where up to sixteen railway tracks and extensive yards built on reclaimed land separated the downtown area from Lake Ontario.

Very different is the situation in central London where, in the nineteenth century, the Victoria Embankment was built along the Thames to accommodate surface vehicular and underground railway traffic as well as a major sewer. This project, which involved the reclamation of a strip of land from the river also provided a pleasant waterfront promenade for pedestrians. Different again is the much more recent multi-purpose reclamation seaward of Montego Bay's central area which was also undertaken largely to improve traffic conditions. Here a by-pass road was built on the reclaimed land to divert through traffic from the congested central area. The steep, rocky and largely built-up hills above Montego Bay made reclamation from the sea a more attractive means of providing a route for the by-pass road and adding space for future urban development; but it is not only Nature that imposes barriers to urban expansion.

Urban space: physical and political constraints

There are many cities where the natural setting imposes physical limitations which tend to encourage reclamation. However, in some places, it is the artificial constraint of political boundaries which make this form of urban expansion attractive to developers. Hong Kong's urban development problems have been caused largely by the steep, rugged terrain and the fragmented nature of the British Colony comprising some 200 islands and an irregular peninsula, but the small total land area of little more than 1,000 square kilometres has added greatly to the difficulties of the populous territory. In contrast, Singapore is essentially a single compact island with relatively flat and easily developed terrain, but the total land area of this city state is only 570 square kilometres, and much of its urban development has involved the reclamation of land from the sea (Wong, 1985).

Very much smaller, and severely constrained by both physical conditions and political boundaries, is Gibraltar. Little more than a precipitous limestone rock on the Mediterranean coast, this tiny colony of 6.5 square kilometres and home to some 25,000 people is politically isolated from its Spanish hinterland. Here, site formation has included quarrying and even extensive tunnelling into the rock itself to create usable space for a variety of purposes, many of them associated with the colony's military and naval functions. Fill from these excavations contributed to the reclamations which have added to Gibraltar's land area, including the extension of the airport runway and a project on the North Front during World War II (Miles, 1947).

Also on the Mediterranean coast, and probably the most extreme example of urban development constrained by political boundaries as well as by problems of a difficult site, is the principality of Monaco. With a total area of 1,188 hectares, less than two square kilometres, and a resident population of 30,000, one of Monaco's major economic development problems is lack of space. More than 20 per cent of the land area has been reclaimed from the sea, much of it in the Fontvieille district, site of a major reclamation scheme in the 1970s. Twenty years later increasing development pressures led to the resiting underground of the principality's railway station, thus releasing more land for building, but now plans are being prepared for a further major extension into the sea off Fontvieille. This may possibly take the form of a 220,000 square metre island city supported, like an offshore oil platform, on legs resting on the sea-bed (Lloyd's List, 1994).

Physical and political constraints of a different kind encouraged land reclamation in Lagos, Nigeria. Built on an insular site among mangrove swamps, this former national capital, still one of Africa's most populous cities, found itself severely constrained by the boundary which separated it from the adjacent Western Region of Nigeria. The latter political subdivision was unwilling to permit the expansion of the capital at the expense of losing some of its own territory and, partly for this reason, Lagos, in the early 1960s, undertook some ambitious reclamation schemes to accommodate urban development. Much of this new building land was created by landfill operations using sand dredged from the adjacent shallow lagoons (Adejumo, [n.d]; Peil, 1991).

Reclaimed land has provided space for a wide variety of urban and related purposes. Land uses which have been accommodated in this way include a variety of commercial, residential, industrial, defence, recreational and transport related activities as well as waste disposal sites. Solid waste disposal has long played a major role in the reclamation of littoral areas, and waste material of all kinds still provides a major source of land fill.

This chapter has already referred to the disposal of harbour dredgings on reclamation sites, a practice which puts to use otherwise often worthless waste material by creating land which can be developed for some practical purpose. In many cases, however, dredge and fill operations are planned as complementary aspects of projects designed to create land with deep water frontage.

Typically, such projects are for the construction of docks where the depth of water permits ships to berth alongside at all states of the tide. For centuries, the creation of permanent deep water frontage for this and other purposes, including the improvement of public health and environmental enhancement, has been one of the major reasons for reclaiming littoral wetlands and shallows. Continuing the analysis of the motivation for reclamation, the next chapter discusses deep water frontage and environmental and amenity improvement as reasons for reclaiming land in urban areas.

5

Deep Water and Green Waterfronts

Deep water frontage: docks and berths

Deep water frontage can be created without reclamation, just by dredging the bed or excavating into the shores or banks of the water body. London's wet dock system was formed largely by excavating land enclosed within the meanders of the lower Thames. With this method, however, there are two important disadvantages: the need to find convenient means to dispose of the excavated material, and the loss of land, which might have been used for building or other purposes, by the conversion of terrestrial space into an aquatic area.

In some ports, the depths of navigable channels have been maintained or increased by the construction of training walls or by reclaiming foreshore areas, thus effectively constricting the width of the water body and increasing the strength of the current and tidal scour. The most common methods, however, involve dredging which is very often combined with foreshore reclamation. Reclamation which extends the land to beyond the low water line ensures that there is always some depth of water on the sea-, river- or lake-front, but dredging is usually required to ensure sufficient depth at all states of the tide or however low water levels fall. The main purpose of this is to enable ships to lie alongside the quay for efficient loading and unloading. Where the process of extension into the water proceeds haphazardly, an irregular waterfront commonly results, and increased silting may occur particularly in the embayments. These can also become foul with refuse and pollutants swept in by currents and trapped in eddies and dead water. Such conditions, unwholesome as well as unfavourable for shipping, have often encouraged the affected waterfront owners to reclaim the filthy, choked foreshore, a matter to which we return later in this chapter.

With the trend for ships to increase in size and draught, and for port operation to require more space, there has been a tendency for harbour fronts to advance further and further into deeper water, often by a sequence of reclamation schemes. In old established ports, this is a process which may have extended over many centuries, often leaving, as we have seen in Chapter 1, 'tidemarks of time' in the form of historic structures, street patterns and place names.

The earliest vessels were commonly beached on the shore or strand, a practice common in many places until the nineteenth century; but, with the increase in the size of ships, special facilities such as jetties and quays were provided. Seagoing ships of ancient and medieval times normally ranged in size between 100 and 1000 tons, but much smaller vessels were common. For example, the double-ended undecked Viking merchant ships of the twelfth century, like most cargo vessels of northern Europe at that time, were craft of 50 to 80 tons. Even as late as the eighteenth century, while the typical East India Company ship was a vessel of 1000 tons, the average size of ships of that period was less than 300 tons.

Rapid developments in ship building occurred in the nineteenth century, but sailing ships did not exceed 5,000 tons. As sails were replaced by the steam engine, and, in hull construction, timber gave way first to iron and then to steel, ships increased in size very rapidly. Nevertheless, the average cargo ship of the nineteenth century did not exceed 6,000 tons, and the 18,000 ton steamship the *Great Eastern* remained the largest ship in the world for nearly fifty years. The size of passenger ships increased until the heyday of the trans-Atlantic liner in the 1930s when the *Queen Mary*, the *Queen Elizabeth*, and the *Normandie*, each over 300 metres in length, became the only liners ever to exceed 80,000 tons.

After World War II, with increasing competition from air transport, requirements of economy and efficiency necessitated the construction of smaller passenger vessels, mostly cruise ships, and by the 1970s their average size was 20,000 tons. By this time, the largest ships afloat were cargo vessels, particularly oil tankers, with hundreds exceeding 200,000 tons and many over 300,000 tons. The Japanese-built Universe class tanker which came into service in the early 1970s is of 326,000 tons deadweight. These enormous vessels are 345 metres in length with a 53 metre beam. Even larger oil tankers, of over 450,000 tons deadweight, are now in operation, and offshore mooring and servicing systems have been developed which are capable of handling all ships now built or contemplated, including vessels of 1000,000 tons deadweight.

Whereas, a century ago, ships typically had draughts of less than six metres, many of today's vessels draw fifteen metres or more, which, together with other factors relating to the changing nature of ships and shipping, has had serious implications for the location and design of port facilities. This, in turn, has encouraged dredge and fill operations and the reclamation of land from the sea, partly to provide deepwater berths and partly to create the necessary space for handling the huge quantities of cargo which modern ships carry.

Perhaps the most dramatic change occurred with the introduction of container ships in the 1950s. In many ports, long rows of finger piers fell into disuse as general cargo operations moved away from the congested city to more distant high volume container facilities which needed relatively few berths but plenty of land space adjacent to deep water.

Despite the construction of many new ports and the enormous growth in cargo volumes this century, the total number of ports has actually declined. In part, this is due to competition from improved land and air transport but, in many cases, locational or site disadvantages have made it difficult for older ports to respond to the changing demands of ship technology and economics. On the other hand, because there are relatively few ports which are accessible to very large ships, there are many more smaller vessels in service, allowing for greater flexibility in operation, particularly for general cargo. For economic reasons, however, the trend towards larger and more specialized ships is likely to continue, although environmental considerations may impose some limitations on their design (Barker, 1991; Bird, 1971; Clearwater, 1985; Couper, 1972).

Among the best known of the long-established ports which have successfully responded to technological changes in ships and shipping is Southampton. In its 1,000-year history as one of England's major ports, this city has pushed its waterfront into the Test and Itchen rivers largely to create the deepwater frontage necessary to accommodate increasingly large ships. A memorial park close to the old city walls now marks the place from which the 180 ton, 27 metre long *Mayflower* set sail for America in August 1620. It was from Southampton, too, that the *Titanic*, a passenger liner of 46,328 tons gross, set out on its ill-fated maiden voyage in 1912. Southampton was also the home port of the Cunard liners *Queen Mary* (81,000 tons) and *Queen Elizabeth* (83,000 tons). It was for huge ships such as these that the New (or Western) Docks were built, providing a water frontage 1.75 kilometres in length with a 10 metre depth of water alongside at low tide. While the construction of these port facilities, begun in 1927, was by the usual means of extensive dredging and landfill operations, Southampton was unusual in that these works were undertaken upstream from the old port rather than nearer to the open sea as is more common (Coughlan, 1979). Nevertheless, the location of the Fawley Power Station and the nearby Esso Oil Refinery near the mouth of the estuary reflects the common trend for waterfront industries which require deepwater berths for ships to be built downstream from the old port, closer to the open sea. Today, the visitor to Southampton may stand on the surviving western section of the medieval city walls and look across a large tract of reclaimed land towards the line of modern docks. The distance separating the ancient walls from the modern waterfront may be regarded as symbolic of the difference in size and draught between the little medieval sailing vessels which used to moor beneath the battlements and the twentieth-century ocean liners which made Southampton so famous.

As the case of Southampton has illustrated, reclamation undertaken to create deep water frontage inevitably yields new land space, a valuable additional benefit. Indeed, landfill projects of this kind are normally designed to meet demands for both deep water frontage and for adequate usable space adjacent to it. When port development occurs in cities where sites for development are scarce, there is even greater incentive to extend the land area into the water. This certainly has been the case with port development in Hong Kong, but even here, while pressure to reclaim has come largely from the need for building sites, records show that demand for a deep water frontage, too, has played an important role in the reclamation history of the territory.

Early nineteenth-century prints of Hong Kong suggest that quay construction by the landfill method was certainly undertaken there before its acquisition by Britain, and deep water access was seen as one of the most important advantages in the colony's earliest reclamation proposals (*Canton Register*, 1842). When the British arrived on the island, the construction of wharves and jetties did not await the implementation of a comprehensive waterfront plan, but each marine lot-holder improved his own access to deep water by extending his lot into the harbour. It was clearly to the lot holders' advantage to gain deep water frontages by reclamation which enlarged their land area rather than to sacrifice parts of their lots by excavating berths.

Despite the government declaration of 1842 that such reclamation was illegal, by 1855 most of the foreshore in front of Victoria had been reclaimed to low water mark and beyond (Tregear and Berry, 1959). Contemporary views of Hong Kong confirm that at least some of this reclamation work provided deep water berths for ships. Collinson's line drawing of Hong Kong Harbour viewed from a hill above Causeway Bay (1845) shows very clearly the artificial promontory of Jardine Matheson's wharf, at East Point, and Bruce's 'View of Jardine Matheson's' (1846) shows fairly large vessels for that time moored beside it.

The first government-sponsored comprehensive reclamation scheme to be executed was that at Bonham Strand in 1852. The primary object of this project was the orderly development of the Lower Bazaar which had been destroyed in the fire of 28 December 1851, but improved access to the harbour was also an important consideration. The provision of 'praya' with a landing place at the end of each cross street was included in the proposal (Hudson, 1978). In Hong Kong, the word 'praya' was formerly used much as the word 'embankment' is in London, to mean a waterfront or quayside road. It is derived from the Portuguese 'praia', meaning 'beach' or 'strand', probably inspired by the Praia Grande in nearby Macau.

Access to deep water was also a matter which received serious attention from the Bowring Praya Commission a few years later. Of the several reasons given in support of the Bowring Praya reclamation scheme, that of improved access to deep water for the movement of passengers and goods received the greatest attention in the commissioners' report. Another advantage of having ready access to water was the facilitation of fire-fighting in a town which had already suffered numerous disastrous conflagrations.

While the Colonial Treasurer felt that the proposals were on too large a scale, the commissioners advised the consideration of a praya even wider than the one proposed. In support of their suggestion, they quoted an 'intelligent witness' who thought that the praya should be constructed so far into the harbour as 'to enable steamers and ships to lie alongside, and passengers and goods to pass to and fro without being obliged to use boats' (Bowring Praya Commission, 1856:5).

Neither the Bowring Praya proposals nor the subsequent scheme advocated by Sir Hercules Robinson in 1863 came to fruition (Eitel, 1895). Nevertheless, an improvement to the colony's deep water berthing facilities was achieved by Governor Robinson. After the acquisition of the tip of the Kowloon Peninsula in 1860, the Governor succeeded in retaining, for commercial development and wharves, the south-western portion nearest to deep water, despite strong military and naval claims to the area (Endacott, 1964; Mayers *et al.*, 1867). Although deep water came quite close inshore on this stretch of coast, it was still found necessary to make substantial reclamations into the harbour to provide berths for large ships. This strip of waterfront was developed by the Hong Kong Wharf and Godown Company which established itself on the north side of the harbour in 1875. By this date Wanchai, site of the company's original godown (warehouse) and jetties, was suffering from progressive silting which, it was believed, had contributed to the commercial decline of the Eastern District. Here, because of the insufficient depth of water, harbourfront lots, which normally commanded much higher rents than those inland, were worth little more than inland lots (Hudson, 1970).

Landfill reclamations for wharves in Hong Kong Harbour has continued into the present century, notably for the container port facilities at sites on the north side of the harbour, and much of the extensive reclamation work envisaged in current development plans is for deep water port development (Hong Kong Planning Department, 1991).

The creation of dry land with a well-defined permanent water front in place of tidal foreshore or littoral swamp is often desirable for reasons other than port improvement, although provision of berths and channels for small boats and pleasure craft is commonly an important feature of some of these forms of development. Reclamation for high-class residential development enjoying deep water frontage (instead of an often unsightly and smelly muddy foreshore exposed at low tide) has a long history, notable examples including London's Adelphi begun in 1771, and Hong Kong's Spring Gardens, built in the 1840s. Developments such as these often had their own waterfront entrances with moorings and access steps which facilitated private transport by water. Today it is water-oriented leisure and recreation that has led to the creation of the marina and the canal estate in which residential lots offer the advantage of both a road frontage for vehicular access, and water frontage for pleasure craft.

Public health, amenity and environment

In recent decades, environmentalists have accused canal estate developers of the widespread destruction of ecologically important wetlands including mangrove forests and tidal flats, notably in the USA and Australia. For centuries, however, swamps and muddy foreshores have been commonly regarded as ugly, smelly health hazards (Mitsch and Gosselink, 1986). To a considerable degree the unsightly, foul smelling and unwholesome character which many of these areas undoubtedly possessed was due to their use as dumping grounds for all manner of filth and garbage from nearby human settlements. Reclamation was commonly suggested as a solution to this problem. Ideally, the offending area would be infilled sufficiently far into the water as to maintain a reasonable depth against the edge of the reclamation at all times, thus avoiding periodic exposure of a muddy foreshore.

The accumulation of sediments together with filth and rubbish on the waterfront was often aggravated by the irregularity of the sea-wall and the construction of piers and jetties which impaired the action of waves and currents, reducing their power to sweep away material deposited in the harbour. In early nineteenth-century America, as in Europe and elsewhere, the waterfronts of ports such as Boston, New York and San Francisco were characterized by haphazard development and frequently squalid conditions. By about 1800, Boston's Town Dock was little more than a rubbish dump and it was infilled as part of the scheme for a new market place with flanking warehouses today known as Quincy Market. In the case of nearby Back Bay, the construction of a tide mill dam exacerbated the problem of foreshore pollution, turning the area into an unsightly and stinking nuisance, thus providing one of the reasons for reclaiming the shallow inlet (Whitehill, 1975). In New York, finger piers prevented the free flow of currents, encouraging the accumulation of refuse and sewer dirt on the waterfront, and it was found more profitable to allow the rubbish and filth to remain than to remove it. Because dredging costs were as high as the selling price of a single lot, the water between Vesey and Dey Streets was allowed to fill with silt and garbage, facilitating the early nineteenth-century Washington Market development (Buttenwieser, 1987). On the Pacific coast, San Francisco's Yerba Buena Cove had nine projecting wharves by 1850, one of them nearly 300 metres in length, and these, together with a number of abandoned hulks cluttered the waterfront where sand and garbage accumulated (Vance, 1976). Here, too, reclamation from the bay, undertaken mainly for speculative purposes rather than public health and amenity reasons, soon helped to solve this particular problem (Figure 5.1).

Speculation and public health, sometimes linked in ways discussed in the next chapter, played important roles in Hong Kong's reclamation history. The unwholesome condition of the Hong Kong foreshore was due partly to the dumping of refuse, noted earlier, but perhaps more importantly to the discharge of sewage along the Victoria waterfront. The sewer outfalls terminated at or even far above low water mark so that for much of the day badly fouled mud-flats were exposed to the air. This was a major concern of Hong Kong residents during the first decades of the colony and, as early as 1843, a letter to the *Friend of China and Hong Kong Gazette* contained the suggestion that this problem should be solved by reclaiming the foreshore as far as the low water mark. Later, in 1856, supporters of the unsuccessful Bowring Praya reclamation scheme put forward as one of their arguments: 'The state of the shore, so alarming to public health' (Bowring Praya Commission, 1856:2). Other perceived causes of disease were the overcrowded condition of the city and nearby swamps, recognized as a source of malaria although the role of the mosquito which bred there was not at first understood. Reclamation was seen as a solution to these problems, too, the first by providing additional land space for better housing, the second by infilling and draining the frequently waterlogged areas (Hudson, 1970; 1978; 1979).

The suppression of mosquito-borne diseases such as malaria has long been advanced as a reason for reclaiming wetlands by drainage and landfill. In the tropical world, especially, the reclamation of mangrove swamps has often been undertaken at least partly for this reason, particularly where they lie in close proximity to urban centres as in several Caribbean islands (Hudson, 1983; 1989b).

On the West African coast, too, the reclamation of wetlands adjacent to towns and cities has been widely undertaken for the reasons already discussed, including public health. Banjul, formerly Bathurst, founded in 1807 on an island at the mouth of the Gambia River, provides a typical example. Banjula Island on which the British settlement was established, was a low, nearly deserted sandbank that was largely under water in the rainy season. Like many other tropical river-mouth swampland areas it was malarious, and urban development there contributed further to its unhealthiness. Professor Yorke, writing in the *West African Review* of 1937, compared parts of the island

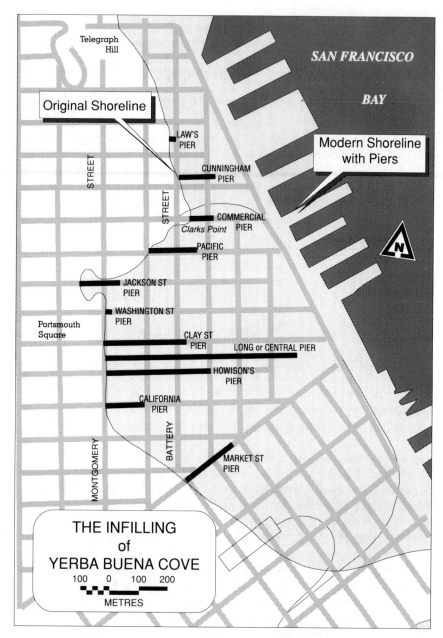

Figure 5.1 Much of downtown San Francisco stands on the site of the former Yerba Buena cove.
Source: Vance (1976)

(renamed St. Mary's Island) to 'a waterlogged sponge, floating in a sea of its own excreta' (quoted in Jarrett, 1951:105). Serious problems of drainage and ill-health remained into the second half of the twentieth century, and together with the increased pressures on land for development, these have been important reasons for reclamation works undertaken in Banjul (Jarrett, 1951).

In the latter part of the twentieth century, the tendency to regard wetlands as wastelands and sources of nuisance and disease gradually changed so that, today, these areas are widely recognized as valuable resources and essential parts of the ecosystem. Instead of seeking to convert wetlands into developable dry land by reclamation, we now try to preserve them. Increasingly, too, former wetlands are being restored and artificial ones created. Almost paradoxically, reclamation methods such as dredge and fill are often used for this environmental restoration and enhancement work. Dredged material is now widely used to restore degraded wetlands and to create artificial habitats for wild life. This is now common in the USA where wetland habitat development using dredged material includes the creation of artificial islands. Over 2,000 artificial islands are distributed throughout the USA in coastal, lacustrine and riverine areas, most the result of dredging operations by the US Army Corps of Engineers, together with some state agencies and private industry. Of various sizes and ranging in age from about fifty years to very recent, many of these islands are owned by other federal agencies, state governments, conservation organizations or private citizens. Their role as wildlife habitats is vital in many areas, particularly where natural island environments have been destroyed or greatly modified (Palermo, 1992).

Reclamation for habitat creation is similarly undertaken in other highly urbanized countries, not least in Japan where severe environmental degradation and loss of wildlife habitats have been unfortunate consequences of that country's remarkable economic growth and urban development. In Chapter 3, reference has already been made to Tokyo's Kasai Seaside Park with its artificial wetlands and islands representing a variety of habitats all on land which was reclaimed from the bay. On Tokyo Bay, there are several other artificial nature reserves established on made land, some of it reclaimed especially for the purpose, and similar projects can be found elsewhere in Japan. Hiroshima's Itsukaichi project is an interesting example which is described in Chapter 9.

Most of the artificial wildlife habitats created in highly developed areas such as the Japanese examples just mentioned are also intended to serve the related purpose of improving the urban environment for human residents by providing green open space and opportunities to observe nature. While nature was hardly a consideration in reclamation projects before the middle of this century, some of them, as we have seen, were intended to improve the urban environment by eliminating polluted foreshores and providing much needed space for orderly development. Developers have often put forward strong arguments such as these in support of reclamation schemes probably inspired more by the profit motive than by genuine concern for the public good. The following chapter, therefore, examines the important role of the real estate business in urban development involving land reclamation, often speculative schemes on a grand scale. To understand this topic properly, however, it is necessary to consider first the frequently vexed questions of title to, and jurisdiction over, the foreshore and sea-bed, areas commonly regarded as submerged real estate.

6

Submerged Real Estate

In a paper entitled 'Legal problems of tidal marshes' which focuses specifically on California and especially San Francisco Bay, Briscoe (1979:387) observes that a full treatment of this topic 'would require volumes'. Here it is possible to include only a very brief examination of ownership of and jurisdiction over submerged and reclaimed lands, particularly in relation to the role of the real estate business in advancing the urban littoral frontier. The discussion focuses on three of the places most frequently cited in this book – Teesside, the San Francisco Bay area and Hong Kong – and examines in some detail the activities of one particularly influential businessman whose speculative reclamation works have left an indelible mark on Hong Kong's cityscape.

Title and jurisdiction: the River Tees

The earliest recorded reclamations from the lower Tees and its estuary date from the eighteenth and early nineteenth centuries. The land thus gained was mostly used for farming, although the river bed reclamations of 1810 and 1831 were essentially by-products of navigational improvements achieved by cutting through the necks of the Mandale and Portrack meanders. The latter development provoked legal wranglings over ownership of the land reclaimed from the Tees involving owners of the river frontage affected by the works, the Lord of the Manor on the Yorkshire bank and the Bishop of Durham on the other (Fallows, 1878; Le Guillou, 1978).

The privately owned Tees Navigation Company, which had been formed to undertake improvements on the river, was replaced by a public body, the Tees

Conservancy Commissioners, by Acts of Parliament in 1852 and 1858. These empowered the Commissioners to restrict the navigable channel of the river to a permanent course marked by beacons or other appropriate means, to reclaim large tracts of foreshore on both sides of the estuary, and to raise the funds necessary to undertake these works. Negotiations were held with the Commissioners of the Woods and Forests, a body which claimed all reclaimed land on behalf of the Crown which, in Britain, is the ultimate owner of tidal foreshore areas. The ensuing agreement arranged for the division of ownership as follows: the Tees Conservancy Commissioners were to receive half as compensation for the expenses of reclamation, and a quarter each was awarded to the Crown and to the frontagers. Details of the reclamation schemes themselves had to be agreed with the Board of Trade and the Admiralty who were among those with interests in the development of the river (Fallows, 1878).

The Tees Conservancy Commissioners continued until 1966 when, following the 1962 report of the Rochdale Committee which recommended the formation of the National Ports Council and the creation of independent estuarial port authorities, a private Act of Parliament was passed establishing the Tees and Hartlepool Port Authority. This independent organization replaced the public body which had been responsible for operations on the lower Tees for more than a century. With the creation of the Tees and Hartlepool Port Authority the procedure for the allocation of rights to the reclaimed land remained basically unchanged. The Crown continues to receive one quarter, half goes to the Port Authority, and the remaining quarter belongs to the ancient frontagers which may include the Tees and Hartlepool Port Authority itself (Auty, 1993).

Title and jurisdiction: Hong Kong

The concept of Crown ownership of the foreshore and sea-bed was carried overseas to the British colonies. One of these, Hong Kong, is of particular interest for the way in which the nineteenth-century private frontagers challenged government authority by undertaking unauthorized reclamations and by refusing to permit the development of a continuous waterfront esplanade for public use.

The law of Hong Kong is based on that of England where the rights to the foreshore and sea-bed are vested in the Crown. This has applied to Hong Kong's coastal margins ever since the territory was acquired by Britain and, even before then, the law in this respect was not very different. In old Chinese law, the ownership of land was vested in the Emperor as representative of the State. This applied equally to land formed by marine and alluvial accretion or by artificial reclamation, and such areas had to be reported to the local officials for tax assessment (Alabaster, 1899; Jamieson, 1921; Jernigan, 1905). Artificially created land was not always declared, however, and when the British acquired the New Territories in 1898 they found that most, if not all of the agricultural areas reclaimed from the sea had probably never been reported to the Chinese government (Lockhart, 1900). In his Public Notice and Declaration of 1 May 1841, Hong Kong's first Administrator, Captain Elliot, stated clearly that land in the Colony would be allotted in accordance with 'the principles and practice of British laws', and unequivocally reserved the rights of the Crown (Elliot, 1841). This was followed in 1842 by the ruling of Elliot's successor, Sir Henry Pottinger: 'the reclaiming of land beyond high water mark, must be deemed an infringement on the Royalties of Her Majesty, and it is positively forbidden by any private person' (1842, Pottinger).

For many years, however, the situation with regard to foreshore rights in the colony remained confused, not so much because of any ambiguity in the law, but because the powerful merchants were reluctant to abide by it. The marine lot-holders were under the impression that they could proceed with reclamations from the harbour despite the pronouncements of Elliot and Pottinger. Their argument was based on the unofficial encouragement which members of the government were said to have given them, and on the terms of the first land sale in 1841 which included the statement: 'Each lot will have a sea frontage' (Morrison, 1841).

The marine lot-holders jealously held on to their supposed private rights to the waterfront and, for many years, confounded the government's attempts to construct a public praya along the front of Victoria. The government suffered major set-backs in the defeat of the Bowring Praya Bill in 1859 and in the result of the Great Praya case of 1868. It found itself responsible for the maintenance of sea-walls protecting private marine lots and yet was unable to reclaim in front of them (Eitel, 1895; Endacott, 1964). Under Governor Kennedy in the 1870s, it was the unco-operative naval and military authorities together with a temporary fall in land values in the Eastern District rather than private lot-holders' opposition which defeated government efforts to construct a praya linking Central District and Wanchai.

The long-awaited Praya west of the Naval Yard was eventually built when it suited the marine lot-holders who, under the scheme proposed in 1887, received portions of the reclamation opposite their waterfront properties. During the discussion of this proposal, the Colonial Secretary again made the government's attitude to the matter clear when he said that the Governor did not at all assent 'to the principle that marine lot-holders have a priority right to the foreshore in front of their lots' (Hong Kong Government, 1888). The Praya Reclamation Ordinance, No. 6 of 1889, reserved the absolute right of the Crown to land, foreshore and sea-bed to be reclaimed under the ordinance.

Since then, government legislation has dealt exhaustively with the problems of these rights. Now, while the Crown rights to foreshore and sea-bed are strictly reserved, provision is made for objections to proposed reclamations and for payment of compensation to those whose properties are injuriously affected by reclamation works.

All land in Hong Kong, including that below the high water mark, is vested in the Crown, and none is sold freehold. Some Crown land is disposed of by private treaty grants, especially for educational and religious purposes, and there have been many grants for various housing and welfare projects. Public utility companies, too, can obtain land by private treaty at full market value if this is essential to their particular undertaking. Such land grants and private treaties, however, though common, are by no means typical.

The general procedure in the disposal of Crown land is to hold a public auction in which the lot up for sale goes to the highest bidder as long as the offer equals or exceeds the upset price. This procedure dates from the very first land sale under the British in Hong Kong, held in June 1841, two years before the formal establishment of the colony. Shortly after this, arrangements were made for sale by private treaty, but these were suspended when further land grants were temporarily prohibited in May 1842. The principle of sale by auction was finally established by the Royal Charter and Instructions of 5 April 1843 and, to the disappointment of the earliest purchasers, who had hoped for freehold ownership of their lots, the British government ruled that, in Hong Kong, land would be sold on a leasehold basis only.

While the basic principles governing the disposal of Crown land applied equally to coastal areas which are permanently or periodically submerged, the particular importance of waterside sites to commerce and industry, and the confusion which arose in the nineteenth century over foreshore rights, led to special legislation in the form of the Foreshores and Sea Bed Ordinance of 1901.

This Ordinance empowered the Governor to grant Crown leases of foreshore and sea-bed, but demanded a special procedure in such cases. Before the lease could be granted, the terms of lease together with a description of the property had to be inserted in every ordinary issue of the *Hong Kong Government Gazette* for a period of three months and be published in Chinese by proclamation posted near the site in question. The notices also invited those who wished to object to the granting of such lease and those wishing to claim compensation for interference with access to the sea to submit their objections and claims within the three-month period. In addition, every Crown lease made under the ordinance had to specify the purposes for which the land was leased. Government reclamations and other works of a public nature over and upon Crown foreshore and sea-bed is provided for under separate legislation.

Despite some modification, the procedure for the disposal of Crown foreshore and sea-bed areas has remained broadly the same. It remains to be seen what changes in procedures may occur after Hong Kong returns to Chinese rule in 1997.

Title and jurisdiction: San Francisco Bay

As in Hong Kong, the laws of the British colonies in North America were generally based on those in England, but this was never the case in California which was under Spanish and then Mexican rule before it was acquired by the USA, becoming a state of the Union in 1850. After this, owners of land, including marshland, which had been granted by the previous Spanish and Mexican governments, required confirmation of title by a specially created board, and many established rancheros suffered from the inroads of American squatters (Briscoe, 1979; Scott, 1985).

In US cities land under water adjacent to the shore originally belonged to the state, but the history of San Francisco Bay as submerged real estate begins even before Mexico formally ceded California to its victorious northern neighbour. In March 1847, the military governor of the newly occupied territory, Brigadier General Stephen W. Kearny, granted beach and water lots in Yerba Buena Cove to the town of San Francisco. Although he probably had no authority to do so, the general gave orders for the lots to be sold by public auction, the proceeds to be used for the benefit of the town. Hundreds of lots that were completely submerged at high water were sold into private ownership under the terms of Kearny's grant, many to be reclaimed by landfill, others to be used as wharves built on piles. Even after California attained statehood, however, the validity of titles to these bay lands remained in doubt. While it was unclear whether the new state had taken possession of San Francisco Bay from the federal government, it acted as if it owned the water lots. In 1851, it granted an area of land below high water mark to the city of San Francisco for a 99-year period in return for the payment into the state treasury of 25 per cent of the income from the sale of lots. Nevertheless, the ownership of the bay lands remained an unclear and vexatious matter until 1880 when the US Supreme Court confirmed that the State of California alone had the right to dispose of bay lands, not only the intertidal shores but also wholly submerged areas (Scott, 1963).

Less than a century later, the state retained only about 50 per cent of the bay, 23 per cent having been granted to the cities and counties on its shores, and 22 per cent being claimed by private interests, although title to many areas was disputed. The federal government held the remaining five per cent (Odel, 1972). With few exceptions, submerged areas lying below 'ordinary low water mark' were never made available for private purchase and 'purported purchases of these lands are void' (Briscoe, 1979:391); but statutes enacted by the California legislature in 1850 included provisions for the sale of two legal categories of wetland. One category, 'swamp and overflowed lands' had passed from federal to state ownership under an act giving the California government the right to alienate completely such areas. 'Tidelands', a separate category of land which had become state property in consequence of California's achieving statehood, were subject to more restrictive conditions of sale. These areas could be sold but only subject to conditions which protected public interests such as access to land and use of the bay, including navigation and commerce. Problems arise because 'swamp and overflowed lands' commonly merge imperceptibly into tidal flats, and the boundary between the two areas, called in law the 'ordinary high water mark', can rarely be clearly defined. Moreover, the boundary may change by natural process or by human intervention, further complicating the legal status of the areas thus affected. In San Francisco Bay, problems are exacerbated by fragmentation of ownership and control.

San Francisco Bay, including the Sacramento – San Joaquin Delta estuary, has a total surface area of some 4,200 square kilometres. Around this huge estuary system, there are more than one hundred cities, and twelve counties; many commissions, special purpose agencies and districts have been established to help manage and regulate activities in the region. Because of the dynamic nature of a water body such as this, actions in one part can have significant effects on others, and yet there is no one multi-purpose regional government body administering the metropolis on the bay. Three regional planning bodies are responsible for preparing advisory plans for regional use, however. These are the Association of Bay Area Governments, the Sacramento Regional Planning Council of Governments, and the San Joaquin Council of Governments. In addition, there are many federal and state government regulatory and management bodies whose activities influence the use and the development of the bay and its margins. The San Francisco Estuary Project (1992a) *State of the Estuary Report* lists nine state government bodies whose work directly affects the estuary, including the San Francisco Bay Conservation and Development Commission which has responsibilities for regulating shoreline development such as new reclamations. Of the seven federal government bodies listed in the report, the US Army Corps of Engineers has a particularly powerful role in relation to reclamation because it regulates activities that affect the navigability of waterways and controls the disposal of dredged and fill material in US waters including adjacent and contiguous wetlands. Against this background of complex ownership and jurisdiction, and the poorly defined, often impermanent nature of the bay-shore, let us now consider the activities of the realtor and the speculator and their roles in the reclamation of land from San Francisco Bay.

James Vance (1964) asserted that the impact of land speculation in the shaping of American cities is more easily discernible in California than in most other parts of the USA and, in the San Francisco Bay area, this influence is well seen in the large-scale conversion of wetlands and shallows into dry land. 'In the 1850s *land* in the Bay Area was a commodity to be traded for profit fully as much as it was a site for the metropolis' (Vance 1964:16). It was the speculative value of land, 'which in early San Francisco must be defined as any area too shallow to sail a freighter across' (Vance, 1964:33), that led to the rapid sale of lots on the mud flats east of Montgomery Street, real estate which even before reclamation commanded very high prices; (Figure 5.1). Speculative pressures quickly led to the infilling of these tidal flats and other shallows off North Beach.

The state itself treated the shallow margins of the bay as real estate, selling off these areas to private interests, sometimes for as little as a dollar an acre, occasionally 'under shady circumstances' (Odell, 1972:8). Indeed, the sale of tidelands by the state was linked with many abuses. For example, some unscrupulous speculators purchased tide lots in San Francisco Bay and then tried to force owners of the abutting dry land to pay extortionate prices for mud flats in order to gain access to the bay, while in Los Angeles County the Central Pacific Railway bought up all the bay frontage at San Pedro, preventing other companies from erecting wharves there without its consent (Scott, 1963). Some conniving officials stretched the definition of 'tidelands' areas between the high and low tide marks, to include large parts of the bed of the bay covered by permanent water up to 5.5 metres in depth. This 'piece of skulduggery ... throws into question even some present-day titles to underwater lands' (Gilliam, 1969:39).

Writing in the early 1960s, before the San Francisco Bay Plan was prepared, Mel Scott (1963:27) explained how economic or psychological and political pressures, as well as physical ones threatened further reclamation of the already greatly reduced estuary:

> As land close to the centres of metropolitan activity is built upon, as orchards and vegetable fields all of fifty miles from San Francisco or Oakland give way to tract houses, space near the geographical centre, especially, becomes ever more desirable and ever scarcer: space for factories; for luxurious marina dwellings, with mooring docks just beyond wide terraces; for waterside restaurants and motels; for private as well as municipally operated small craft harbors, with related concessions and huge parking lots; for heliports and airports for private planes as well as commercial carriers. To private owners of lands in the bay and to cities holding grants from the state, the compulsion to utilize the bay for expansion is well-nigh irresistible. The private owners have visions of substantial profits; the cities, desperately seeking revenue to improve or broaden municipal services, hope to increase their tax rolls.

Today development of San Francisco Bay is much more strictly regulated, but developers continue to encroach on the water area with landfill schemes. The Bay Conservation and Development Commission, which has authority to issue permits for such projects, also has the task of monitoring the area under its control, and its annual reports record numerous cases of violations including unauthorized reclamations.

Speculation and reclamation: business and politics in Hong Kong

The profit motive and the activities of the land speculator have had their impact on Hong Kong Harbour no less than on San Francisco Bay, both areas of water having been considerably reduced since their rapid development began in the 1840s, one based on gold, the other on opium (Figures 3.1 and 6.1). The 'skullduggery' which often characterized development in the Californian boom town was equally rampant in the British colony. In Hong Kong, as in San Francisco, politics and business were often inextricably intermixed, and not all government officers were averse to using their positions to advance their own private interests. Hong Kong's Colonial Treasurer, R.M.

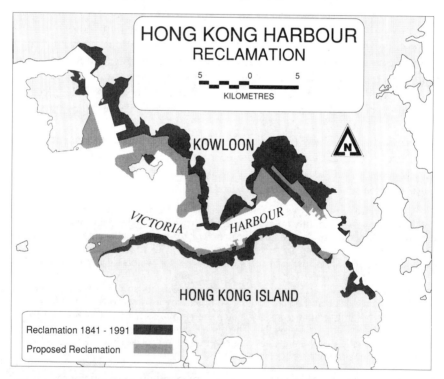

Figure 6.1 Reclamation has played a major role in Hong Kong's urban development, considerably reducing the area of the harbour and changing the configuration of the coast. This process is expected to continue into the twenty-first century.
Reproduced with permission, Hong Kong Government Information Services.

Martin, alleged that almost everyone connected with the government engaged in the buying and selling of land in the colony, and some felt that speculative dealings in land were being encouraged by official negligence in the enforcement of conditions of sale and the collection of Crown Rents (Martin, 1847; Eitel, 1895). Among those who were accused of corruptly using their official position in land development projects was Assistant Magistrate and Sheriff, Charles Holdforth, who fled to San Francisco in 1850 having made what is thought to have been a small fortune from his illegal practices in Hong Kong (Endacott, 1962).

Business opportunities in nineteenth-century Hong Kong attracted ambitious people from all over the world, among them Catchick Paul (later Sir Paul) Chater, a businessman and politician who played a major role in the promotion of two of the colony's most important reclamation schemes. The following account of Chater's activities is drawn from my published study (Hudson, 1978) which is based largely on official Hong Kong government records, notably the *Hong Kong Sessional papers, 1888*, comprising documents relating to the Praya Reclamation Scheme, and the *Sessional papers, 1904*, which include the *Praya East Reclamation Final Report* (Hong Kong Government, 1888).

Hong Kong had seen a considerable amount of reclamation from the harbour before Chater's arrival from India in 1864, but it was not until the 1880s that renewed private and government interest led to several major waterfront projects including the first of the two Praya Reclamation Schemes promoted by the Calcutta-born financier. Chater had risen from an assistant in the Bank of Hindustan to an exchange and bullion broker, then to one of the most successful real estate operators in the colony, eventually becoming a member of the Legislative Council. As a private developer, he had already been responsible for reclamations in Kowloon, Shek Tong Tsui and Kennedy Town, but he now recognized that the time was ripe to revive the scheme for a continuous reclamation along the Victoria waterfront, a goal of the Hong Kong government long frustrated by the private owners of waterfront lots. In 1887, the year of his unanimous election to the Hong Kong Legislative Council, Chater submitted his Praya Reclamation Scheme to the Acting Colonial Secretary.

Chater advocated this ambitious project mainly on the grounds of public health which, as we have seen, was a very serious problem in Hong Kong, one which many felt might be ameliorated by reclaiming the Victoria foreshore to the low water mark or beyond. For over half a century, however, the public health argument had failed to sway marine lot holders who vigorously opposed proposals for a comprehensive waterfront reclamation scheme which they claimed would interfere with their private access to the harbour.

Opposition to a comprehensive reclamation scheme for the Victoria waterfront did not abate until the 1880s, when the marine lot holders agreed to co-operate with the government in such a project. By this time, it was the lot holders themselves, led by C.P. Chater, who were urging the scheme on the government. Under the terms of the Praya Reclamation Scheme put forward by Chater, the cost of the project was to be borne by the marine lot holders. In return, they were to receive the land reclaimed from the sea in front of their properties, less the space required for public roads and open space. The public areas, including the seventy-foot (21-metre) wide praya itself, accounted for about half of the 57 acres (24 hectares) reclaimed.

Although the Praya Reclamation Scheme proposed by Chater came at a time of renewed concern about the sanitary conditions of Hong Kong and new recommendations for reclaiming the foreshores on public health grounds, there can be little doubt that private profit was the principal motive for this waterfront scheme. There is a clear connection between the Praya Reclamation Scheme and the founding by Chater of the Hong Kong Land Investment and Agency Company. The company's brief official history draws attention to the link between the two enterprises when it states that 'it is fair to assume that the idea of promoting a land investment company in Hong Kong grew out of the great interest in property development which came in 1887 with the reclamation of the foreshore between Des Voeux Road and Connaught Road in the Central District' (Hong Kong Land Investment Agency, n.d.: 6).

Chater is reported to have given up his other business in order to devote his time and attention to 'his pet scheme': the land investment organization. This and the Praya Reclamation Scheme were, apparently, complementary parts of Chater's grand plan. In the words of the company's brief history: 'Mr Chater foresaw that the development of the new land and indeed the urban areas of Hong Kong generally would call for a very substantial amount of capital and that the people who mobilise that capital should do well for themselves' (Hong Kong Land Investment Agency, n.d.: 6). It was to this end that Chater went into association with one of Hong Kong's leading business houses – Jardine, Matheson and Company – to promote the colony's largest land investment organization.

In a letter to the Acting Colonial Secretary, in which he outlined his Praya Reclamation proposal, Chater dwelt on the public advantage to be gained by the scheme and, in particular, he drew attention to 'the enormous benefit to the Public Health which would accrue from the removal of so grave a danger to the Community as that presented by the actual condition of our Praya foreshore' (Hong Kong Government, 1888).

The public health argument was little more than a facade, and the underlying profit motive is clearly revealed in the recorded discussion of the project. This is confirmed by Chater's support for the marine lot holders when, on grounds of expense, they requested a reduction in public health standards to be applied to buildings erected on the reclaimed land. One cannot but agree with the pier owners who, in 1888, thought it 'reasonable to suppose that if the value of the land reclaimed did not greatly exceed the cost of reclamation, the undertaking would never have received serious consideration' (Hong Kong Government, 1888).

By the time of his Praya Reclamation proposal, Chater had acquired some choice properties on the waterfront of Victoria's Central District. In May 1889, he owned over 100 metres of this valuable strip. The areas of the proposed reclamation assignable to the lessees of these lots under the Praya Reclamation Ordinance of 1889 amounted to 14,336 square metres in Victoria's Central District.

The government of Hong Kong, as one of the participants in the scheme, also stood to gain from the development. Apart from the anticipated profits arising from those parts of the reclamation belonging to the Crown, there were the new building sites which would be created by the excavation of earth for use as fill material, and the prospect of increased rents and rates from the large area added to the town.

But Sir William Des Voeux, who took office as Governor of Hong Kong in 1887, felt that too much of the profit from the Praya Reclamation was going into private pockets. His attempt to change the terms of the original agreement in order to obtain a larger share for the government had little effect, however. Chater thwarted the governor's efforts by successfully arguing the case for the private participants at the Colonial Office in London, and the previously agreed plan was only slightly amended.

Understandably, real estate owners involved in the Praya Reclamation Scheme wanted to be sure that the property market would not be depressed by such a large development. It was, no doubt, to reassure property owners that the Surveyor General, J.M. Price, explained how such a fall in the value of land was unlikely in view of the flow of immigrants. These were arriving from China at a rate of about 8,000 persons annually. Price pointed out that the total population of 39,000 which the reclamation was expected to accommodate was equivalent to only five years' immigration. As the project was expected to take at least five years to complete, the Surveyor General was able to give the encouraging assurance that 'notwithstanding the reclamation with its 1,320 new dwellings we shall be in precisely the same plight that we are at the present moment' (Hong Kong Government, 1888).

The estimated cost of the Praya Reclamation Scheme, nearly three million Hong Kong dollars, proved to be remarkably accurate despite the great increase in costs which occurred during the construction period. The money which the lot holders, including the government, had paid into the reclamation fund, together with the interest which had accrued on that sum, actually exceeded the total cost of the reclaimed land allotted to the participants in the scheme. The cost of the reclamation was not uniform along its length, however, and there was a slight debit balance on some sections. Nevertheless, in no section was this more than a small percentage of the original estimated cost, and the surplus refunded to lot holders on the other sections far exceeded the deficit called up.

The original estimate for the average cost of the entire scheme was about two to three Hong Kong dollars per square foot, but prices fetched for the reclaimed land in some cases exceeded the most optimistic estimates, even when adjustment is made for the fall in the value of the dollar. Before the whole scheme was actually completed, plots of land at the western end of the reclamation realized nearly nine dollars per square foot, while those in the central portions were sold for twenty dollars per square foot. Chater's 'great health reform' had proved to be very profitable indeed.

The successful promotion of the Praya Reclamation Scheme after so many abortive efforts has been largely credited to Chater. Even Governor William Des Voeux, who claimed some credit for the project, admitted that this reclamation scheme 'owed its conception to the fertile brain of Mr (now Sir P.) Chater' (Des Voeux, 1903:249). There can be no doubt that Chater's business acumen and his ability to deal tactfully with objectors to the scheme played an important part in the project's success, but the underlying reasons depended on economics rather than personalities.

While marine lot holders obtained advantage from the possession of direct private access to and from the harbour, they were likely to oppose any scheme which could interfere with their business. With the exception of Jardine, Matheson's deepwater berths at East Point, the early period of the development of the port of Hong Kong was characterized by the use of small junks and lighters to convey goods between ship and shore. Cargoes being transferred to or from the 'godowns' or warehouses in this way passed over the sea-wall or quay in front of the merchant's premises.

As ships and cargoes increased in size and sail gave way to steam, larger and more efficient port facilities were required. Godowns began to move from the central portion of the Victoria waterfront to less developed and relatively uncongested areas such as West Point and Wanchai. Meanwhile, continued immigration and the economic development of Hong Kong increased pressure on the limited space available in the city. Moreover, the Central District, where most of the original merchant premises had been established, gradually acquired the functions of a modern central business district (CBD) with its characteristically inflated property values. Thus, by the late nineteenth-century, shipping and cargo-handling practices had changed in a way which reduced the importance of direct waterfront access for businesses in the Central District, while rising land values had made the idea of reclamation there more attractive to them.

Chater recognized this opportunity. In 1887, he noted that: 'In Hong Kong, land has now attained such high values in consequence of the increased prosperity of the Colony and the influx of population, that it is now found remunerative to even reclaim sites from the sea at great expense to the owner' (Hong Kong Government 1888). It was because of this that Chater was able to convince the marine lot holders of the advantage of the Praya Reclamation Scheme.

Thus, with the consent and support of the business community, the colonial government was at last able to proceed with the comprehensive waterfront development which it had long advocated. As leader of the property owners involved in the Praya Reclamation Scheme and member of the government which implemented it, Chater was in the ideal position to pilot this large-scale property development project to its profitable conclusion.

In 1902, shortly before the completion of the Praya Reclamation, the managing directors of the Hongkong Land Investment and Agency Company formed a new organization called the Hongkong Land Reclamation Company. Shareholders in the parent company raised objections to this, but it was not until 1923 that these were finally met and the two companies' interests were merged. By this time, the Praya East Reclamation was in progress.

The idea of a continuous praya along the waterfront from West Point at the western end of the Central District to East Point at the eastern end of Wanchai had long been mooted, but the Naval authorities which occupied a section separating the two areas had been unco-operative. Nevertheless, in 1887, during the discussion of the Central Praya Project, a scheme for a separate waterfront development at Wanchai, known as Praya East Reclamation, had been mentioned. Chater advocated the scheme in 1900 and subsequently, but it was not until 1921 that the Praya East Reclamation was begun, Chater having persuaded the government to resume Morrison Hill to make it available as a source of fill material.

Although he had retired from the Legislative Council, Chater still had very great influence in the colony, and he remained a member of the Executive Council from 1896 until his death in 1926. While strongly influencing the colonial government's policy on Hong Kong's urban expansion, Chater, at the same time, made judicious speculative purchases of property in parts of the city where future developments might be expected to increase values. He was, of course, in the best position to know about the government's plans for the future of Hong Kong. Indeed, he help to formulate them. Both the Praya and the Praya East Reclamations were schemes which he had successfully urged on the government, and Chater and his land investment company prospered greatly from them.

Just as the start of the earlier Praya scheme had found Chater in possession of valuable pieces of waterfront in the Central District, so had the later development been preceded by the same man's similar speculative activity in the eastern part of the city. Much of the Wanchai waterfront property which

Chater bought for the company consisted of warehouses which, in themselves, were poor investments, for competitors in the Western District and Kowloon soon put them out of business. Chater, however, was more interested in the profits to be made from these holdings when the Praya East Reclamation Scheme received government approval and support.

Like the earlier praya development, the Praya East Scheme was a contributory enterprise under government supervision, the cost being borne by the marine frontagers including the government itself. At that time, the colony was experiencing another land boom, and during the years 1921 to 1924, the Hongkong Land Investment and Agency Company (n.d.: 13) sold large areas of land and reclamation rights in the Eastern District 'at a handsome profit'. The company's dividend rate, which in 1919 increased from seven to eight per cent, was doubled to sixteen per cent in 1924 when there was also a ten per cent bonus.

In 1924 the contractor reported that he could not carry through the work at the contract rate agreed to because Morrison Hill, from which most of the fill was being obtained, contained a much larger proportion of solid rock than had been anticipated. Subsequent strikes and economic depression further hampered the project which was eventually completed at a cost of nearly five and a half million Hong Kong dollars, more than two million dollars above the original estimate.

The completion of the scheme coincided with a slump in the property market which the development at Wanchai greatly aggravated. Rents in the colony fell on average by 25 per cent, drops of 65 per cent being recorded in some cases. The influx of Chinese refugees fleeing before the Japanese advance from 1937 onwards reversed this trend, but soon Hong Kong was to suffer destruction and depopulation under enemy occupation.

After World War II, Hong Kong was to experience its 'economic miracle', the colony's dramatic growth stimulating further large-scale reclamations. This in no way diminished the importance of the land reclaimed in Hong Kong's Central and Eastern Districts under the powerful influence of C.P. Chater. To this day, despite the enormous changes wrought by redevelopment which has replaced the original late nineteenth- and early twentieth-century buildings by modern skyscrapers, much of Hong Kong's busy central area still bears the stamp of Chater's enterprise.

As Hong Kong and other examples show, even in what are generally regarded as free-market, non-interventionist economies, the public sector may play a major role in the planning, commissioning and implementation of land reclamation. This is true of Japan, where the responsibility is dominantly that of the prefectures under the general supervision of the national Ministry of Construction. In Singapore, land reclamation is now entirely a public sector matter, the Housing and Development Board being involved in all stages, from planning to completion (Pinder and Witherick, 1990).

While institutional arrangements for the land reclamation process vary according to the economic and political systems of the countries where the developments take place, the techniques employed and the problems encountered depend more on the physical conditions, although other factors, such as economic activities, may be important, too. Reclamation methods may vary according to the level of technology available locally, but increasingly techniques are being applied globally. Indeed, there are many individual coastal engineering and reclamation companies which operate all over the world, shifting their plant and human resources to wherever there is a demand for their services.

The following chapter on techniques and problems discusses these aspects of the reclamation process in general terms, referring to specific examples as illustrations which also demonstrate changes over time and variations from place to place.

7

The Reclamation Process: Techniques and Problems

Reclamation methods

Just as the numerous specific motives for undertaking reclamation projects can be reduced to a few general reasons, so can the diverse techniques involved in reclaiming areas from the sea and other water bodies be considered as variants of two or three basic methods. As noted by Du-Plat-Taylor (1931:1), in his classic work on the subject: 'Reclamation may be defined as the conversion of marshland or foreshores into properly drained lands for any purpose, either by enclosure and drainage, or by the deposition of material thereon.' Wetlands may also be reclaimed by drainage alone, the excavation of channels often serving to lower the watertable sufficiently to create useable dry ground. In addition, natural processes of accretion along the shore may be artificially accelerated by, for example, cutting sedimentation channels, erecting groynes or planting colonizing vegetation, notably spartina grass.

On some shores, accretion has been the unintended result of human activity inland such as deforestation and poor farming methods resulting in soil erosion, and mining practices which increase the load of rivers. A notable example of the latter is provided by California where large deposits of clay and silt up to a metre thick have infilled parts of San Francisco Bay, the result of hydraulic mining in the Sierra Nevada between the mid-nineteenth and early twentieth centuries (San Francisco Estuary Project, 1992a).

In terms of total land area, most reclamation has been undertaken for pastoral and agricultural purposes for which simple drainage or, more usually, enclosure and drainage are appropriate methods. For most forms of urban development, however, the raising of levels by some type of landfill is required. Even in large areas reclaimed by empoldering, involving the construction of enclosing dikes, individual buildings and entire villages, towns and cities are usually built on artificially raised sites to provide adequate drainage and security against flooding.

The method of reclamation selected depends partly on the intended use of the new land and partly in the physical conditions of the site, including geology, landforms, depth of water, currents, tidal range and weather experienced there. Three very different examples will serve to illustrate this. Stokke Lake in Norway was an unusual case of reclamation achieved in 1906 by drainage alone. This was possible because the 400-hectare shallow water body was near the coast, the lake-bed sufficiently elevated above sea-level for the water to be drained off by gravity. To do this, a tunnel was driven through the rocky ridge which separated the lake from a nearby fjord (Du-Plat-Taylor, 1931).

In contrast, the South Pacific provides many examples of artificial islands built of coral rubble raised manually from the sea-bed to form sites for offshore villages. This practice is facilitated by the shallowness of the lagoons commonly found in that area and the presence of coral reefs which both afford protection against heavy seas and break up to form suitable material for the construction of the artificial islands using simple techniques (Parsonson, 1966).

Where a low-lying coast affords little or no natural protection, and especially where frequent severe storms whip up destructive seas that can endanger human settlements, reclamation and coastal defence usually involve formidable engineering works. Perhaps nowhere better illustrates this than the Texas city of Galveston, built on the aquatic lowlands fringing the Gulf of Mexico, a region well-known for its violent storms. The hurricane which struck Galveston on 8 September 1900 generated a storm surge estimated higher than 4.57 metres, killed more than 6,000 people and caused property damage in excess of US$25 million. At least 3,600 houses were destroyed in an area of over 600 hectares, 10,000 people of a population of 38,000 being made homeless. It was amply demonstrated that here was a littoral settlement occupying an area which had not yet been securely won from the water. This challenge was met with an extraordinary engineering scheme which not only protected Galveston with a 20.9 kilometre concrete sea-wall, but which also literally raised up the city using over eight million cubic metres of dredged sand and 3,324 cubic metres of mainland soil as fill, laid to an average depth of 2.28 metres. Over 2,000 buildings, some of them large edifices, were raised up bodily to allow for fill to be placed underneath them in a project of a kind never previously attempted in the USA, and which some prominent contractors pronounced absurd (Davis *et al.*, 1988).

A detailed technical account of engineering methods used in land reclamation is outside the scope of this book, but to understand the patterns and problems of development of cities on the shore and the environmental impacts of the reclamation process, it is necessary to have some knowledge of the various techniques employed and the circumstances in which they are used.

Where reclamation is undertaken for urban development, the landfill method is normally used. The enclosure and drainage method is generally regarded as less suitable for several reasons including the very high capital costs of dike construction and pump installations, and the recurrent costs of pumping. The maintenance of the protective dikes and the pumping equipment would be a source of constant concern, and a low-lying site prone to dampness might be a perceived, if not an actual, health hazard. Even where, as often happens, development occurs on land previously reclaimed for agriculture or other non-urban purposes by enclosure and drainage, it is usually necessary to raise levels in order to create suitable building sites, and it is common to strengthen and heighten the protective dikes as a precaution against inundation. The landfill method of reclamation permits the formation of sites which are elevated above flood levels, are self-draining and are thus more suitable for urban development. Moreover, in many cases, the excavation of material for fill creates more sites for development.

Revetments and sea-walls

While avoiding the necessity for massive dikes, the landfill method of reclamation normally involves the construction of some kind of revetment or sea-wall to retain the fill material and to provide protection against erosion (Figures 1.2 and 8.2). In sheltered waters, land may be reclaimed by dumping coarse material without a bund or revetment to retain the fill, but the seaward or riverfront face of a reclamation normally requires protection from the destructive forces of waves and currents. Furthermore, because of the low angle of rest of dumped spoil, a marginal quay wall is necessary if boats or ships are to come alongside.

To avoid unnecessary repetition, the terms 'sea', 'sea-wall', 'coast' and 'coastal' are used in the following discussion and no reference is made to river- and lake-front sites. The reader should be aware, however, that reclamation on inland waters involve similar processes although the problems tend to be generally greater in coastal areas which are affected by tides and rough seas.

Where there is no great difficulty in obtaining suitable fill material, the sea-wall is usually the most expensive item in a land reclamation project. In general, therefore, the most economic reclamation is that in which a relatively large area is enclosed by a short sea-wall. The depth of water at the reclamation site is also very important because the greater the depth the more massive the sea-wall required and the greater the amount of fill needed.

Further, the absence of large tidal fluctuations and strong currents greatly facilitates reclamation work, particularly sea-wall construction. The ideal reclamation site, then, is a sheltered, shallow bay with a narrow entrance where a short sea-wall could enclose a relatively large area. This is how most urban reclamations begin. With the growth of coastal cities, however, these readily reclaimed sites are usually soon infilled, and pressures for development not only encourage the reclamation of inlets further along the coast but also lead to landfills in deeper waters, even where the configuration of the coastline necessitates a relatively long sea-wall.

Methods of sea-wall construction vary according to site conditions and availability of building materials as well as to the purpose for which the reclamation is intended. Among the critical site factors is tidal range. A large tidal range, particularly where it generates powerful currents, can make even a modest reclamation scheme difficult. Apart from problems caused by strong tidal currents, the large rise and fall in water levels may necessitate a correspondingly high and massive sea-wall, especially where the reclamation extends to or below the original low water line. Seasonal, as well as diurnal, variations in tidal conditions may have significant effects on the reclamation work. In the past, considerable delays were incurred when it was necessary to wait for exceptionally low tides in order to work at the base of the sea-wall. There are also times when tidal currents are too strong for divers to work underwater. Nowadays, with more advanced technology for the mechanical placement of construction materials underwater and the use of specially designed concrete blocks, work on the sea-wall is less susceptible to the vagaries of the tide.

A wide variety of building materials has been used in sea-wall construction. Especially in the more distant past this has generally reflected the local geology and vegetation. In the absence of readily available suitable stone, fascines and timber revetments were commonly used, and even where stone walls were constructed, timber piles were often driven into the substratum to support them. On some urbanized alluvial coasts, large quantities of solid waste material from local industries made a cheap substitute for natural stone, slag in particular being used extensively in the construction of retaining walls in landfill reclamation schemes.

Today concrete and steel are universal building materials widely employed in sea-wall construction although stone is still commonly used, sometimes in rip-rap form, sometimes, often decoratively, as ashlar. Concrete is commonly used in sea-wall construction in the form of large pre-cast concrete blocks piled in rows one on top of another, sometimes relying on friction for their stability, sometimes designed to key into one another. Steel sheet piling is widely used in bulkhead developments where they form vertical protective edges to the landfill which they retain. Other forms of coastal protection often found in association with sea-wall construction for reclamation schemes include sloping seaward faces designed to reduce wave impact and prevent overtopping, and concrete tetrapods laid in front of the sea-wall to dissipate wave energy.

However sturdy the sea-wall itself, its stability depends on the strength of its foundations. The ideal foundation is solid bedrock or stable sand but, on many coasts, deep layers of mud or silt, commonly up to ten metres or more in depth, add to the construction difficulties. In order to avoid possible subsidence and collapse in reclamation schemes where the sea-bed is blanketed with a deep layer of soft, oozy material, the line of the sea-wall may be dredged and provided with a firm foundation of sand or other suitable fill on which the massive structure may rest.

Raising levels

Where there are no strong currents or destructive waves, infilling to raise levels may begin before the completion of the sea-wall which is to retain and protect the reclamation. If the primary object of a landfill scheme is merely the disposal of waste material the type of fill used and the dumping procedure followed are not of critical importance; but unless the reclaimed land is to remain undeveloped or is intended for some open space use, the poor quality fill or haphazard dumping will probably create problems sooner or later.

The best fill for most urban sites is material which compacts well and allows easy drainage. It should not contain substantial amounts of organic material which may decompose causing subsidence and, possibly, a methane gas hazard; neither should it be toxic and thus pose an environmental threat. Among the materials most suitable for fill are well weathered or crushed rock, sand, gravel, and some industrial wastes including slag and pulverized fly ash. Large boulders, which leave cavities between them when dumped, and silt which has a very high moisture content and often contains dangerous pollutants are generally not suitable although they have often been used as fill, sometimes causing serious problems when the reclaimed area is developed.

An ideal situation is where the reclamation site is in close proximity to the source of fill, particularly where this material is the by-product of another economic activity. In Boston, for example, the demolition of the hills on the Shawmut Peninsula to create building sites in the eighteenth and nineteenth centuries yielded gravel which made excellent fill used in reclamation work at the foot of the slopes being levelled. Similarly, the deeply weathered igneous rock material excavated in site formation work on the slopes which rise steeply from the Hong Kong shoreline has, for over a century, provided a plentiful supply of good fill used in nearby reclamations. In a very different setting, much of Teesside's iron and steel manufacturing plant was built on land reclaimed by dumping on the estuary foreshore vast quantities of slag produced by the industry itself. In many ports harbour maintenance operations can provide a practically inexhaustible source of fill which may be conveniently and economically used to reclaim adjacent foreshore areas. Unfortunately, in many places the dredgings are largely mud and silt which are not suitable for use as fill on sites intended for future urban development. Where the dredged material is gravel or sand, however, reclamation work may be greatly facilitated by the ready availability of excellent fill.

It is not always possible to rely on the supply of fill from other activities, however. Slumps in the building industry or in manufacturing may reduce the supply of fill material, and new uses may be found for by-products previously regarded as little more than waste to be disposed of as cheaply as possible. Whereas, at times, the owners of a reclamation area may be able to make money by charging for permission to dump on their site, at others they may have to pay for the supply of fill needed to complete their project.

In Hong Kong, a considerable amount of reclamation has been achieved by merely opening up parts of the foreshore as public dumping grounds under government supervision. Except during times of recession in the building industry, the provision of these facilities for the disposal of earth and rock from site formation works and debris from building demolition was normally sufficient to assure a steady supply of good fill. In another strategy, Hong Kong's colonial government long took advantage of the demand for fill in private reclamation schemes by assigning certain pieces of Crown land as borrow areas for the supply of the required earth and rock. In this way the purchasers of marine lots which required reclamation might find themselves executing site formation work for the government while in the process of bringing their own properties up to the required levels. The government, of course, benefited both from the creation of development sites on Crown land and from the reclamation of new land from the sea which would increase public revenue from rents and rates. The development of Kowloon at the beginning of the twentieth century owed much to this practice, the government often imposing conditions which specified where the fill was to be obtained and to what levels the borrow areas should be excavated. Such arrangements neatly and profitably dealt with some of the government's own site formation and spoil disposal problems (Hudson, 1970).

In the second half of the twentieth century, the scale of Hong Kong's reclamation schemes increased so much that it became no longer practicable for the government to rely on site formation work for the supply of fill, and a search began for alternative sources of suitable material for use in land fill projects. In Hong Kong today, marine sand is generally used in preference to fill derived from sources on land for several reasons. Development of Hong Kong's central urban areas has extended so far that there are now few undeveloped hillsides conveniently available for excavation of fill. Moreover, the environmental problems associated with the development of large urban borrow areas are generally unacceptable. Fortunately, hitherto unknown reserves of exploitable sand have recently been discovered beneath the sea within the territory, and marine sand has the advantage that it can be dredged, transported and placed more quickly and more economically than fill obtained from the land (Brand and Whiteside, 1990).

Transporting fill

As more distant sources of fill are exploited, transportation becomes an increasingly critical factor in the reclamation process. In the early days, fill material was normally excavated and transported to the reclamation site using large amounts of human labour, often employing carts drawn by animals to carry the heavy loads, but commonly without the assistance of wheeled vehicles. In the early years of the colony of Hong Kong, it was largely human muscle-power that transported the fill to reclamation sites, and the *China Mail* of 15 January 1852 makes an interesting reference to the type of container used in this laborious task when it records that valuable land had been won from the harbour 'by the deposit of rubbish and so many hundred buckets-full of earth from the hillside'. 'The ox cart was the normal means of conveying materials for reclamation in early Boston (Bunting, 1967:366) and, as late as 1851, Herman Melville, in his novel *Moby Dick*, referred to the selling of fill 'by the cartload, as they do the hills about Boston' (Melville, 1988:430).

Boston, however, was more innovative in the technology of transportation and land reclamation than Melville's passing reference might suggest. Claimed by some to be the first railway in America, an inclined plane was built on the western slope of Boston's Mount Vernon at the end of the eighteenth century. Its purpose was to remove material excavated from the hill during site preparation work for a new residential development and to convey it to a new reclamation scheme. Operated by gravity, the laden trucks descended to the Charles River at the foot of the hill where their loads of gravel were deposited on the foreshore to create more land for the developers (Bunting, 1967; Whitehill, 1975).

By the time of Boston's ambitious Back Bay reclamation (Figures 2.2, 2.3 and 8.1), begun in 1858, the gravel hills of the Shawmut Peninsula had been considerably reduced and mostly built over making it necessary to look further afield for fill. The developing technology of steam powered machinery solved this problem, both by facilitating the excavation and loading of fill and by providing the motive power for transporting it to Back Bay. Railway lines already crossed this shallow inlet on embankments, and trains hauled by steam locomotives were by now a common means of transport. For the Back Bay scheme, a special railway line was built connecting the reclamation site, by way of the short Charles River Railroad, with gravel pits at Needham over

14 kilometres away. The gravel was excavated and loaded into railway trucks by steam shovel, two shovels-full filling each truck, each train consisting of 35 trucks hauled by a steam locomotive. Work proceeded by day and night, about 25 gravel trains arriving at the Back Bay reclamation site during each 24-hour period (Bunting, 1967; Whitehill, 1975). A reclamation project on this huge scale would have been impossible before the railway, steam locomotive and steam shovel. A new era of reclamation had begun.

When the Back Bay reclamation was being planned, Boston had already begun to encroach on the Charles River foreshore. Nevertheless, most of the area remained sparsely developed with some residential districts on the eastern and southern shores, a few tide-powered mills, and railway tracks crossing the polluted mud-flats on embankments. Problems of transporting fill and other materials for reclamation schemes are minimal in situations such as this where the development is on the urban fringe. Things may be very much more difficult where a reclamation project is planned for a waterfront site in the heart of an existing urban area. 'How is a hill to be demolished, transported across several streets, and then dumped into the harbour?' asked the *China Mail* in an article describing the proposed Praya East Reclamation Scheme in 1921. 'Given the necessary plant and labour the first and last parts of the question present no insuperable difficulties. Not so the question of transport' (*China Mail* 1921:9). Here, in the crowded Hong Kong district of Wanchai, it was necessary to devise a transport system for the reclamation project which did not interrupt the traffic.

The solution proposed involved the construction of a special railway track which passed under the existing Praya East, a busy tram route, by making use of the Bowrington Canal that had been built to drain an earlier reclamation area in the 1850s. Unfortunately, the distance between the underside of the canal bridge and the high tide level in the channel below was insufficient to permit the passage of a laden truck. The engineer's solution was to construct the track in a concrete trough about a metre below high water under part of the bridge, allowing the canal drainage to discharge through the remaining two spans. Trucks were to be hauled to the top of the incline which passed beneath the bridge, released by the locomotive on the inland side, then coupled to another engine on the harbour side. Although part of the track would be below sea level at high tide, it was thought that shunting could be organized to minimize delay. An alternative solution to the canal route involved the use of overhead transport lines for part of the way, possibly in conjunction with the suggested canal line. The scheme eventually adopted involved the use of the Bowrington Canal route with an additional line laid along one of the cross streets. Reclamation work began by dumping spoil from hand wagons before four locomotives, 50 Decauville wagons and 100 side-tipping wagons together with rails arrived and were put into operation in 1922 (Hong Kong Government, 1922; 1923).

Across the harbour from Wanchai, the original Kai Tak reclamation involved the use of a narrow gauge railway. First intended for a residential development, Kai Tak became the site of Hong Kong's international airport, opened in 1929 and substantially enlarged by reclamation. After World War II it was evident that Hong Kong needed a much bigger airport with a longer runway capable of taking modern aircraft including the new jet airliners. The decision not to build an entirely new airport on a different site meant that this enormous engineering project, involving the extension of the runway into the harbour, had to take place in Kai Tak, an area now engulfed among some of Hong Kong's densest urban development. Again there arose the question of how to transport the large quantities of materials required to the reclamation site while minimizing disruption to city life, including traffic.

One possible method considered was a conveyor belt system, but this idea was rejected as being more expensive and less flexible than lorry haulage which had now become the normal means of transporting fill. An urgent large-scale project such as this, however, required special traffic arrangements to accommodate the heavy flow of vehicles through the built-up area. A route specially selected from the city's road system was closed to general traffic and fenced off to form an access road for the haulage of fill. Overbridges were provided to allow the passage of normal traffic underneath where two major roads crossed the route, and ten footbridges were provided for pedestrians. Just enough room was allowed between the lorry route fences and the adjacent buildings on either side to permit access for the fire brigade. At two places on the route, there were gates which were constantly attended, to enable the fire brigade to cross the road in emergencies. Lorry sizes and loads were limited to those used on normal roads. This was because of the restricted width of the access road, particularly at two right-angle bends which were only slightly widened, and because abnormally heavy vehicles might have damaged underground services such as drains and sewers. Over a period of about eighteen months between the permitted working hours of 7.30 a.m. and 10.00 p.m. with one hour's break for lunch, a total of nearly three million cubic metres of fill was hauled over three kilometres through Kowloon, laden vehicles arriving at the Kai Tak reclamation site at a rate of about one every 40 seconds. Accidents were relatively few and casualties light, the greatest problems being mud and silt on the road in wet weather and dust in fine (Henry *et al.*, 1961; Wilson, 1967).

Since that time Hong Kong's reclamation schemes have used proportionately less earth and rock derived from the hills around the harbour, sand from the sea-bed in various marine areas of the territory now being the preferred fill. Among the important advantages of this material is that it can be easily and economically transported from its source to the reclamation site. In particular, it is usually transported by water and thus avoids many of the problems associated with the haulage of fill on land, especially in heavily built-up areas.

Water transport of fill is a very old practice, rafts and barges long having been used for the purpose. Ships' ballast has also been used to reclaim land, and in many ports there are areas, former ballast dumps, which are largely composed of fill transported by sea from sources thousands of kilometres away. The most characteristic modern form of water transport of fill, however, is the pipe-line through which dredged spoil, typically mud or sand, is pumped in slurry form to the reclamation site. Excavated and raised to the surface by suction dredger, the material is then either pumped to the site directly, or, if the distance is too great, prevailing weather conditions are unsuitable, or if floating pipelines would interfere with shipping, taken by barge from which it is then pumped out through a shore delivery pipe. Flexible self-floating pipelines are sometimes used for transporting the fill material, but these are very costly, and articulated steel pipes on small pontoons are more commonly employed. Where heavy seas are a problem, a sunken pipeline on the sea-bed is one solution. Using booster pumps, dredged spoil has been transported by pipeline for distances of up to 12 kilometres, but expensive long distance pumping of fill is economical only in long-term reclamation projects (Du-Plat-Taylor, 1931; Webb and van Gulik, 1979).

The pumped dredged spoil arrives on site in slurry form and, as the water drains off leaving behind the solid fill, compaction and settlement occur at rates which depend on the type of material. With gravel and coarse sand the water drains away freely and the fill compacts well so that the site is relatively soon ready for development. With finer materials such as mud and silt very much longer waiting periods may be necessary before the site can be developed and, even then, expensive soil compaction techniques or special construction methods such as piled or raft foundations may be required.

Depositing fill

It is not only the type of fill, but the way in which it is deposited on site, which is important in land reclamation schemes. Where depths are sufficient, fill may be deposited on the sea-bed by bottom dumping from hopper barges or it may be transferred by the use of grabs. Alternatively, it may be pumped on to the reclamation site behind a retaining wall, the enclosed water area gradually being infilled by the accumulating solid material as the slurry water drains away. The pipeline outlet can be moved to direct the supply of pumped fill to where it is most required on site. Commonly, the reclamation is extended seawards by end-tipping whereby fill material arriving on site by land is dumped at the water's edge, progressively advancing the landfill area into the water. Fill may also be dumped from the enclosing sea-wall, thus enabling the reclamation to advance on two or more fronts.

Where the sea-bed is of solid rock or is formed of stable deposits of sand or gravel, these methods may proceed without difficulty, but in many reclamation areas the presence of deep layers of soft mud or silt raises serious problems. When end-tipping extends a landfill area over deposits of this kind the weight of the dumped spoil may squeeze the soft material from beneath the layer of fill forming a 'mud wave' in front. Eventually, as the reclamation is extended, the front of the landfill may advance over the mud wave and become very unstable. Consequent slippage creates an irregular intermixture of dumped spoil and bottom mud which later can lead to irregular settlement and subsidence.

It is often impracticable or uneconomical to remove the soft sea-bed deposits prior to reclamation and there are several techniques which avoid or minimize the problems where fill is deposited on top of this type of material. Special dumping procedures such as layer tipping from barges can reduce the problem. Another method involves dumping spoil on the soft sea-bed layer in a grid pattern of bunds then infilling the spaces between them. This compresses the mud fairly evenly and results in an even settlement without catastrophic collapses. Where the rate of reclamation exceeds the demand for land, in places where spoil disposal is a major reason for coastal landfill for example, it may be possible to allow long periods to elapse before developing the site. During this time, the reclaimed area can be put to temporary use such as recreation, open storage or car parking. Permanent development may not occur until several years later, after the made ground has been allowed to consolidate and settle under its own weight, helped, perhaps, by the passage of vehicles over the reclaimed area.

In situations where there is more urgent need for the reclaimed land, and especially where reclamation is extending into deeper water with thicker marine deposits, special techniques may be used to accelerate the site preparation process. Although potentially damaging to the marine environment over a wide area, the partial or complete removal of sea-bed deposits can be an effective but expensive method. It was used in Hong Kong's Kai Tak runway extension and Kwai Chung container terminal, for example, both large reclamation projects undertaken for very specific purposes with considerable time constraints imposed on the completion of the developments. Other methods which do not involve the removal of sea-bed material include preloading the reclamation fill with surcharge, and the installation of vertical drains in the marine deposits to accelerate consolidation. More recently, the use of geotextile has been found effective in reducing mud wave problems and uneven settlement, the fabric being laid on top of the soft sea-bed deposits prior to the dumping of fill. Settlement may also be accelerated by vibrocompaction, a technique involving the use of large vibrating probes applied to the made ground after the reclamation area has been infilled, prior to its development (Ng, 1991; Wong *et al.*, 1987).

Appropriate design, suitable methods and careful monitoring can minimize the problems of reclamation, but difficulties are still likely to be experienced both during the execution of a landfill project and afterwards, when the made land is developed. The excavation, transportation and deposition of fill can cause serious nuisance and environmental problems including dust and noise generation, increased water turbidity, and the disruption of traffic on both land and water. Most of these problems are of a temporary nature but, in places where reclamation is a major means of creating land for development, they may become a normal part of daily city life. Where inconvenience caused by reclamation work amounts to serious disruption of business, the often vexed question of compensation may arise. This becomes even more important where the harm to business, property values or to quality of life is permanent. Typically, in coastal reclamation schemes, this occurs where frontages are deprived of direct physical or visual access to the waterfront.

Drainage problems

Among the problems caused or exacerbated by reclamation, particularly where successive schemes extend the land area progressively further into the water, is drainage. A widening strip of level land along the coast raises the problem of maintaining sufficient fall gradients in drains and sewers. A common solution is to raise ground levels inland from the new reclamation scheme, not unusually in an area developed on land reclaimed in an earlier project. This work, involving the modification of the existing drainage system, can be very expensive. In Hong Kong's Praya East Reclamation of 1921–1930, the cost of reconstructing drainage works on the back areas, which was required to provide satisfactory gradients for the discharge of storm water and sewage into the new drains, amounted to nearly seven per cent of the cost of the entire scheme. The work entailed raising the ground floor levels of some of the old houses as well as the existing roads with all sewers and storm water drains (Anderson, 1931). The difficulties encountered in such a project, and the enormous inconvenience and dislocation caused during its execution, can be imagined.

Development problems

With the completion of reclamation, problems may not be at an end. Difficulties can arise which delay the start of development, and troubles may be encountered during and after completion of construction work on the site. Development of the first phase of Teesside's Seal Sands Reclamation, completed in 1953 after more than two decades of interrupted work, was delayed for several reasons. These included a relatively inaccessible location, lack of good deepwater frontage, and the poor load-bearing capacity of the fill which was largely silt derived from maintenance dredging operations in the Tees estuary (Hudson, 1962). Failure or delay in development may not necessarily be due to any intrinsic fault in the reclamation itself, however.

Commonly, a large reclamation scheme takes years to complete, even, as we have seen, several decades, and being a costly long-term investment, such a project can involve considerable financial risk. A speculative scheme which is launched during a land boom period may be completed at a time when prices are falling with declining demand for property. This occurred in the Praya East Project which was begun during a building boom in the early 1920s and finished, after unforeseen and costly delays, just in time for the Great Depression of the 1930s. By this time, the reclaimed area had been developed, but the properties became difficult to let and rents fell dramatically (Hudson, 1978).

Fluctuations in the property market affect all types of urban development, not only those that occur on reclaimed land, but there are problems which, if not confined to projects on landfill, are especially characteristic of them. Subsidence has already been mentioned and, although much can be done to minimize this by using appropriate landfill methods and materials, it is normal for further settlement to occur after a reclaimed area is developed, sometimes with very unfortunate results, including structural damage and drainage problems. The breakdown of organic material in landfill not only contributes to the dangers of irregular subsidence, but may also create a methane gas hazard, particularly when wells or other excavations are required in connection with development on former refuse dump sites. Wells sunk for water extraction may also contribute to the subsidence problem by lowering the water table, the imperviousness of the built-up land surface retarding the replenishment of groundwater. This is a very serious problem in some highly urbanized coastal areas such as parts of Japan where landfill rests on deep alluvial deposits.

To obviate some of the problems of development on land which has a low load-bearing capacity or is liable to subsidence, buildings are normally designed with foundations which either 'float' like rafts on top of the fill or are supported on piles which extend to the more stable substratum. Piling on landfill can have its own problems, however, particularly in old reclaimed areas where the precise nature of the fill is not known and obstacles such as unexpected boulders or even sunken ships may be encountered. In many parts of the world, there is a lack of complete records. Often, especially where reclamation was illegal, no records were kept and, sometimes, recorded information has been lost or destroyed.

Not only is the detailed composition of the old landfill frequently unknown, but sometimes long-forgotten buried structures, such as old sea-walls, hamper excavation and foundation work. In the past, when a sea-wall was to be superseded by a newer structure seawards, it was commonly dismantled, the cut stone and rubble being removed and sometimes cleaned for re-use. Nevertheless, portions of old sea-wall often remained and were swallowed up by landfill as the reclaimed area was extended further into the water. The presence of these old stone structures in the ground can hamper piling operations, and the seepage of sea water through the rubble may increase the difficulties of making deep excavations on building sites close to the water-front. In Hong Kong, for example, some major developments near the harbour have encountered groundwater levels which rose and fell with the tide, so freely did the sea water flow through the portions of old sea-wall which lay buried in the landfill (*PLA Monthly* 1960; Lumb, 1966).

Threat of earthquakes

In regions of seismic activity, the landfill which underlies buildings and the poorly consolidated deposits on which it rests make urban areas developed on reclaimed land particularly susceptible to earthquake damage. The most serious damage caused by the two major earthquakes which have struck Jamaica, in 1692 and 1907, was due to the failure of unstable ground, notably where development involved coastal landfill. In the Kingston area, much of the urban development is underlain by thick alluvial deposits, and water-logged ground lies close to the surface in several low-lying districts near the harbour (Figure 7.1). This has been the site of considerable landfill reclamation since the seventeenth century. In these circumstances, ground liquefaction whereby loose water-saturated deposits lose their shear strength, is a major earthquake hazard, and it is this which caused the dramatic destruction of Port Royal in 1692. Here the earthquake shock caused the liquefaction of the waterlogged silts, sands and gravels which underlay the flourishing port, two-thirds of which slid beneath the sea, including the waterfront area built on land reclaimed from the harbour (Pawson and Buisseret, 1975; Wright, 1976).

It is not only in coastal areas that urban development on reclaimed land may be at risk from earthquakes. In the destructive Mexico City earthquake of 1985 the most severe damage occurred in those districts built in areas formerly occupied by the waters of Lake Texcoco, now almost entirely infilled. Stratigraphically, Mexico City may be divided into three zones, each with its own characteristic superficial deposits: the very soft and wet clays typical of the ancient lake area, compact sands and silts found in the more elevated surrounding districts, and transitional deposits consisting of soft clay with lower water content interbedded with lenses of sands and gravels. It was in the west of the lake zone where firm ground lies far below the surface that the greatest damage occurred. Here the destruction was caused mainly by the filtering and amplification of the seismic waves coming from the distant epicentre, resulting in almost harmonic, long duration, high amplitude motion (Meli, 1988; Navarrete *et al.*, 1988).

Soft lacustrine, alluvial and marine deposits can amplify seismic ground motion relative to the solid bedrock, the extent of damage to the buildings depending largely on the amplitude and frequency of the shaking. Most geologists and engineers agree that for soft deposits such as mud and silt maximum amplitudes are reached at low frequencies. It is not certain, however, whether such amplification would occur during a strong earthquake because the physical structure of very soft deposits may be too weak to transmit large amounts of deformation (Josselyn and Atwater, 1982). Technical matters such as these are of the greatest importance in many large coastal cities in seismic regions where much development has occurred in areas of soft alluvial deposits, especially where these are overlain by poorly consolidated fill. Much of the research on this topic has been done in the San Francisco Bay area where citizens live under constant threat of a major earthquake, a hazard greatly increased by the extensive urban development which has involved landfill on the estuary margins.

An official report issued after the disastrous San Francisco earthquake of 1906 described its physical effects as the displacement of the earth's surface in areas which had been reclaimed from the water or swampy ground by landfill;

Figure 7.1 The satellite town of Portmore, near Kingston, Jamaica, in the early stages of development (1972). The housing estate under construction in the centre of the photograph is built on land reclaimed by the infilling of mangrove swamps near the entrance to Kingston Harbour. Just off the photograph, to the left, lies Port Royal which was destroyed by an earthquake in 1692. There are fears that recent urban developments around the harbour may also be vulnerable to seismic activity, especially where they are underlain by poorly consolidated alluvial or marine deposits (author's photo).

collapse of buildings in weak condition; fracture of underground pipes, especially in marshy or filled ground; and the outbreak of fire caused by broken gas connections and electricity wires, overturned stoves and the like. Although not understood at the time, liquefaction of sandy fill used in reclamation from the bay caused much of the earthquake damage. This not only had the direct effect of causing structural failure and collapse in streets and buildings, but also contributed to destruction by fire by rupturing water mains, thus depriving many areas of the means of extinguishing the flames (Josselyn and Atwater, 1982; McGloin, 1978).

Similar forms of destruction occurred in Japan's Great Kanto Earthquake which devastated Tokyo in 1923. The city's worst damage was in the Koto area which had developed on very soft alluvial soils between the mouths of the Ara and Sumida rivers. Here nearly 30 per cent of all the houses were demolished by the tremors and more destruction was caused by the fires which followed (Cybriwsky, 1991). More recently, in the 1995 Kobe earthquake, much of the severest damage was in the port area where development was largely on land reclaimed from Osaka Bay. Here, too, liquefaction caused ground failure and subsidence which contributed to the widespread destruction.

The metropolitan areas of Tokyo, Osaka-Kobe, San Francisco and Mexico City are among the world's greatest urban agglomerations and they, like Kingston and many more smaller centres, live in the near certainty of future severe earthquakes. Consequently, buildings today are designed and development is controlled in order to minimize the effects of earthquake damage. Even where urban development lies over soft alluvium or similar poorly consolidated deposits modern design and construction methods, though not always able to avoid damage from earthquakes, can often prevent collapse and so save life. Much of the severe damage and consequent loss of life which occurred in recent earthquake disasters resulted from construction which, because of age or default, was not up to modern standards. Nevertheless, the widespread devastation caused by the 1995 Kobe disaster has seriously undermined confidence in the capacity of modern building technology to withstand severe earthquakes. The ultimate test of the efficacy of these standards will come when the inevitable 'big one' strikes a major city on the shore.

Threat of the sea

In some low-lying coastal areas, even in places outside the regions of major seismic activity, earthquakes may bring disaster in the form of tsunamis. These sometimes huge sea waves can traverse enormous oceanic distances wreaking havoc far from the epicentres of the earthquakes which generate them. Much more common are storm surges and waves which can cause extensive coastal flooding and serious erosion. These events remind us that land·won from the sea has to be held against an enemy which never tires and, on exposed shores, massive sea defence works may be required to protect urban areas which are developed on reclaimed land.

Problems of this kind are exacerbated where coastal land is subsiding, something which can often be attributed to human activities including reclamation. Subsidence in reclaimed wetland areas may be caused by compaction resulting from the placement of fill, but other important contributors to the depression of the ground surface include lowering the water table with resultant consolidation, compaction and densification of previously saturated sediments, and oxidation of organic matter and minerals in the soil. These are factors which need to be taken into account when trying to assess and forecast sea-level rise. In the Port Adelaide estuary, for example, three-quarters of the secular rise in mean sea-level of 2.5–2.9 millimetres per year indicated by the gauge records can be attributed to land level changes which are largely due to human activity. Many of the world's historic tide gauge sites can be expected to be similarly affected and thus their data should be used with caution when attempting to draw conclusions regarding global or local eustatic sea-level changes (Belperio, 1993).

Nevertheless, despite present uncertainty regarding the so-called 'greenhouse effect' and its possible influence on the oceans, there is widespread concern about rising sea-levels and the possibility that this might accelerate as global temperatures rise. Already, many coastal cities are beginning to take precautions against this eventuality, preparing and implementing policies aimed to reduce the harmful effects of a possible sea-level rise. Apart from improving coastal defence and land drainage systems, these measures include planning policies which range from requirements for higher ground floors in new buildings to restrictions on the use of low-lying land (O'Neil, 1990; Titus, 1986). Over time, the effect of these policies on urban development could be considerable, particularly in terms of land use. For example, areas which otherwise would have been developed for residential or commercial purposes may now be restricted to open space uses such as parks and golf courses. Other uses which might be suitable in vulnerable areas include car parking and some types of storage.

The advancing sea has had significant, sometimes drastic effect on the morphology of many coastal settlements, some formerly important towns, such as medieval Dunwich and Ravenspur on England's North Sea coast, having disappeared entirely beneath the waves. In modern times, however, despite some temporary marine incursions, coastal cities have generally been able to hold the sea at bay. Indeed, as we have seen, very many settlements have made substantial advances into the sea, and this reclamation process has had a significant effect on the urban morphology of coastal cities around the world.

8

Reclamation and Urban Morphology

Reclamation shapes the city

Reclamation shapes cities in several ways. This can be simply illustrated by an Australian example which might be described as the 'squaring' of Circular Quay. When the British first settled on the shores of Port Jackson, New South Wales in 1788, the site they chose for Sydney was a small cove into which flowed a stream with a funnel-shaped mouth. The shape of the inlet was considerably modified between 1837 and 1847 when convict labour was used to reclaim over 4 hectares of mudflats and construct a curving stone sea-wall which became known as Semi-Circular Quay. In the 1850s, the quay was extended over the stream, the Tank Stream as it was called, connecting with Campbell's Wharf, and it was about this time that the name Circular Quay came into use (Andersons, 1988). Remodelling of the quay between 1903 and the 1950s gradually straightened the arc of the sea-wall, creating the roughly rectangular shape we see today, 'but the old name of Circular Quay remains in use, a romantic misnomer' (Stephensen, 1966:139).

The most obvious morphological impact of reclamation on a city, then, is to alter the configuration of the waterfront and to increase the urban area. Buttenwieser (1987) notes that, because of landfill, Manhattan south of City Hall is today 33 per cent larger than when the Dutch bargained with the Indians for possession of the island, but landfill wrought an even greater transformation in Boston (Figures 2.2, 2.3 and 8.1). According to Drake (1972) the Massachusetts city had trebled its initial area by reclamation. He estimated the area of the original peninsula site as 253 hectares, but others have put the figure higher, up to 400 hectares or more, depending, no doubt, on where the line is drawn between land and water on maps of the early seventeenth-century coast. Whitehill (1975:4) is rather more cautious when he states: 'To visualize the limits of Boston in 1630, one must imagine away considerably more than half the land that appears on a modern map.'

In the case of Hong Kong, a landform analysis indicates that 3,698 hectares, or 3.4 per cent of the colony's total area, may be described as 'reclamation' (Styles and Hansen, 1989:29), but this refers to the whole territory, not just the urban parts. At the end of the 1980s, it was estimated that reclaimed land represented some 24 per cent of developed terrain within the territory, a proportion which is likely to increase as reclamation continues at an increasing rate (Styles and Hansen, 1989:97). Several of Hong Kong's post-war towns, such as Tsuen Wan-Kwai Chung (Figures 8.2 and 8.3), Sha Tin and Tuen Mun, have been built largely on land which was reclaimed from the sea for that purpose. Other parts of these urban areas were developed on sites created by hillside excavations yielding fill used in the reclamation work.

While much of the downtown and other city 'core' areas have developed on reclaimed land in many urban centres, elsewhere it is often not the city proper

Figure 8.1 The Charles River, Boston, viewed from the Prudential Center. In the foreground is part of the Back Bay district developed on land reclaimed during the second half of the nineteenth century. On the other side of the river lies Cambridge where the waterfront is occupied by the Massachusetts Institute of Technology, also built on reclaimed land. This portion of the Charles River was tidal until the construction of a dam in 1910 excluded the harbour tides (author's photo).

which has expanded by reclamation but related developments such as industrial areas, docks and airports. This is particularly true of Teesside where some 95 per cent of the intertidal mudflats, an area of about 2,000 hectares, has been reclaimed, mostly for industrial and related port development (Evans, 1990a), but where Middlesbrough and its satellites are built on land which was not previously submerged. The reclaimed areas of the Tees estuary represent about 14 per cent of the non-agricultural land in the county of Cleveland, together forming an extensive tract used mainly for industry. This is comparable in size to the built up area of Stockton-on-Tees, a town of over 170,000 people.

The direction of urban growth by reclamation and its consequent effect on the physical shape of the city depends largely on the site of the original settlement and its position in relation to the water. For reasons discussed in Chapter 7, reclamations are generally more readily undertaken in shallow, sheltered inlets; hence settlements on bays tend to advance into the water between the two protecting headlands as in early Auckland (Figures 1.1 and 1.2). Settlements on promontories or peninsulas tend to expand into the bays on each side, as in the case of Boston (Figures 2.2 and 2.3). With the growth of large towns and cities along the littoral, the urban waterfront commonly embraces a variety of landforms including bays, peninsulas and even islands,

Figure 8.2 The reclamation of Gin Drinker's Bay, Hong Kong, in 1967. In the foreground, hills are being terraced to create building sites and to provide fill material, while the bay below is being infilled behind an enclosing sea-wall. Hong Kong Island can be seen at the top left of the photograph (author's photo).

as in Hong Kong, Bombay and Rio de Janeiro (Figures 1.3 and 6.1). In this way, the city not only increases its area at the expense of the water, but alters the shape of its water boundary, often completely transforming the original configuration of the shoreline.

While it is normal for rivers and streams to enter the sea by debouching into bays, estuaries and deltas must be regarded as distinct types of site for urban development. Unlike small rivers and streams which can be put into underground culverts and built over like London's Fleet River and Sydney's Tank Stream, large rivers with estuaries or deltas are in themselves considerable bodies of water which normally remain as surface streams albeit often much modified by training and reclamation. Hence, they remain significant barriers to development and major influences on urban morphology.

In the case of estuaries, reclamation normally extends the urban area downstream, frequently on both sides of the inlet as it typically widens towards the sea. Very commonly, reclaimed areas correspond largely to former intertidal foreshore areas, including mud- and sand-banks, the deeper channels usually being preserved for river discharge, tidal flows and navigation. In deltas, too, it is generally the lobe-like intertidal mud- and sand-banks which are first reclaimed, a process which is often little more than the artificial acceleration of natural geomorphic processes. Normally, the earliest

Figure 8.3 This photograph was taken in 1993 from the same spot and in the same direction as that in Figure 8.2. In the intervening quarter of a century, the satellite city of Kwai Chung has developed on the reclaimed land and terraced hillsides. The hills of Hong Kong Island are obscured by haze (author's photo).

reclamations in estuarine and deltaic areas are for agricultural or pastoral purposes but, in many places, fish ponds or salt pans are the first uses to which these converted wetlands are put. Urban development may spread on to these areas later, usually requiring the raising of levels to create sites suitable for building.

A similar process has occurred in the two most celebrated canal cities of Europe – Amsterdam and Venice – both created where rivers enter shallow coastal lagoons formed behind offshore sandbar islands. Venice and the other island towns of the Venetian Lagoon reflect in their general outline the original patterns of the muddy islands and tidal creeks on which the first inhabitants established their homes probably about AD 400. When fishing, salt production and limited agriculture gave way to trade as the dominant economic activity, the rise of Venice as a wealthy commercial centre led to the conversion of the half-tamed wilderness of marshy islands into urban streets, squares and canals lined with splendid buildings. Reclamation involved the deepening of the channels and the deposition of the excavated material on the low-lying islands to raise their levels; hence the present form of the multi-insular city with its intricate pattern of winding canals dominated by the inverted S-shape of the Grand Canal. Examined in detail, most of the canals are seen to be in the form of a series of straight segments following a generally curved alignment. Similarly, the Venetian waterfront, though character-istically curvilinear in general outline, mostly comprises innumerable stret-ches of straight embankments and sea-walls. The urban morphology of Venice, then, preserves much of the original overall pattern of islands and channels, but the natural curvilinear forms of nature have been modified as the land areas have been consolidated and expanded, and the channels deepened and narrowed. In more recent times, some of the canals have been infilled, and the street name element, 'Rio Terra', generally signifies the site of a former canal.

Amsterdam's urban morphology is very different from that of Venice, the Dutch city's very artificial arrangement of concentric semi-circular canals contrasting sharply with the more natural reticulated pattern of waterways found in the Italian city. The form of Venice is largely determined by the original system of channels in the Lagoon. That of Amsterdam derives from a more drastic alteration of the natural pattern of drainage, being a classic example of the 'dike and dam' settlement described by Burke (1956). The two cities have much in common: the dredging of canals and the use of fill to raise levels behind retaining walls; the extensive use of piles driven into the ground to support buildings; and waterways which serve both as drains and streets. Unlike Venice, however, Amsterdam does not have an insular site, and its expansion has taken place in the form of concentric rings created by dividing the Amstel River and diverting the bifurcations around the city. The semi-circular extensions are defined by a series of encircling canals which served the additional function of defence as well as means of draining the marshy site and of transport. The insular site of Venice gave it a good natural defensive position, but Hazlitt (1900) notes that, in 1339, the Puncta Luporum, a headland on the opposite shore, was cut away to increase the width of the channel separating the city from the mainland. The soil thus obtained was used for embanking and levelling.

Other canal cities established in wetland areas include the eighteenth-century Russian capital, St Petersburg, and Bangkok, similarly founded in the sixteenth century and enlarged when it became the Thai capital in the late eighteenth century. In recent years, many of Bangkok's 'klongs' or canals have been infilled, being replaced by roads as the motor vehicle increases its dominance over city transport formerly carried largely on the waterway system. In Tokyo, also, many of the old canals have been filled in, but their influence on the modern city can still be traced in the pattern of highways and parks, the clockwise spiral of former inner city moats being largely preserved in the roads round the Imperial Palace (Cybriwsky, 1991). Early Tokyo, or Edo as it was then called, developed in a way which closely resembled that of Venice and Amsterdam, its excavated canals providing fill which was used to raise the level of land between them (Mogi, 1966). Other Japanese cities, too, expanded into the sea in this way, much of the urban development occurring on artificial islands separated by canals crossed by numerous bridges. A map of Osaka published in 1707 illustrates this, the pattern of developed islands and canals apparently a modification of the natural arrangement of sand-banks and channels still to be seen on the seaward side of the city (Zusho, 1707).

The more recent artificial islands and channels which characterize Japanese ports such as Tokyo, Yokohama and Osaka, are generally larger and more rectilinear in outline than their precursors, a reflection of the greater control over nature which modern technology bestows (Figures 8.4 and 8.5). Venice, too, clearly displays the differences which the advance of time and technology have impressed on the artificial landforms and urban morphology in cities that have developed on reclaimed land. A glance at the recent map of Venice reveals the contrast between the more organic reticulated forms of the ancient parts and the obviously artificial rectilinear outlines of the later additions. The latter include the reclaimed areas associated with the railway terminal and adjacent modern docks, and the residential Sacca Fisola. Not all modern canal and artificial island developments are characterized by rectilinearity and lack of reticulation, however. The residential canal estates so typical of the Florida and Queensland coasts display innumerable variations of the interdigitated dendritic or trellis patterned street and canal systems. While the layout of these developments commonly breaks away from the regular grid which often characterizes the street plan of adjacent urban areas, in most cases, these littoral landforms can be easily recognized as artificial by their 'unnatural' shapes and regularity.

Anthropogenic coasts

Artificial littoral landforms are by no means confined to urban areas, but even those formed by reclamation for agricultural purposes are usually found in areas of dense human settlement such as The Netherlands and the China

Figure 8.4 Tokyo Bay is an excellent example of an anthropogenic coast. Here the coastal plain has been enlarged by reclamation and many artificial islands created. *Source*: Pinder and Witherick, 1990.

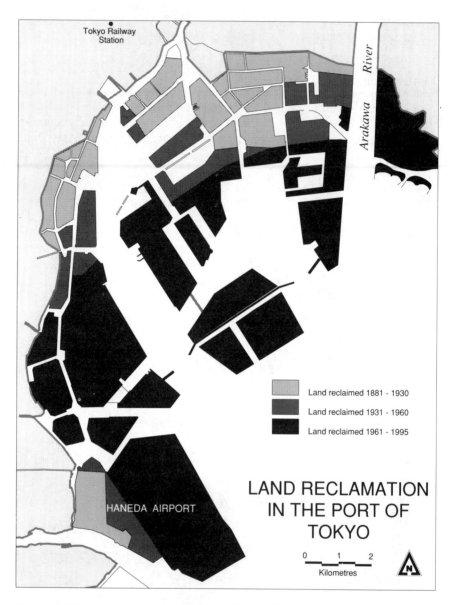

Figure 8.5 The geometric shapes which typify coastal landforms created by reclamation are clearly seen in this map of the Port of Tokyo. The two artificial islands east of the Arakawa rivermouth are examples of the more natural forms which characterize some recent reclamations.
Source: Bureau of Port and Harbour of the Tokyo Metropolitan Government.

coast. These polderlands contain many substantial villages and towns (Wagret, 1968). It is in highly urbanized areas, however that anthropogenic coasts achieve their most advanced forms of development (Hudson, 1980).

No longer is human modification of shores and coasts confined to small details. Today whole estuaries, large bays and considerable lengths of coastline bear the characteristic stamp of human modification in the form of extensions of land in a variety of configurations. In the Tees estuary very little remains of the original shore and its once extensive tidal flats save the 130-hectare remnant of the Seal Sands now under the protection of English Nature. The river, which formerly entered the North Sea through several winding and shifting courses, is now confined to one straighter permanent channel, a relatively narrow ribbon of water where a century ago the high tide inundated a tract of sand banks and mudflats up to five kilometres across (Figure 9.1).

The scale of change has been much more dramatic in San Francisco Bay, reduced in area by about 600 square kilometres in little over a century (Figure 3.1). While this encroachment on the bay has inevitably altered the configuration of the shore, the distinctive pattern of human modification of the coastline is nowhere more pronounced than in Tokyo Bay (Figure 8.4). Here, most of the 170-kilometre coast comprises geometrically shaped artificial landforms including coastal plains of made land and rectilinear peninsulas and islands separated by angular channels. Similar anthropogenic coasts occur on other highly urbanized parts of the Japanese coast and elsewhere in the world, especially in the more developed regions. On the Dutch coast, well known for its agricultural polders, much reclamation has been carried out for urban uses, including the huge development of Europoort near Rotterdam. On the coast of California, not only in San Francisco Bay, but other major ports have made extensions into the sea. Notable among these are San Diego, where the resort and marina areas of Shelter Island and Harbor Island were created by dumping harbour dredgings, and Los Angeles whose port, San Pedro, has advanced over 6 kilometres into the ocean.

Internal structure: patterns of streets and lots

The creation of large areas of urban land by reclamation, though now more commonly achieved by single massive schemes, has in the past been mainly the result of sequential developments. Each new reclamation made an addition to the urban waterfront land in a gradual process which has often left its distinctive mark on the physical form and layout of the city as described in Chapter 1. Here, the influence of the reclamation process on the internal structure and form of the city is considered in more detail with particular reference to the pattern of streets and lots.

Rural settlements in areas of reclaimed land generally reflect, in their distribution and morphology, patterns of artificial landforms associated with embanking and drainage. In the Low Countries of North-west Europe and on the alluvial margins of the China Sea coast, for example, settlements commonly take advantage of the better drained and relatively flood-free sites afforded by dikes and embankments; hence the typically pronounced linearity of the Dutch dike towns (Burke, 1956) and their equivalents in other parts of the world. The use of the tops of dikes for roads, across often muddy terrain, further encouraged linear development along them, and the importance of canals transport as well as drainage has had a similar influence on the growth of settlements which commonly became very elongated and attenuated. The use of main drainage channels as transportation routes strongly influenced rural settlement pattern on land reclaimed from Japan's Kojima Bay where houses were built in a dispersed fashion along the canals (Eyre, 1956). Here, as is common in reclaimed areas, the pattern of development displays a marked rectilinearity.

In creating new rural landscapes as well as cities, normally 'man works with regular squared and geometric forms unless nature diverts him from his straight path' (Abercrombie, 1959:20), and this pattern is often preserved in the subsequent street and lot layout when such an area becomes urbanized. This can be well seen on the coast of Guyana where the early Dutch colonists applied their traditional knowledge and skills and used African slave labour in the tropical swamps to create elongated rectangular polders for plantation agriculture (Daly, 1975; Rodney, 1981). The Guyanese capital, Georgetown, is of British and French origin, but the landscape in which it developed is largely a Dutch colonial creation, one which had a marked influence on the layout of the town. As Georgetown grew from the late eighteenth-century nucleus of Stabroek on the Demerara River front, it absorbed the surrounding sugar plantations. The rectilinear property boundaries defined by the enclosing embankments, and the grid system of drainage canals are largely preserved in the street plan of modern Georgetown which developed by the subdivision of the original long narrow blocks extending inland from the river and ocean fronts.

An interesting variant of this type of development is seen in New Orleans where, like Georgetown, the street pattern predates urban development to the period of sugar plantations when property lines, and often field lines, extended back from the river at right angles to the levee. Here, the only good land in the swampy deltaic environment was the better drained natural levee, and the value of the land beside the Mississippi was further enhanced by the property owners' need to have access to the river for transport. Away from the river, land values fell to almost nothing in the back swamp. In response to this situation, the three-kilometre band of natural levee was divided into narrow strips, the long lots laid out at right angles to the riverfront. Because New

Orleans developed within a meander of the Mississippi, the strips of land here were not parallel but converged in a fan-like pattern. As in Georgetown, these lot lines were reinforced by the excavation of drainage channels along the boundaries, and with subsequent urban development main streets were often put along property lines following the banks of the canals. As open drains in an urban development, these water courses commonly became smelly nuisances and were later lined with concrete then eventually covered to form wide boulevards. Intersecting the radial roads are cross streets built in concentric curves roughly parallel to the river in sections of straight tangents allowing the formation of piecemeal grids within the overall web-like pattern. The typical wedge shape of New Orleans city blocks is largely a consequence of the fan–like radial pattern of streets but, in places, it is caused where grid layouts do not accord exactly with old property lines (Lewis, 1976).

In like manner, many Japanese cities have expanded over former agricultural land which was reclaimed by drainage. Here, too, features and patterns of the old rural landscape often survive in the urban fabric which replaces it. Most obvious are the canals and embankments, the former being preserved for drainage and transportation purposes within areas converted to urban use. This is well seen in Tokyo, east of the Sumida River, where the original earth levees and embankments often remained, some of them being reconstructed after the urban development of the area in response to the threat of flooding (Mogi, 1966).

The ever-present threat of inundation in dike-protected polders encouraged those who live within such low-lying areas to raise their dwellings, sometimes on piles, often on artificial platforms of earth. Subsequent urban development usually requires raising levels on a large scale, often using fill material brought in from considerable distances. Nevertheless, former agricultural polders, now built up, often lie at a markedly lower level than other districts of the city of which they are part. Normally, of course, land slopes upwards on the inland edge of the old reclamation areas, the original shoreline; but, in many urbanized areas, newer land on fill seawards of the former polders is considerably higher, too.

Hiroshima, on the delta of the Ohta River, exemplifies this well (Figure 1.4). Between 1589, when the building of Hiroshima Castle was begun, and 1911 about 18 square kilometres of land were reclaimed by drainage; between 1912 and 1984 over 32 square kilometres were added to this by landfill reclamations which extended the delta southwards into the deeper water of Hiroshima Bay (Hori, 1984). Reclamation by landfill has continued, and while many of the older parts of the city remain at or only slightly above normal sea-level, some of the newer areas have developed on twentieth-century reclamations on the seaward side where the made land is generally two or three metres higher. Hence there is a general rise in land levels from some of the important residential and commercial areas of the city to the major industrial zones and new urban developments to the south. Protected by dikes, the low-lying areas of the city, which developed on early reclamations, have remained vulnerable to inundation, especially during typhoons, and work is under way on strengthening and heightening the river embankments.

The boundary between parts of Hiroshima reclaimed by drainage and those won from the sea by landfill can usually be distinguished quite easily, particularly where it is crossed by streets which often show a marked break of slope. Irregular subsidence of the landfill has given the surface of some of the more recently reclaimed areas a slightly undulating character and, in places, the foundations of buildings have been exposed as the surrounding levels have sunk. For some buildings, additional steps have had to be added to provide access where entrances now stand awkwardly high above the road level.

In some of the older areas of Hiroshima, streets are built along old dikes and side streets and alleys slope down from them in a fashion reminiscent of the better-known examples in Amsterdam. Burke (1956) has drawn attention to the fact that the streets on the old dikes of Warmoesstraat and the Nieuwendijk are much higher than the surrounding streets. 'The narrow lanes which cross them were formerly field paths leading up from the marshy meadows, and it is noticeable that those approaching the steeper dike, the Nieuwendijk, do not meet it at right angles, but at such an angle as to secure an easier ascent across the slope from the meadows' (Burke, 1956:141). Here patterns of an early medieval rural polder landscape survive in a seventeenth-century townscape which has been preserved as part of twentieth-century Amsterdam.

The growth of modern Amsterdam and other Dutch cities has involved the conversion to urban uses of large areas of former agricultural polderland, and raising of levels with fill, mainly sand. The landfill method of reclamation is usual where the intended use of the site is urban. Hence the expansion of towns and cities into large water bodies rather than into areas already reclaimed for non-urban purposes has generally involved depositing fill directly on to the natural wetland margins, shores and beds of the adjacent sea, lake or river. Starting in places reached only by the highest tides or exceptional floods, the advance of the urban littoral frontier pushes the waterfront into progressively deeper water, often in a sequence of projects which may span decades, even centuries. In many cities, the original shore-line and the subsequent positions of the waterfront established by later reclamations can be traced in the modern street plan. As we have seen, the names of the streets often remind us of their former waterfront positions, but this is by no means always so. The names of Hong Kong's Queens Road, on the original shoreline, and Des Voeux and Connaught Roads, both along the lines of former waterfronts created by subsequent reclamation, reveal nothing of their origins apart from a hint of their approximate dates. Similarly, nothing in the name of Boston's Beacon Street suggests that its Back Bay section is built on the line of the former Mill Dam which once cut off the inlet from the Charles River.

The layout of streets and lots in reclaimed portions of cities may not be noticeably different from that in other parts of the same urban area. Where the level surface or gentle slope of a natural coastal plain gradually merges with the flat extension created by reclamation, the street pattern is not likely to change significantly at the boundary of the made land area. Indeed, in some cases, the pattern of streets already established on dry land may be continued in the water even before reclamation is completed. In Guayaquil, for example, the grid layout of streets and lots is extended into the un-reclaimed tidal flats by the squatters who build their flimsy dwellings on piles, linked by a grid system of light timber catwalks which establishes the future street pattern (Crooke, 1971).

Similarly, in early San Francisco, the grid pattern of streets established on the land beside the bay was extended seawards as Yerba Buena Cove was reclaimed for urban development. Here the two different grids, on different axes, which were laid out on either side of Market Street, were both continued on land reclaimed from the bay (Figure 5.1). As in San Francisco, the grid system of streets in Auckland's central business district is imposed equally on level and steeply sloping land, in areas that have been reclaimed from the sea and in others which were dry land from the start. True, some details of downtown Auckland's street pattern, notably the curve of Fort Street, reflect the original position of the shore and the subsequent history of reclamation, but within the rectangle defined by Quay, Nelson, Wellesley and Princes Streets variations in the predominantly rectilinear grid pattern usually relate to factors other than reclamation. There is no essential difference in layout between those areas developed on reclaimed land and those which are not (Figure 1.1).

The same cannot be said of Hong Kong. Here, most of the level land in the city is reclaimed and the streets of this area are generally laid out in a series of rectilinear grids, the main roads roughly parallel to the coast. In contrast, urban development on the precipitous slopes above has taken place along sinuous roads which tend to follow the contours as far as possible. Never-theless, in Hong Kong, too, the strong tendency for humans to impose regular geometric patterns on the landscape, even where nature appears to dis-courage this, has led to the development of grid systems of streets on many of the lower slopes immediately adjacent to the reclaimed areas. Hence the boundary between those parts of the city which are on reclaimed land and those which are not cannot be distinguished precisely by an examination of the street map. It is often very obvious on the ground, however. Whereas streets on the reclaimed land are all quite level, many of those immediately inland rise very steeply, especially where the layout is a strict rectilinear grid.

In some places, these streets take the form of long flights of steps such as the appropriately named Ladder Street.

In Boston, where over half of the city is built on reclaimed land, the overall street pattern varies considerably, but this does not appear to have much to do with the three and a half century history of reclamation except in some of the more detailed features. The old town expanded from its nucleus beside the Town Dock, long since infilled. As it grew, Boston spread in all directions, covering the original Shawmut Peninsula and the surrounding reclaimed mudflats and shallows with an irregular spider's web pattern of streets. Eighteenth- and nineteenth-century extensions were generally laid out in the regular rectilinear grids typical of their periods, but these were applied without obvious variation to natural and made land alike. On Beacon Hill, for example, the grid of elegant streets laid out in the late eighteenth and early nineteenth centuries extended without noticeable changes onto the land below which was reclaimed from the Charles River.

The much more regular grid and larger blocks of the northern portion of Back Bay distinguish this major reclamation area, but its standard rectilinear layout, more typical of other US cities than of Boston, is mainly a reflection of the influence of the state government on this particular section of the former tidal inlet (Kennedy, 1992). Back Bay is worth closer examination for the way it illustrates how significant variations in layout can develop within areas of reclaimed land. While most of the former bay is laid out on the rectilinear grid pattern, marked variations in the direction of streets and sizes of blocks are evident. The grain of the northern part of Back Bay was set by Beacon Street which here became the successor to the road built across the Mill Dam. The main streets of this area were built parallel to this, with the broad Commonwealth Avenue forming the major axis (Figure 8.1). Further south, however, the orderly development of Back Bay was complicated by the presence of two railway lines. These crossed the shallow inlet and fringing marshes on embankments which intersected in the form of a St Andrew's cross, strongly influencing the street pattern which developed in this part of Boston during the second half of the nineteenth century. 'South of Boylston Street the railway lines not only prevented any symmetrical continuation of Back Bay streets, but created a dreary kind of no man's land that was unconducive to handsome treatment' (Whitehill, 1975:158). This triangular 'no man's land' formed by the intersection of two differently oriented grids has since been redeveloped. Formerly devoted mainly to railway yards, most of this area is now occupied by the high rise Prudential Center development, 'a windy world of its own where one can work or shop, live briefly or permanently' (Whitehill, 1975:225). For a detailed discussion of the evolution of the layout of Back Bay, the reader is referred to Bainbridge Bunting's (1967) *Houses of Boston's Back Bay*, especially Chapter 8, 'The Back Bay area as an example of city planning'.

For very different reasons, interesting variations in urban layout developed on reclaimed land in Hong Kong. Particularly noticeable is the contrast between the city blocks on the north side of Queens Road where the first reclamations were made, and those on the seaward side of them which developed on later reclamations (Figure 8.6). The older blocks are typically narrower than the later ones and their long axes are oriented differently. The width of the early waterfront lots was determined by the original conditions of sale, each parcel of land having 'a sea frontage of 100 feet, nearly' (Morrison, 1841). Their length is the result of uncontrolled and mainly illegal reclamation carried out by private lot holders who thus more than doubled the original area of their properties between 1841 and 1855 (Eitel, 1895). Because of the importance of trade and shipping in Hong Kong, land beside the harbour attracted most economic activity, and waterfront lots were in great demand, commanding the very highest prices. Waterfront lots, therefore, tended to be narrower than those elsewhere, and the high price of land in this location encouraged owners to expand by reclaiming the foreshore of the harbour, thus also gaining better access to deep water.

In this way, there developed a coastal strip of reclaimed land divided into elongated narrow blocks typically separated by even narrower lanes, generally oriented with their long axes roughly at right angles to the waterfront. Some of the blocks diverge from the normal rectangular form, however, often tending to be wedge-shaped. Comparison of the modern street and city block layout with old maps of Hong Kong suggests that this pattern reflects minor irregularities of the original shoreline to which boundary lines were drawn roughly at right angles. As those lots which were on convex stretches of coast advanced further into the harbour, their water frontages tended to increase because their side boundaries diverged seawards. Conversely, those on concavities of the coastline would tend to lose frontage as their boundaries converged towards the harbour, a situation likely to have caused inconvenience and complaint.

The later reclamations – the two comprehensive Praya schemes promoted by Paul Chater – were undertaken between 1887 and 1930, after the main port activities of Hong Kong had moved away from the central districts to less congested, less expensive sites that could better accommodate the increased size of ships and their cargoes (Chiu, 1973). By this time, water frontage was less important in the city centre and the emphasis was on the maximization of use of building space consistent with adequate traffic circulation. For this reason, the new areas were laid out with larger building blocks served by a well-spaced regular grid of wide roads. The main streets were built parallel to the waterfront facilitating communication between the eastern and western portions of the city, but the presence of a military base and naval dockyard between Central District and Wanchai continued to be a hindrance to east–

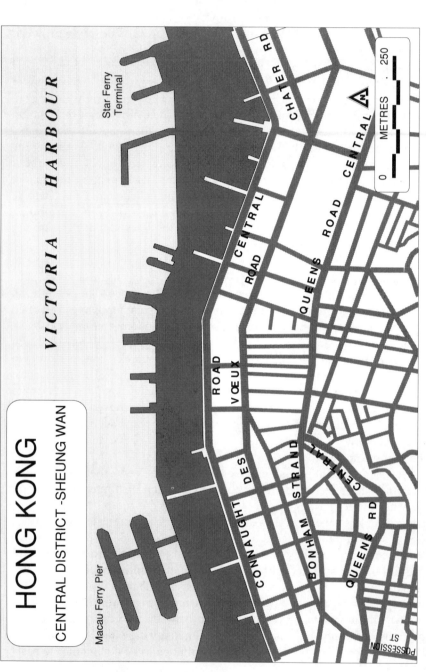

Figure 8.6 Part of Hong Kong's central business district showing variations in the street pattern. Queens Road marks the approximate line of the original shore. The area indicated by the dark tone was reclaimed between 1914 and 1970.

west traffic movement until the 1960s when the government acquired part of the site for highway construction.

Site formation

Hong Kong's Praya and Praya East Reclamations transformed the city, not only by enlarging the level coastal strip to accommodate new urban development, but also by the excavations which yielded the necessary fill, at the same time creating more level sites for building. This is a process which had been going on since the very beginning of the colony and which had already levelled several hills that formerly overlooked the harbour. Much of the fill for the Praya East Reclamation came from Morrison Hill, a remnant of which survived for many years because its hard, rocky core was unsuitable for use as landfill material. Today, only the name of the hill and a circular pattern of roads on its levelled site remind us of the former landmark.

After World War II similar cut and fill reclamation projects continued on an even larger scale, especially in Hong Kong's New Territories where the sites of several new towns were formed in this way. Hence the reclamation process in Hong Kong, including the excavation of fill, has had a major impact on the physical features of the territory and the topography of the urban areas (Figure 8.2).

Reclamation projects using the cut and fill method have modified the physical landscape in many urban areas apart from Hong Kong. Although it is a technique which became increasingly effective, first with the application of steam power, later with the use of more modern machinery, remarkable feats were achieved with much simpler technology. The flat topography of Tokyo's Kanda district was formed by the removal of a hill in the early seventeenth century, the material obtained from the excavation being used to infill part of Tokyo Bay. In this way, building sites were created for the expanding city both inland and seawards, a process which continues to this day (Cybriwsky, 1911; Mogi, 1966). At about the same time, Boston, a much younger and then more primitive settlement than the Shogun's city, began to transform its natural topography by a process in which 'the tops of hills have literally been taken off to fill the valleys and coves' (Whitehill, 1975:2). Consequently, the site of Boston is not only much larger but is also much flatter than it was before reclamation and associated excavation began to alter its topography. Boston's early European settlers named the hills which formerly dominated the Shawmut Peninsula, Trimountain or Tremont because of their three prominent summits, Mount Vernon, Pemberton Hill and Beacon Hill. Of these, only a decapitated remnant of the latter survives, shorn of about 18 metres of its original height. These hills and two smaller ones, Fort Hill and Copp's Hill, were all levelled to create building sites and provide gravel for use as fill in nearby reclamation schemes.

By the same process, offshore islands such as Castle Island and Deer Island in Boston Harbour became joined to the mainland, something which has occurred in many coastal cities. Salman Rushdie (1982:92) recalls the time 'when Bombay was a dumbbell-shaped island ... when Mazagoan and Worli, Matunga and Mahim, Salsette and Coluba were islands, too. In short, before reclamation' which converted the original archipelago with its fishing villages into an urbanized peninsula, the core of one of the world's largest cities (Figure 1.3).

Reclamation, urban morphology and environment

Around the world, reclamation has been a major influence on the morphology of cities large and small where patterns of streets and lots commonly reflect this widespread process. The effects of reclamation and associated works are often clearly seen in the size and shape of the developed area, and in the modified relief of the site on the original land as well as on that won from the water.

In recent decades, the scale of reclamation and associated excavation and dredging for fill has increased enormously with consequent impact on the environment. Writing in the early 1960s, when environmental awareness in the USA was just beginning to grow, Mel Scott (1963) illustrated the threat to San Francisco Bay and the surrounding area with a discussion of landfill proposals for one of the counties on the shore. At that time, there were plans for San Mateo County which, if executed, would involve the development of 60 square kilometres along 42 kilometres of shoreline. The estimated amount of fill required for these huge works was expected to rise from about 25 million cubic metres between 1962 and 1970 to 185 million cubic metres in the last decade of the century. The latter figure alone was 'equivalent to a mass of earth two square miles in area and 100 feet high' (Scott, 1963:29) (over five square kilometres in area and more than 30 metres high).

One possible source of fill considered for the proposed San Mateo reclamation schemes was the San Bruno Mountains which were near enough to the shore to facilitate earth haul transportation, possibly involving a conveyor-belt system. Thus, with the serious possibility that the San Bruno Mountains might be cut down and dumped into San Francisco Bay, there was a threat to both a scenic inland recreation area and an extensive tract of the already much diminished natural harbour. The protests and opposition to these proposals were part of the now celebrated struggle to save San Francisco Bay which played a pioneer role in the environmental movement of the 1960s and 1970s.

Concern about the environmental consequences of land reclamation was largely related to the growing awareness of the ecological value of wetlands and coastal waters whose degradation and destruction by dredging, landfill and pollution were beginning to provoke public outrage. Damage to littoral ecosystems, the hydrological effects and other potentially detrimental consequences of reclamation are matters considered in the following chapter.

9

Reclamation and the Environment

Opposition to reclamation schemes is by no means new. The nineteenth-century Hong Kong waterfront lot holders who frustrated government reclamation projects and the seventeenth-century fishermen, fowlers and reed-cutters who sabotaged drainage works in the Fens were probably not the first of their kind to take a strong stance against threats to their livelihood posed by reclamation. Similar opposition is voiced today. In the north Queensland city of Cairns, for example, plans for a reclamation scheme in front of the Esplanade have been opposed by owners of sea-front properties and by others more concerned about its possible detrimental effects on local fisheries (Hudson, 1989a). In Australia, as elsewhere, however, while individuals, small groups and companies may still be moved to oppose what they perceive as threats to their private interests, it is a growing public concern for the environment which has made the conservation of wetlands and littoral areas a major national and international issue.

Reclamation impacts on the environment in many different ways, including, as we have seen, the modification of the physical landscape by conversion of aquatic areas into dry land and by excavation and dredging for fill, operations which drastically alter topography. The ecological consequences of these works include the destruction of aquatic ecosystems directly affected by reclamation and the less direct but often very serious environmental effects felt over much wider areas. Other effects include the reduction in area and volume of water bodies, and changes in the characteristics and behaviour of waves and currents which can have serious consequences for navigation and coastal protection as well as pollution. These and other changes brought about by reclamation are commonly detrimental to the scientific and amenity values of the sea, lakes, rivers and wetlands, including aesthetic quality and recreational opportunities. All of these matters are linked with the ecological health of the aquatic environment, and it is to the impact of reclamation on ecosystems that our discussion now turns.

Littoral ecosystems

Reclamation is undertaken most readily in shallow waters and areas of periodic inundation, commonly in estuaries and sheltered bays. Here, it is the littoral wetlands which are most likely to be reclaimed, and these areas are generally the first to be infilled before extensions are made into deeper water (Figure 7.1). Definitions of wetlands vary according to the objectives and field of interest of the user (Mitsch and Gosselink, 1986). For our purpose, it should suffice to note that 'wetlands are lands transitional between terrestrial and aquatic systems where the water table is usually at or near the surface or the land is covered by shallow water' (Cowardin *et al.*, 1979, cited in Mitsch and Gosselink, 1986:18), and that the term embraces a variety of ecosystems including permanently and periodically inundated swamps, mud flats and marshes of all types, some of them in freshwater, others in tidal salt water environments.

Formerly widely regarded as unpleasant, even sinister and forbidding wastelands, wetlands have acquired a new popular image since the 1960s, largely through the work of ecologists and conservationists. An extensive wetland literature at both the technical scientific and popular levels has now made widely known the important ecological functions and values of wetlands and here it will suffice to mention briefly some of the main points, drawing partly on summaries which I have published elsewhere (Hudson, 1974, 1983, 1989a).

Wetlands provide major habitats for a wide variety of flora and fauna, including birds, mammals, reptiles and amphibians but especially fish and shellfish. Today, most commercial and recreational fishermen are probably aware of the vital role of wetlands as fish habitats, breeding grounds and nurseries. Writing particularly of North America, Mitsch and Gosselink (1986) note that about two-thirds of the fish and shellfish species that are harvested commercially are associated with wetlands as are over half of the US total of threatened or endangered fish species. Throughout the world, many species of fish spend at least part of their lives in coastal wetlands, and other valuable marine creatures go through their entire life cycles there. The large quantities of organic matter generated in wetlands, particularly among the extensive root system of mangrove forests, form a rich protected substrate in which a variety of organisms live. These serve as a food base for marine flora and fauna, some of which, crabs and oysters for instance, may be directly harvestable. While some commercially important fish live in the wetlands, many more spend part of their life cycle there, especially for breeding and spawning and during early growth. Many other salt-water fish are indirectly dependent on coastal wetlands which produce nutrients on which they feed out at sea. Wetlands are thus valuable as 'sources, sinks, and transformers of a multitude of chemical, biological and genetic materials', and their function as natural processors of waste products have earned them their description as 'the kidneys of the landscape' (Mitch and Gosselink, 1986:3).

All this gives some idea of the enormous ecological damage which is caused by reclamation, especially when it involves landfill for urban development. The term 'fill' is applied to several forms of artificial extension into water bodies, all of which have serious consequences for the aquatic environment. The San Francisco Bay Conservation and Development Commission (1987) has published a brief inventory of the environmental impacts of fills of different types which it may be useful to summarize here.

Floating fill is designed to float at all or most states of the water level, and includes floating breakwaters, pedestrian walkways on floats, dry docks, boat docks, historic ships and other vessels moored for extended periods. These structures and vessels block sunlight, thereby reducing photosynthesis and eliminating aquatic plants. They also reduce wave energy which can increase the rate of siltation and affect tidal circulation and currents, and reduce oxygen exchange by decreasing the amount of water surface area available.

Submerged fills include the underwater placement of dredged materials, storm water outfall pipes, pipelines, rip-rap, breakwaters and some public access facilities such as tidal stairs and boat launching ramps. Fill of this type can cause changes in substrate which can significantly affect the number and type of benthic organisms living in an area. By creating underwater mounds and other submerged structures they affect water volume, circulation and currents thus possibly affecting the rate of sedimentation. Rip-rap, bulkheads and breakwaters alter the natural processes of shoreline erosion and accretion.

Pile-supported fills are structures supported above water on piles, including the piles themselves. They include wharves, piers, board walks, bridges and a variety of buildings which project out over the water on piles. The adverse environmental impacts of pile-supported fill are generally similar to those of floating fill, including the displacement and disruption of existing benthic communities. By creating shade, pile-supported fill can affect water and soil temperatures, thus influencing an area's plant and animal communities, while animal use of an area affected by this type of fill can be disrupted. The piles dampen wave energy and create eddies which may alter water circulation and increase the rate of sedimentation.

Most of the reclamations undertaken for urban development involve landfill or the use of earth fills. These are solid fills placed in aquatic areas to create dry land and more than any other type of fill they can have drastic effects on the natural environment. Most obvious is the destruction of fish and wildlife habitats and the disruption of the ecological balance of a water body and its environs. The diminution of water surface area and volume reduces a water body's ability to moderate the local climate, including the generation of sea and land breezes, thus increasing the possibility of air pollution. Similarly, a water body, reduced by reclamation, may lose its capacity to maintain adequate oxygen levels and assimilate waste, adversely affecting the ecology and contributing to problems of water pollution. The latter may be further exacerbated in marine inlets such as estuaries when reclamation significantly reduces the tidal prism that flushes out wastes.

Hydrology and hydraulics

The maintenance of water quality is one of the functions of wetlands which act as filters for run-off. They trap silt brought down by rivers and, on many coasts, their destruction has led to increased marine turbidity. In some tropical and sub-tropical areas, this has caused the destruction of coral reefs which thrive only in clear water and which are important sources of sand for many beaches. The deterioration of protective reefs, and the depletion of sand supply, increase the threat of marine erosion so that the chain effects of a reclamation scheme may include ecological damage and coastal erosion. This can more than offset the gain of land for development. Similarly, the reclamation of inland water bodies – such as lakes, river margins and fresh-water wetlands – reduces their ability to moderate rainfall run-off and river flows, making water supply more erratic and increasing flood problems.

In enclosed bodies of water (such as lakes, estuaries and bays) reclamation, particularly where it involves the loss of extensive shallows and fringing wetlands, can have serious effects on the character and behaviour of waves and currents. A reduction in the area of an enclosed water body may reduce wave amplitude by shortening fetch, but constriction of channels by reclamation tends to amplify waves and tides and increase current velocities. Sometimes, the increased scouring caused by accelerated flows has the beneficial effect of reducing silting in navigation channels but, equally, there may be harmful erosion, and dangerous currents and waves may jeopardize ships and other craft. By changing the configuration of the shoreline, reclamation can not only divert current flows but may also alter wave refraction patterns, possibly resulting in the concentration of wave energy on some shores. Furthermore, coastal reclamation, by removing extensive areas of shallow water and littoral vegetation which are capable of absorbing and dissipating the force of storm waves, can increase the destructive power of rough seas. Reclamation does not necessarily increase the velocity of currents and heights of waves, however, and the extension of land into the sea or other aquatic area can create areas of stagnant water which may have undesirable consequences such as silting and pollution.

Amenity

Water pollution does serious ecological damage, often with unfortunate economic consequences such as the destruction of fisheries. Commonly, harmful pollution effects are most noticeable when they detract from the amenity values of the shore and adjacent waters, by triggering offensive algal blooms and fouling beaches, for example. It is not only through pollution that the amenities of the riverside, lakeside, and seaside may be damaged by reclamation. All over the world, land reclamation has played a major role in the reduction of the aesthetic, recreational and scientific value of the shore. Reclamation has destroyed thousands of kilometres of natural coastline, much of it of very high landscape quality; it has buried beaches and infilled inlets formerly used for recreational purposes including bathing, boating and fishing, and it has degraded and obliterated wetlands formerly enjoyed by naturalists.

Development involving reclamation commonly reduces public access to the waterfront although, in recent years, much greater attention has been given to the provisions for public amenity when planning new waterfront projects. Indeed, as we noted in Chapter 3, the latter part of the twentieth century has seen a revolutionary change in attitude towards the use and abuse of the environment, one which has led to a greater concern for the management and conservation of wetlands, littoral areas and even the seas themselves. To illustrate the way in which this heightened awareness and change in outlook has been reflected in management policies and practices, the following section discusses three areas where land reclamation has had a major environmental impact: San Francisco Bay, Teesside and Japan's Inland Sea.

San Francisco Bay: conservation and development

As we have seen (Chapter 3), the San Francisco Bay campaign was a milestone in the modern conservation movement, and much has been achieved since the early 1960s when reclamation threatened to reduce the Bay to little more than a channel. Although human activities of many kinds were having adverse effects on the San Francisco Bay environment, 'More than anything else, the threat of a Bay fill galvanized public opinion' (Wilmar, 1982:100).

Reduced from its original 1,760 square kilometres to about 1,000 square kilometres by the mid 1960s, the Bay was shrinking at an accelerating rate as development pressures encouraged further diking and filling (Figure 3.1). The

Bay was especially vulnerable for several reasons including physical characteristics which facilitated reclamation, notably the shelter afforded by its enclosed natural setting and its shallowness, about two-thirds of it less than 3.5 metres deep at low tide. Among the human factors which contributed to the Bay's physical decline were its fragmented ownership and control, and apathy which reflected a long-held perception of the Bay as real estate (see Chapter 6).

In an atmosphere of awakening environmental awareness this changed dramatically, and growing public concern became channelled into an organized force: the Save San Francisco Bay Association. This put pressure on the California Legislature which responded first by establishing a temporary San Francisco Bay Conservation Study Commission that recommended the setting up of a permanent planning body to control development of the Bay. In the face of bitter opposition from local as well as state government sources, the San Francisco Bay Conservation and Development Commission (BCDC) was created in 1965: 'Its primary objective ... to prevent unneeded filling of the Bay' (San Francisco Bay Conservation and Development Commission, 1992?).

It should be noted that the BCDC was not established to put a complete halt to reclamation, and in its *San Francisco Bay Plan* of 1969 are listed six categories of what is termed 'justifiable filling'. Three of these relate to making provision for sea, air and land transport, two to recreation and amenity development, and one to creating sites for waterfront industry. Filling for these specified uses will be approved if deemed to be in the public interest and where the same benefits cannot be achieved equally well without filling or by appropriate siting elsewhere. Projects which may receive favourable consideration by the BCDC include port terminals needed to meet the requirements of modern shipping technology, airport terminals and runways, and new freeway routes constructed on piles, not solid fill. Other acceptable water-related uses are industrial developments requiring access to shipping channels for transportation of raw materials or manufactured products, and developments which provide new recreational opportunities, wildlife refuges, improved public access to the waterfront, or aesthetic enhancement of the shoreline.

The aim is clearly to provide for necessary and appropriate development in a way that minimizes damage to the Bay environment; and to this end the BCDC has developed a mitigation policy which it has applied since 1974 in an effort to lessen the impacts of approved Bay fill projects. When granting a fill permit, therefore, the BCDC imposes conditions which may include a mitigation programme in accordance with the following established policy:

1. Benefits from the mitigation should be commensurate with the adverse impacts on the resources of the Bay, and consist of providing area and enhancement resulting in characteristics and values similar to the characteristics and values affected.

2. The mitigation should be at the fill project site or as close as possible.
3. The mitigation measures should be planned and controlled to assure their long-term success and permanence.
4. The mitigation should, as far as possible, be provided concurrently with those parts of the project causing adverse impacts.
5. All affected local, state and federal agencies should be involved in developing each mitigation programme to ensure that it satisfies the policies of all agencies concerned.

(San Francisco Bay Conservation and Development Commission, 1987; 1988).

Mitigation requirements vary according to the nature of the development and the type of fill used, but they typically involve removal of existing fill at the project site or the creation or enhancement of tidal marsh equal or greater in size to the proposed fill area. There is also provision for contributing funds on a pro-rata basis to a mitigation bank where the amount of the contribution is directly related to the cost of acquiring, restoring, monitoring, and maintaining an area as tidal wetland habitat (San Francisco Bay Conservation and Development Commission, 1987). In consequence of mitigation, San Francisco Bay is now slightly larger than it was before the establishment of the BCDC. Between 1970 and 1992, new surface area added to the Bay has exceeded that lost to new fill by a little over three square kilometres (San Francisco Bay Conservation and Development Commission, 1993). Where the required work has been carried out adequately, most mitigation programmes have been successful in creating and enhancing Bay resources ranging from increasing the Bay's surface area and tidal prism to creating diverse wetland plant and animal communities. Nevertheless, tideland restoration involves considerable uncertainty and risk, and levels of success have varied. Reasons for this include difficulty in identifying and acquiring suitable tidal restoration sites and incomplete execution of the stipulated mitigation work (San Francisco Bay Conservation and Development Commission, 1988).

In 1974 the California Legislature directed BCDC to prepare a protection plan for the marshes around Suisun Bay which is connected to San Francisco Bay by the Carquinez Strait and, in 1977, the Commission's authority was extended to include the conservation of this, the largest remaining contiguous wetland in California. These marshes were an important addition to the area under the control of the BCDC whose work has greatly reduced the loss of tidal wetlands along and immediately adjacent to the shore San Francisco Bay and its Suisun Bay extension.

Nevertheless, wetland losses continue. Considerable areas of wetland away from the present shore remain outside the BCDC's jurisdiction, and seasonal and riparian wetlands in particular are under threat from development. Projected urban expansion in the estuary basin could affect at least 1,400 hectares of wetlands and 4,000 hectares of stream corridor, although mitigation could offset some of the losses. Most of the region's urban expansion is expected to occur upstream of the Carquinez Strait, but there will be considerable development around much of San Francisco Bay as well, much of it involving the loss of wetland. Many highway projects, airport expansion schemes, and residential, commercial and industrial developments which are now proposed involve the use of fill and consequent loss of wetlands (San Francisco Estuary Project, 1992a).

The lack of a comprehensive approach to the environmental problems of the San Francisco Bay estuary system and its basin has long been a matter of grave concern. Recognizing this, in 1986 the Regional Administrator of the US Environmental Protection Agency's office in San Francisco called together elected officials along with representatives of agriculture, industry, environmental groups, user organizations and government agencies to begin to address these problems. This was the origin of what came to be called the San Francisco Estuary Project, part of the US National Estuary Program launched in 1987 to provide US$60 million in federal funding over a five-year period 'for developing comprehensive plans to address the environmental problems facing the Nation's most significant bays, sounds, and harbors' (San Francisco Estuary Project, 1992a:xiii). Included in the San Francisco Bay Estuary Project area was the 4,000 square kilometre Sacramento–San Joaquin Delta through which flows 90 per cent of all fresh water entering the Bay.

Whereas the BCDC *San Francisco Bay Plan* of 1969 was largely concerned with the use of the shore and loss of water surface area and wetlands through reclamation, the *Comprehensive Conservation and Management Plan for the Bay and Delta* (CCMP) submitted by the San Francisco Estuary Project participants is much broader in scope.

> The CCMP is a blueprint for restoring and maintaining the chemical, physical and biological integrity of the Bay and Delta. It seeks to achieve high standards of water quality, to maintain a balanced indigenous population of fish, shellfish and wildlife, to support recreational activities, and to protect the beneficial uses of the Estuary (San Francisco Estuary Project, 1992b:3).

The CCMP was approved by Pete Wilson, Governor of California, and Carol Browner, US Environmental Protection Agency Administrator, in late 1993, after which an Implementation Committee was established. This committee 'convened three geographic subcommittees to oversee implementation on a regional basis: the South Bay, North Bay, and Delta geographic subcommittees. The purpose of these subcommittees is to involve the local players and government officials and to determine a strategy to implement CCMP actions on a local basis. Membership in these subcommittees is open to any interested party' (Sokolov, 1995).

Environmental awareness and conservationist policies came in time to save much that is of great value in San Francisco Bay's natural environment. One reason was its great size which meant that, despite the depredations of well over a century, the ecosystem was not yet destroyed beyond redemption and that considerable remnants of its diverse natural environment survived. Comprising the 3,000 square kilometre Sacramento–San Joaquin Delta and the 1,238 square kilometre San Francisco Bay, the Bay/Delta estuary is the largest estuary on the west coast of North and South America. San Francisco Bay is also one of the largest and most beautiful harbours in the world. An important reason for the early and relatively successful popular movement to save the Bay was probably because it was a highly valued resource possessing qualities of romance and charisma (Odell, 1972). This could not be said of the Tees estuary.

Teesside: nature–industry partnership

The estuary of the River Tees, on England's North Sea coast, is small by world standards. Originally some 30 square kilometres in area, it is now reduced to little more than a channel 300 to 500 metres wide, with over 90 per cent of the formerly extensive tidal marshes and mudflats reclaimed (Figure 9.1). Heavily

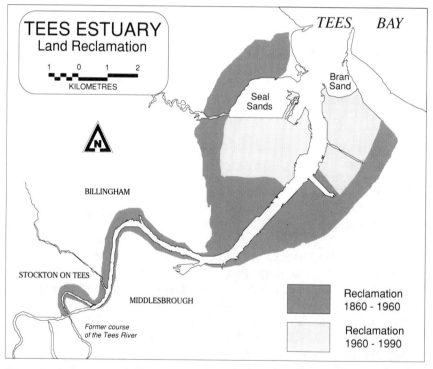

Figure 9.1 With the urban development of Teesside since the mid-nineteenth century, reclamation has transformed the estuary of the Tees. Most of the reclaimed land is used for industry and port facilities.
Source: House and Fullerton (1960), Tees and Hartlepool Port Authority.

industrialized for over a century, by the 1970s the lower Tees had become 'grossly polluted' and 'visually repulsive' (Porter, 1973:1). Nevertheless, the Tees estuary has been identified as a site of 'international importance' under the Ramsar/Cagliari Convention for the conservation of wetlands which was ratified by the British government in 1976. It is particularly important for its populations of waterfowl and is notable for the remarkable recolonization of the industrial estuary by an animal species which had become extinct there: the common seal (Evans, 1990b; Wilson and Jackson, 1990). It is this animal, once numerous in the estuary, which gave its name to the Seal Sands, a formerly extensive intertidal area which has played a prominent role in the environmental and reclamation history of the Tees.

The earliest recorded reclamation on the Tees estuary shore dates from about 1723 when embankments were made enclosing part of the West Coatham Marsh for pasture. This was followed by other reclamation schemes, including one begun in 1777 by Sir James Lowther which ended disastrously when a storm destroyed the unfinished embankment (Le Guillou, 1978; Pattenden, 1990). At this time, there were probably about 2,400 hectares of intertidal land at the mouth of the Tees (Davidson, 1980), and it was not until the nineteenth century that the estuary environment began to undergo major transformation. In little over a century, it was turned from a marsh-fringed expanse of tidal mud and sand banks threaded by several shifting river channels into an artificially trained channel bordered by made land composed of industrial waste and harbour dredgings. Iron and steel works and chemical plants with their associated waste dumps replaced the pristine wetlands and abundant wildlife.

Early in the nineteenth century, two meander loops were cut off at Mandale and Portrack, thus straightening the river as it entered the estuary. In the second half of the century, much of the river foreshore was reclaimed, largely by the deposition of slag from the iron industry; but it was in the twentieth century that reclamation began to make significant inroads into the extensive intertidal areas of the Seal Sands and the Bran Sands, major feeding grounds for transient and migratory birds (Figures 4.1 and 9.1). By 1969, Seal Sands, the main intertidal area on the northern side of the river and the most important feeding ground for shore birds in the estuary, was reduced by reclamation to about 400 hectares and further reclamation in 1973 left little more than 140 hectares. Similarly, reclamation on the southern shore reduced Bran Sands to about 60 hectares (Davidson, 1980).

While the despoliation of the landscape, including the coast, had long been a popular concern in Britain, it was the protection of beautiful countryside such as Teesdale rather than the rehabilitation of already spoiled industrial areas such as Teesside that attracted most public attention. It is significant that a Liverpool University planning study of reclamation in the Tees estuary, written in 1962 under the supervision of a distinguished landscape architect, does not treat environmental degradation and conservation as major issues, the chapter on Seal Sands containing no reference whatever to the ecological value of the area (Hudson, 1962). This reflects the common official attitude of the time. Writing at the end of the 1960s, the Director of Planning and Development of the then Teesside County Borough Council stressed the importance of the River Tees for industrial development, noting that: 'The growth demands of heavy industry in the estuary area are expected to result in the investment by 1991 of £220 million for reclamation and development of Seal Sands and Bran Sands for industry' (Fairbank, 1970:445). In this economically vulnerable old industrial area, the emphasis was understandably on development rather than conservation.

The 1960s were a time of stiffening environmental attitudes in Britain as in the USA and elsewhere, however. It was during this period that conservationists struggled, unsuccessfully as it turned out, to defeat the Cow Green Reservoir scheme which submerged part of a botanically important site near the source of the Tees in the wilds of upper Teesdale. River pollution was now beginning to receive greater attention, and the Tees estuary was one of four chosen for study by a Royal Commission on Environmental Pollution (Porter, 1973). There was also growing concern about the possible environmental impacts of further reclamation in the Tees estuary.

The Teesside Structure Plan proposed by the Cleveland County Council in 1975 made provision for the conservation of the remaining 148 hectares of Seal Sands on the grounds that the area was a site of special scientific interest which was of major importance to nature conservation. The Secretary of State, however, modified the Plan, expressing the view that:

> despite the importance of nature conservation considerations, it is of great importance to employment in the region and in the overall economic interest that the plans should make provision for the potential need for deep-water facilities by making this land available for port and port-related industry (cited in Davidson, 1980:4).

Nevertheless, the Secretary of State conceded that the impact of development should be kept to a minimum and that, as far as possible, compensation for damage should be made. He suggested: 'It may be possible to bring forward other sites, with rather different types of scientific interest, to fulfil at least some of the scientific and educational roles played by Seal Sands at the present time' (cited in Davidson, 1980:4). In consequence, the Teesside Structure Plan was modified to allocate the remaining area of Seal Sands to development, while including a policy which expressed the Cleveland County Council's commitment to the protection of Sites of Special Scientific Interest (SSSI) of which Seal Sands was a particularly important example. The County Council expressed its intention to co-operate with the Tees and Hartlepool Port Authority and other relevant bodies to assist in the study of the likely effects of development on SSSI, and where proposals were expected to have serious environmental impacts, as in the case of Seal Sands, to develop compensating provision. As far as possible, this was to maintain an equally high level of conservation interest although it would not be of the same kind as that lost to development (Davidson, 1980).

In making provision for landfill schemes to create new sites for 'necessary' water-related uses such as port facilities and related industry, the Teesside Structure Plan resembles the BCDC San Francisco Bay Plan; but while there are some similarities between the Cleveland County Council's policy of compensating site provision and the BCDC's mitigation policy, on Teesside it is not regarded as feasible to attempt to replace the lost wetland values with identical or closely similar ones. With only about five per cent of the original 2,400 hectares of intertidal area remaining, scope for mitigation is extremely limited should further reclamation occur.

With the threatened loss of the remaining area of Seal Sands, an investigation was undertaken in 1978–79 into the possibility of developing alternative sites as a compensatory measure. Jointly financed by the Nature Conservancy Council and the Cleveland County Council, the study sought to identify sites which could be modified to provide feeding areas for the internationally important populations of those species of shorebirds which were dependent on Seal Sands. The main challenge was to provide feeding areas for wintering birds that are available during three stages of the tide – low, mid and high – because different species feed at different times of the tidal cycle. One potentially suitable area, Bran Sands, was not investigated because it, too, was scheduled for development, and the study noted that modification of other possible sites could affect some of their special environmental qualities. Nevertheless, it concluded that appropriate modification, which would involve excavation, could greatly enhance their conservation value (Davidson, 1980).

The development of the oil terminal and chemical works at Seal Sands and an iron ore terminal and blast furnace complex at Bran Sands involved reclamation which left only very small remnants of the once extensive tidal flats at the mouth of the Tees, but these were, nevertheless, still considered important local, national and international environmental resources. Towards the end of 1989, there was launched the *Cleveland Wildlife Strategy*, prepared by the Cleveland County Council and the Nature Conservancy Council, which refers to 'a complex of sites known collectively as 'Teesmouth Flats and Marshes' comprising Seal Sands, Seaton Dunes and Common, South Gare and Coatham Sands as well as Cowpen Marsh SSSIs' (Cleveland County Council and Nature Conservancy Council, [n.d.] 20). The *Strategy* notes that the Seal Sands SSSI remains one of international ornithological importance, that Bran Sands and Coatham Sands, too, provide important winter-feeding grounds and roost sites for various bird species, and that the whole area is of considerable importance for its flora and fauna. This official advisory document, prepared mainly to guide Cleveland's four constituent Borough Councils, emphasizes that the 'complex of sites around Teesmouth forms part of the same ecological system and as such it should be thought of and managed as one large integrated site'.

Thus, although reduced to small, fragmented and degraded remnants, the Tees estuary wetlands were still of considerable ecological importance, and stronger measures were now being taken to maintain and enhance their environmental value. Emphasizing the County Council's conservation policy, the *1990 Cleveland Structure Plan* proposes a Teesside International Nature Reserve which includes the Seal Sands SSSI and adjacent marshlands on the north side of the estuary, a proposal that has received support from quarters not previously considered to be allies of the conservationist cause (Ault, 1992; Gillis, 1990).

Until this time, Teesside conservationists had continued to face considerable opposition from industrial interests in an area where economic development and job creation were widely seen as the major priorities at both the local and national levels. In 1990, however, the Chairman of the Teesside Development Corporation was able to announce that Teesside industry had suddenly gone green!

> The change has been so rapid that it is hard to remember that a little over a year ago Teesside was a battleground of entrenched positions.
> A year later, we are able to publish an Annual Review that includes initiatives by eight major Teesside companies, which demonstrates that these major employers and providers of wealth have an understanding and commitment to the protection and enhancement of the environment (Norman, [1990?].)

The development which occasioned these jubilant remarks was the formation in 1989 of the Industry Nature Conservation Association (INCA) both nationally and in Cleveland. Teesside industry, it seems, discovered that it was good to be green. This new attitude is exemplified in a publicity document for a proposed European Chemical Centre on Teesside which makes much of the environmental qualities of the site at Seal Sands which is 'separated from residential areas by a 2,000-hectare nature reserve, where wildfowl and rare plants and flowers live in harmony with modern industry' (Teesside Development Corporation, [n.d.]: 1). Nature, we are told, contributes to the year-round appeal of Teesside,

> an appeal that is heightened by sharing shoreline and skyline with one of the most important and striking looking petrochemical complexes in Europe ... [and] further enhanced by Teesside Development Corporation's initiative to develop the Tees estuary site as a World Wetlands Park of over 20 square kilometres ... one of the largest nature reserves in the UK' (Teesside Development Corporation, [n.d.]: 7).

Elsewhere reference is made to the abundance and variety of wildlife, including common and grey seals and an 'exotic plant life of orchids and other rare species', some of which have actually benefited from 'industrial operations such as slag dumping' (Teesside Development Corporation, [n.d.]: 7).

Similar industrial concern for nature is expressed in a Phillips Petroleum Company publication, *Oilport Teesside*, which describes the Norsea Oil Terminal development. While a 'major land reclamation programme was necessary at Seal Sands to build the Teesside Terminal' and 'twelve million cubic metres of sand and silt were pumped from the River Tees to enable construction of deepwater loading berths' (Phillips Petroleum Company, no date: 7), care was taken 'to avoid any harm to wildlife in the area and it appears wildlife has increased since the tank farm was built' (Phillips Petroleum Company, [n.d.]: 24).

This apparent change in attitude towards the environment coincides with important developments in international politics which have enormous implications for the British economy. The name European Chemical Centre on Teesside reminds us of the increasing role that Europe is playing in British affairs, and this has serious implications for environmental aspects of economic development in the UK. A report prepared for companies operating in Cleveland and published in 1990, observes that the signing of the Single European Act (SEA) in 1986 committed the twelve signatory member states of the European Community to the maintenance of a high level of environmental protection, and warned that firm action would be required to ensure that degradation of the environment does not accompany the expected economic development. This report notes that landfill engineering standards in the UK could be tightened considerably by environmental regulations emanating from Brussels, warning that 'the outcome will be that industry will face increasing environmental pressures in the future' (Clayton and Peppin, 1990:29).

In terms of environmental planning and conservation, Teesside in the 1990s appears to have reached a position similar to that achieved in the San Francisco Bay area twenty years or so earlier, and the threat of environmental damage from further reclamation is now greatly reduced, at least for the present. Industrial waste continues to be dumped on land already reclaimed from the estuary, but harbour dredgings are disposed of at sea, one reason being that silt and sand from the Tees are too contaminated with heavy metals and other industrial pollutants to be safely deposited on the shore (Palmer, 1993). As noted by some representatives of industry, there are instances where industrial waste dumping on the Tees estuary shore has had beneficial effects on certain types of plant life. Of particular interest is the colonization of basic slag dumps at the mouth of the Tees by calcareous plants including the Northern Marsh Orchid. Here also, breakwaters built of slag have caused the accumulation of sand on which has developed a rich and varied flora (Cleveland INCA, [n.d.]: Quayle and Bellamy, 1988).

Little of the Tees estuary foreshore remains to be reclaimed, and the environmental importance of that which survives is now well recognized. Strong protective measures have been taken recently with the much publicized support of industry which is co-operating in several wetland conservation initiatives. One proposal involves reopening a part of the Seal Sands reclamation area to the tidal process. Nearby, the Cleveland Wildfowl Trust has undertaken wetland restoration work which has returned part of the Greenabella Marsh to a wetland habitat. With the new alliance between industry and conservation on Teesside, there is now hope for the future of the precious remaining five per cent or so of the original tidal flats of the estuary, and some restoration work has been started in the enclosed marshes near the river mouth.

While the growing strength of the environmental movement has certainly done much to change attitudes to littoral wetlands and reduce pressures to reclaim them, other factors probably include economic downturns and over-estimation of future needs for land for industrial development together with de-industrialization in some areas (Pinder and Witherick, 1990). In the 1980s, demand for land for development eased considerably both on Teesside and in the San Francisco Bay area, and there are fiscal advantages to be had by businesses which contribute to environmental conservation programmes (Crawford, 1993; Tomlinson, 1993). In other parts of the world, such as Hong Kong and Japan where population pressure and economic growth maintain a heavy demand on land for development, particularly in coastal areas, reclamation seems likely to continue on a large scale despite increasing awareness of its environmental impacts.

Japan's Inland Sea: economic miracle; environmental disaster

In Japan, public concern over the environmental costs of post-war economic development there eventually led to the establishment of a number of citizens' groups seeking to protect the coast where degradation caused by industrial, commercial and related urban developments was particularly severe. Large-scale landfill projects and extremely high levels of pollution together with loss of public access to the sea caused by coastal development began to arouse local opposition which, in the 1970s, grew into a vigorous national movement. Shapiro (1988) has described how the Irahima-ken or Coastal Access Rights Movement, founded in 1973 by a school teacher in the city of Takasago, grew from a local protest group into Japan's first national coastal citizens' organization. The following discussion of coastal development on the Inland Sea and the work of the Coastal Access Rights Movement is based largely on the account by Harvey Shapiro of the Department of Environmental Planning, Osaka Geijutsu University, which draws on a wide range of sources, many of them in Japanese. This is supplemented by my own study and field observations of part of the Inland Sea Coast, particularly in Hiroshima.

Situated on the Seto Inland Sea about 40 kilometres west of Kobe, Takasago, with its steel and chemical works, paper mills and other industries, has long since lost the natural beauty of its pine-covered sand dunes for which it was celebrated in poetry as long ago as the tenth century. Gone, too, are its bathing beaches which became popular a hundred years ago. Takasago's development is typical of that which has transformed much of the Inland Sea Coast. Renowned for its great natural beauty, the Inland Sea is also of vital economic importance, with some 25 per cent of Japan's population concentrated along its coast, many of them in major cities, including Osaka, Kobe and Hiroshima.

With an area of 22,000 square kilometres, the Inland Sea is Japan's largest estuarine water body, but agricultural and urban reclamation have been encroaching on its area for many centuries, the extensive landfill schemes of the twentieth century having made the greatest impact. The Inland Sea's highly indented 6,000 kilometre coastline and the shallowness of its island-studded waters which average about 30 metres in depth, facilitate reclamation. This practice is encouraged by the mountainous nature of the surrounding land and the lack of extensive natural coastal plains. By 1973, about 2 per cent of the surface area had been lost to landfill, all of it in the ecologically productive nearshore areas less than 10 metres deep. A mere decade later, the area lost to landfill had risen to over 13 per cent (Hosomi, A. 1982, cited Shapiro). The adverse environmental effect of this development was heightened by the pollution generated by industrial and other urban activities on the reclaimed land. With its relatively small volume, some 800 cubic kilometres, and linked to the open sea by only three narrow channels, the Inland Sea is especially vulnerable to pollution, the water exchange rate being about sixty years.

The stimulus of World War II and of the post-war economic reconstruction programme which followed encouraged industrial development in Japan's coastal areas. In 1940, the Japanese Government made coastal landfill a key element of its national policy. Immediately after the war much coastal reclamation was undertaken for agricultural production, but from the mid-1950s national economic plans stimulated large-scale coastal landfills for industry, the government subsidizing such developments for heavy industries, petro-chemical plants and the like. Between 1945 and 1977, over 35 per cent of all Japan's landfills were on the Inland Sea, resulting in a drastic reduction in the amount of natural coastline. In three of the prefectures which adjoin the Inland Sea, Hiroshima, Okayana and Kagawa, the proportion of natural coast fell from 34.5 per cent in 1955 to 20.3 per cent in 1970 when 58.6 per cent of the coastline in those areas was artificial and 21.1 per cent classed as semi-natural.

Overshadowed by the nearby Osaka-Kobe metropolitan area, Takasago's modern industrial development dates from the beginning of the twentieth century when the town was successful in attracting the Mitsubishi Paper Manufacturing Company and the Kanebo Spinning Corporation. From as early as 1902, citizens protested against industrial water pollution but the local authorities preferred to tolerate the environmental costs in exchange for the financial advantages which the industries brought to the district. Local governments in Japan are financially weak and highly dependent on central government. To generate revenue without increasing taxes, local governments compete with one another to attract industries which in turn provide financial support for local public works. This practice is encouraged by central government which sees it as a means of stimulating economic growth.

Despite continuing environmental degradation, Takasago remained a popular resort for sea bathing but, after 1930, increasing industrialization with associated rising pollution led to a serious deterioration in the condition of the beaches which were finally closed in 1960. Earlier, in 1954, the fishing unions of Takasago and surrounding towns had begun to receive compensation from both the Mitsubishi Paper and Kaneka Chemical Companies for loss of livelihood due to industrial pollution. This was the year when Takesago achieved city status and began to prepare itself for post-war economic development, 'thus setting the stage for a *permanent* separation from its natural coastline and sandy beaches' (Shapiro, 1988:506).

While the Japanese share with many other of the world's peoples values which make environmental degradation and loss of access to the sea repugnant to them, their traditional relationship with the sea and shore has some unique characteristics which is it necessary to understand when considering the rise of the Coastal Access Rights Movement. For the Japanese, the coast has important spiritual values, being regarded as the interface between 'this' and the 'other world'. Consequently, many Shinto festivals and customs are practised on the coast, often on the beach. Sea water, long considered holy, is believed to have purifying and curative properties, and with Japan's deliberate adoption of 'Western' modernization policies in the Meiji Period (1868–1912), sea bathing was actively encouraged by the government, first for therapeutic reasons and later for recreational purposes. Furthermore, fish and other marine products have long been important in the traditional Japanese diet not only because of the country's limited land resources but also because of the influence of Buddhism which discourages the consumption of meat. To the Japanese, then, 'the coast traditionally belonged to the gods and was a public place freely open to all where they could be blessed by the gods and enjoy each other's company as part of nature' (Shapiro, 1988:496).

This began to change with the emergence of Japan from isolation at the beginning of the Meiji Period and, in 1874, as part of a national land reform policy, the sea and shoreline of the entire coastline were declared to be government property. The government wanted to have absolute control over the sea shores in order to facilitate the implementation of its *fukoku-kyohei* (strong military–rich country) policy and, to this end, major commercial and naval port developments were undertaken.

Government ownership and control of the foreshore facilitated its economic development programmes, particularly industrial expansion of the coast involving extensive landfill schemes. The Japanese legal system took the view that the free use of the sea coast was a privilege which the State had a right to bestow on the public, but that it was not a public right. This view was upheld by the significant Matsuyana District Court ruling of 29 May 1978 which declared that swimming beaches and the water surface are natural properties owned by the State. Disappointed by this court decision, the Coastal Access Rights Movement hastily convened its third National Symposium to discuss the issue of whether the free use of the sea coast was the people's inherent right or a privilege which the state may, at its own discretion, confer on the public.

The Coastal Access Rights Movement had been launched in Takasago when, in 1973, Hiroshi Takasaki, a local school teacher, called a citizens' meeting to prepare a formal complaint about mercury contamination discovered in the harbour. Twenty years earlier symptoms of what became known as Minamata disease had begun to appear fishermen's families on Minamata Bay on the west coast of Kyushu, eventually attracting much international media attention and alerting the world to the dangers of mercury poisoning associated with marine pollution. By now, growing awareness of the environmental costs of coastal urban industrial oriented economic growth in Japan was creating considerable public disquiet reflected in increasingly organized opposition.

Like many other Inland Sea coastal cities, Takasago had been the site of extensive landfill for industrial development, much of it undertaken as a prefectural project begun in 1961, shortly after the closure of all the city's beaches. The land thus reclaimed was occupied by the Kaneka Chemical Company, the Sumito and Kobe Steel Companies, and the Kansai Power Company. In addition to the fills themselves, the public sea-wall and an additional 1.8 metre strip of public sea area bordering the reclamations was sold off to the companies to accommodate the tetrapods used to protect the retaining walls from storm damage. As a result, the city of Takasago was completely deprived of any accessible coast, artificial or otherwise, many regarding this as the inevitable price of progress for which an affluent life would be the reward.

Takasaki (1977, cited in Shapiro, 1988), however, demonstrated that these developments actually incurred substantial financial costs to the public in terms of payments for the use of swimming pools and cost of travel to distant branches, fishing spots and attractive natural environments. The promise of an affluent life in return for the sacrifice of the coast was beginning to sound increasingly hollow. The 1973 meeting, which launched the Coastal Access Rights Movement, concluded that landfill projects for industrial development had ignored and violated public customary rights of access to the coast and also endangered health, safety and welfare by pollution from those industries. The Movement was formed to work for the restoration and protection of Japan's natural environment and the elimination of pollution. Thus the term 'irihama-ken', coastal access right, was born and, in 1976, the first National *Irihama-ken* Symposium was convened in Kobe. The overall objectives of this gathering were:

1. to develop a theory of coastal access rights in a scientific manner and to use the knowledge gained to strengthen and support the resolve of all citizens' movements in Japan aimed at protecting the coastline; and
2. to work toward enactment of laws that eliminate the destruction of the natural coastline and ensure its preservation.

(Kihara, 1978, cited in Shapiro, 1988)

Notwithstanding opposition from environmentalists, the momentum of Japan's commitment to high economic growth policies has continued to take the country further down the path towards environmental disaster with concomitant adverse effects on the quality of human life. Shapiro (1988:515) writes:

Despite the rising sense of crisis and outcries of its environmentally sensitive citizenry, the forces behind the destruction of the nation's vital coastal resources continue to press for still more of the same, giving economic growth priority over everything else, as they have done for the last three decades.

In the last decade of the twentieth century, however, there is some encouraging evidence that environmental concerns have begun to influence Japanese development policies, including those relating to coastal landfill projects. Writing in the 1980s on the subject of coastal land reclamation, University of Hiroshima geographer, Nobuyuki Hori (1984:160), cautiously remarked, 'In the case of Hiroshima Bay, the existing balance between what is desirable for both man and the environment is barely being maintained and perhaps now is the time for serious reflection before it is too late.' Recent coastal projects in Hiroshima indicate that while reclamation continues to play a major role in the economic development of this important Inland Sea city, environmental considerations are now beginning to strongly influence the design of landfill schemes.

A notable example is the Itsukaichi District project undertaken by the Hiroshima Prefecture in conjunction with the State, begun in 1986 and due for completion in 2000. Involving the reclamation of 154 hectares of land from waters ranging from one to ten metres in depth, this project combines port improvement, including the construction of new wharves, with urban development which provides sites for housing, factories, roads, schools and hospitals. It also includes a domestic refuse disposal site. An official brochure describing the project notes that: 'The coastal urban areas have been a magnet for industries and have experienced a rapid increase in population but have fallen behind in providing a good living environment for these people' (Hiroshima Prefectural Government, [n.d.]). This plan, therefore, aims at restoring the degraded natural environment, providing parks and 'green zones' for the enjoyment of the public. Of particular interest is the 24 hectare artificial tidal flat on the eastern edge of the reclaimed area at the mouth of the Yahata River, an important habitat for wild birds, including geese and ducks. Adjoining this, at the eastern tip of the landfilled area is a wild bird sanctuary which together with the artificial tidal flat is designed to protect the birdlife of the region.

The creation of artificial coastal wildlife habitats by landfill is now common practice in many parts of the world and, with the destruction of the global ecosystem by human activity, it has become necessary to act on behalf of Nature which, at least in the short term, appears to be unable to defend herself against the onslaught. In some ways, this making provision for nature in artificially created reserves often resembles what Relph (1976) has termed 'museumization', but instead of preserving and reconstructing an idealized history, commonly in newly created places, it is an idealized 'Nature' which is reconstructed and preserved, again often in environments deliberately created for the purpose. Perhaps the term 'zoofication' might convey some idea of this process, but it is not only animals but plants, too, which are being preserved and exhibited in this way. Since artificial reserves are a means commonly used to preserve nature, 'reservication' is suggested as a possibly more appropriate term.

Not all reserves occupy artificially created sites such as coastal landfills, but even those which are designated areas of relatively undisturbed wild nature are artificial in the sense that their existence depends on active protection and management for human purposes. In the case of the coast and other littoral areas, management entails decisions on where and how to develop and where to preserve the environment in a relatively unchanged state. Reclamation inevitably involves change to the littoral environment although, as we have seen, it may also play a role in environmental conservation.

In some highly developed urbanized areas, Nature may find herself largely confined to artificial reserves, such as specially designed landfills, deliberately set aside and developed for the purpose as part of an overall development strategy. This is what appears to be happening in parts of Japan, Europe and the USA which, perhaps, provide the most likely models of the future urban environment, at least in the developed world. Nowhere is the pace and scale of environmental change greater than on the urban littoral frontier and, in the following final chapter, the role of reclamation in the development of this vitally important zone at the interface of land and water is reviewed.

10
The Urban Littoral Frontier: Model, Alternatives, Future

Like all cities, every city on the shore is unique, but each one shares with others many common characteristics. The same can be said of reclamation for urban development. In an attempt at a synthesis, Pinder and Witherick (1990: 264–5) have suggested a threefold classification of wetland reclamation generated by urbanization, based on the general relationship of the new land uses to the established uses of the old land. 'Expansion', 'clean-break', and 'remedial' reclamations are the proposed categories. Expansion reclamations are those where established land uses have need for more space and simply extend onto new land, maintaining their dominance of the zones from which the colonization occurs. Clean-break reclamations are developments on new land which constitute a complete departure from surrounding established land uses such as a new highway or power station on a hitherto undeveloped stretch of coast. Remedial reclamations are those which provide detached overspill space for the amelioration of particularly severe problems such as slum housing or a congested obtrusive airport. Remedial reclamations may be variations of the expansion or clean-break categories, but pressure on land may well mean that they are physically separate from the mainland. A recent example is Hong Kong's new international airport at Chek Lap Kok which is built, mainly on reclaimed land at an offshore island, to replace congested Kai Tak Airport, now inconveniently, even dangerously, engulfed by high density urban development.

While this classification is useful as a means of synthesizing the diversity of urban littoral reclamations, it does not address the question of the role of reclamation in the development of the littoral city as a whole.

The previous chapters have considered reclamation for urban development as a world-wide phenomenon, examining cities in many different locations and in many different ages. From this discussion, it is possible to make some generalizations about the reclamation process as it affects urban form and the natural environment. Thus, it is possible to devise a model of development evolution for the littoral city, demonstrating the role of reclamation in urban growth. Discussion of the model provides the opportunity to highlight some of the main themes addressed in the previous chapters, setting the scene for a brief consideration of possible future developments, including alternative forms of urban expansion.

This final chapter, then, presents an urban reclamation model after which alternative solutions to urban expansion problems are discussed with reference to their implications for the quality of urban life and the environment. While urban development has had a considerable impact on the natural environment, human settlements also remain vulnerable to environmental hazards to which littoral cities are especially prone. As the twenty-first century approaches, scientists and planners are becoming increasingly concerned about the possible consequences of global environmental change on human settlements, especially those on the coast. Here many cities, great and small, face the threat of rising sea-levels, a danger particularly acute in urban areas developed on reclaimed land. With this forward glance into an uncertain future the last chapter, and hence this study of the urban littoral frontier, is brought to a close.

The model

The purpose of the urban reclamation model proposed here is to illustrate the influence of this type of development on the physical form of cities on the shore, providing a base with which to compare actual examples. The model is intended to help to explain the direction and sequence of development, emphasizing the variables of time and distance as expressed in terms of land use and land value. When discussing urban land use and city structure, Stanford economist, Richard Muth (1969: 47) observed that 'the supply of land with certain spatial characteristics is sometimes increased by filling in areas along waterfronts and more frequently, through investment in transport facilities'. While it is probably true that the expansion or improvement of the transport system is the most common response to increased demand for urban land, this book argues that reclamation on the waterfront has made a major contribution to land supply, one that has had a significant influence on the development of many cities. For the purpose of the model, it is accepted that, historically, most cities have grown from a single nucleus and have expanded annularly, most rapidly along major transport arteries. The assumed basic city form, therefore, is stellate.

For simplicity, the urban nucleus lies at the intersection of two transport routes which are of equal importance. These radiate from the city core across a homogeneous plain in four directions except where the original settlement was established on the unembayed shore of a large water body the depth of which increases constantly with increasing distance from land. Similar water depth gradients occur where the city has developed on the shores of a bay.

Figure 10.1(a) represents the model city on an inland site, showing four stages of growth beyond the original nucleus at the intersection of the two major routes. In general, therefore, the earlier the development, the closer it is to the centre, the later growth being nearer the periphery. Only the more rapid development along the radials formed by the two intersecting transport routes distorts the annular growth rings, creating lobes which convert the circular urban form into one which is more or less star shaped. This is because rapid transport between the central business district (CBD) and the outer suburbs compensates for the greater distance from the city centre, stimulating residential development, and because access to good transport facilities near cities also attracts commercial and industrial development.

Figure 10.1(b) illustrates the form of the city when the original settlement was established beside a large water body. As in the classic case of Chicago whose well-known concentric rings as identified by Burgess (1925) are truncated by Lake Michigan, the annular growth zones of our model water-side city are similarly bisected by the shore-line beyond which no development has occurred. This book, however, has attempted to demonstrate the fallacy of the tacit assumption that urban development in littoral areas occurs only in an inland direction. To simplify the following discussion, the word 'sea' is substituted for 'water body', and the terms 'seawards' and 'sea-wall' are used correspondingly, but the reader should remember that reclamation from large lakes, rivers and swamps can take similar forms.

Figure 10.1(c) shows how the model can be modified to recognize the widespread occurrence of urban expansion by reclaiming land from the adjacent sea. In this instance, the earliest phase of expansion (represented by Zone 1 in the diagram) occurred on existing dry land only. The second phase, however, includes not only expansion on the inland periphery but also a block of reclamation on the shore adjacent to the original nucleus, now the downtown area or CBD. By this time, real estate values in the heart of the city have risen to such levels that it has become economically feasible to create new land for development by reclamation.

While, for the purpose of the model, it is assumed that the city is located on the coastal margin of a homogeneous plain, we have noted that in many coastal cities physical constraints such as encircling mountain slopes or swamps have encouraged reclamation almost from the very beginning. Even without those topographical constraints, however, further reclamation along the original shore occurs as Zones 3 and 4 are added to the first and second

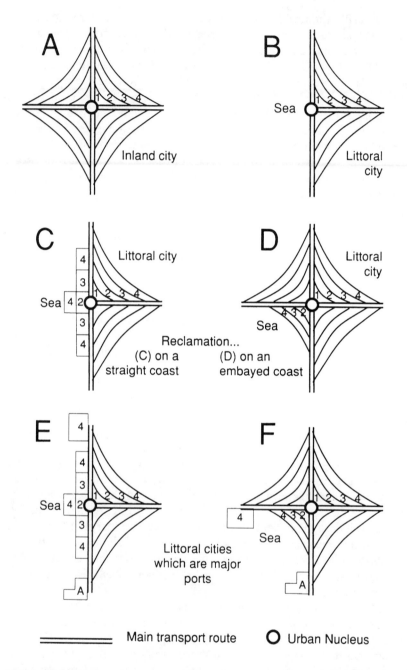

Figure 10.1 Urban Reclamation Model: (a) stages of annular growth of a city unconstrained by an adjacent water body; (b) littoral city where expansion occurs only on pre-existing land; (c) littoral city on a straight coast, showing stages of urban development seawards on reclaimed land as well as inland; (d) littoral city on a bay, showing stages of growth; (e) and (f) stages of urban expansion in littoral cities where major port and airport development have occurred on the shore at the edges of the built-up area. The airport is indicated by the letter A.

belts of development around the central core. It will be observed that development outward from the core occurs more rapidly inland than along the shore on reclaimed land. This is because, in general, it is easier and less expensive to develop on existing dry land than to reclaim an aquatic area and then develop it. It is also generally easier and less expensive to reclaim land from the foreshore and adjacent shallows than from deep water areas further offshore. Nevertheless, as CBD property values increase and reclamation techniques are improved, it may become feasible to reclaim land from deeper water areas beyond the earlier reclamation line close to the city centre. Thus in Figure 10.1(c) reclamations belonging to the fourth phase of urban expansion include one block seawards of the earliest reclamation which was part of the second phase.

Such a sequence of city centre reclamation, as we have seen, is not uncommon. This pattern of growth may continue until the technical or economic limits of reclamation are reached, a situation which has often proved temporary, or until human limitations are placed on this form of development, for environmental reasons for example. It will be observed that a continuation of this sequence of reclamation would lead to a linear form of development along the main routes on the seaward side of the original coast, possibly including a seaward extension of the route ending on the coast. Eventually, this reclamation process could create something like a reduced mirror image of the pattern of development which occurred on the natural dry land. The way this could come about may be better understood when considering the case illustrated by Figure 10.1(d).

For various reasons many littoral cities have grown up on the shores of bays and other inlets. These commonly offer shelter for shipping and for human settlement sites, thus favouring port development, and often occur at the mouths of rivers bordered by well watered fertile agricultural land that encourages the development of a prosperous and densely populated hinterland. The site of the original major coastal settlement has often been determined by the lowest river crossing point on the main route which normally follows the coast and intersects that which leads inland along the valley.

The bay-head settlement is represented in Figure 10.1(d) where one quadrant of the basic model city is occupied by water into which expansion occurs by a sequence of reclamation. As in Figure 10.1(c), major lines of transport follow the shoreline, something which is common in the real world, and probably has been since the dawn of human settlement (see Chapter 2). Because reclamation is usually much easier at the shallow head of a sheltered bay than on an unprotected coast such as that depicted in Figures 10.1(b) and (c), the first stage of reclamation in the bay represented in Figure 10.1(d) might well coincide with the first phase of urban expansion inland. For the sake of consistency, however, the first extension into the bay is shown as part of the Stage 2 urban growth, as in other cases represented in Figure 10.1.

Subsequent reclamations occur in a sequence which corresponds with the sequence of inland growth but on a smaller scale and at a slower pace, reflecting the relative difficulty and expense of reclamation in comparison with development of natural dry land.

The shape of the reclaimed strips reflects several factors including water depth, length of the sea-wall, and the influence of transport routes along the coast. Because it is generally easier and less expensive to reclaim land from the foreshore and adjacent shallows, there is a tendency to undertake reclamation works along the shore before making extensions into deeper water further out. This tendency is likely to be reinforced by the presence of major transport routes along the original shore which encourages urban development. Hence reclamation may be expected to extend along the shoreline and the coastal routes rather than to advance into the deep water normally found in the middle of the bay. Rising central area land values concomitant with urban expansion may offset the costs of reclaiming deep water areas, however, and this may be helped by the relative economy of constructing a straight, and therefore shorter, sea-wall. As was explained in Chapter 7, normally the shorter the sea-wall in relation to the area of land reclaimed the more economical the project. Countering this, however, is the generally greater cost of sea-wall construction in deep-water and the larger volume of fill required in these circumstances.

In the light of all these variables, the model in Figure 10.1(d) shows a sequence of gently curved strips of reclaimed land extending progressively seawards, more rapidly along the shores of the bay than into the middle of the inlet. The resultant pattern of growth in the marine sector of the model city thus corresponds closely to those in the three other, terrestrial, sectors, but on a much reduced scale.

So far the discussion of the model has considered reclamation and urban growth only in terms of centrality and related land use and land value patterns, and other reasons for reclamation, notably access to deep water and port development, have not been taken into account in the model. Figure 10.1(e) is a version of the case illustrated by Figure 10.1(c) in which the city has developed an important port function. In the beginning boats may have been hauled up on the strand, larger vessels possibly anchoring offshore. Early in the development of the port jetties are likely to have been built and possibly the beginnings of an artificial harbour to provide a haven on this exposed coast. The first phase of expansion, represented by Zone 1, then, could have coincided with the construction of a small artificial harbour formed by a mole or jetty, possibly with some marginal reclamation to create a modest quay in place of the muddy and probably unwholesome fore-shore.

In the second phase of urban expansion an area of land is reclaimed on the waterfront as in Figure 10.1(c), but, in this case, a major factor is the demand for docks where vessels can moor in deep water berths. Reclamation area 2 includes the site of the primitive port, the original town dock having been filled in. On this open coast, the new deep water dock will probably require the construction of some kind of breakwater to provide protection for the artificial harbour. The third and fourth phases of urban expansion include further reclamations as in Figure 10.1(c), but with the following differences shown in phase four.

In Figure 10.1(e) the fourth phase of development coincides with major technical developments in shipping and port operation which have contributed to the decline of the obsolescent downtown waterfront area. Larger ships and corresponding changes in cargo-handling demand docks which can accommodate vessels of greater capacity and draught with adjacent areas for the handling and storage of cargo. To meet these demands, a large new dock complex has been developed by a reclamation scheme at the outer edge of the city where land, including submerged land, is available relatively cheaply, and problems of congestion associated with the downtown area are avoided. The need for berths which can accommodate ships of large draught has encouraged reclamation into deep water further out from the original shore beyond the line of earlier reclamations. Technical difficulties presented by this engineering task are now more readily overcome by advances in reclamation technology, which also facilitate development on a far greater scale than was possible hitherto.

Meanwhile, urban renewal in the old waterfront quarter adjoining the downtown area may involve further reclamation, possibly for prestige commercial sites overlooking the water as the CBD expands into the former dockland area. Today, however, other uses are competing for access to the city waterfront where development is increasingly responding to demands of leisure, recreation and tourism. The heritage value of old waterfront districts is now more widely appreciated and is often recognized as an important resource for tourism development. Hence the revitalized waterfront may preserve some of the old buildings recycled for new uses, and at least some of the old dock basins may be converted into pleasure boat marinas. In Figure 10.1(e) therefore, the fourth phase of reclamation nearest the CBD takes the form of the partial infilling of the artificial harbour which has been replaced by new docks on the edge of the city, but part of the old dock remains unreclaimed to serve recreational and leisure purposes.

In the case of Figure 10.1(f) the city lies on a bay which forms a natural harbour, reducing the need for extensive artificial dock construction. The reclamations which extend sequentially from the original city waterfront towards the middle of the bay provide sites with progressively deeper water frontage to accommodate larger ships which can berth alongside the quay. As reclamation advances the waterfront area seawards, CBD expansion may follow in its wake just as it may expand inland, engulfing inner residential districts on its fringe. As in the case of Figure 10.1(e), technical developments in shipping and cargo-handling together with problems of inner city congestion and obsolescence provide the stimulus for developing an entirely new port facility on the edge of the urban area where large areas of land, including foreshore and coastal shallows, can be obtained relatively cheaply.

Reclamations associated with Phase 4 of urban expansion include a large new port development a considerable distance from the CBD, but connected with it by one of the original major routeways which follows the old coastline. In Figure 10.1(f) further reclamation on the waterfront adjacent to the CBD is likely to be at least partly in response to the need for a transport route which by-passes the densely built-up and congested city centre. It may also provide public open space facilities such as an esplanade or waterfront park, reflecting the increased awareness of the amenity value of the waterfront. The design of the new waterfront development is likely to make provision for heritage conservation, and environmental considerations could now begin to impose constraints on the reclamation process which might otherwise have tended to accelerate because of developments in construction technology and increasing economic and population pressures. The future of reclamation is as likely to depend on local environmental, economic, demographic, educational and political circumstances as on technological process.

The model would remain incomplete without the inclusion of the airport which is now found in even very small cities and towns, and which in coastal areas is commonly built on land reclaimed from the sea and littoral wetlands. In Figures 10.1(e) and 10.1(f), the airport is indicated by the letter A. Like the new port development, it lies well away from the city centre, but unlike the modern sea terminal, its development is not closely linked with the evolution of the old urban core where the decline of the historic waterfront and the growth of the new port area were related phenomena.

In many cities, airport development began over half a century ago, often long before the demise of the central city waterfront although decline of the old port area may well have begun. For several reasons, the airport site chosen was usually well outside the built-up area. This avoided buildings which might obstruct aircraft landing and taking off, and also made use of cheaper land on the city outskirts, an important consideration where, as in the case of airports, very large areas are required. A waterside location was often selected for the airport site for cities on the shore. This made possible unobstructed approaches and take-offs over water, and when the need for airport expansion arose the requisite land could generally be created quite easily by reclamation.

In Figures 10.1(e) and 10.1(f), the runway is shown projecting into the water as is often the case in the real world, but runways are also commonly built on reclaimed strips aligned parallel to the shore. The orientation of the runway depends on several factors including the direction of prevailing winds. With increasing air traffic requiring larger terminal facilities and the increasing size of aircraft requiring longer runways, airports have commonly undergone several phases of redevelopment and expansion, frequently involving further reclamation. Meanwhile, urban expansion has often reached and spread beyond the airport which formerly lay far outside the built-up area. Increasing demand for air transport facilities has led to the development of additional airports so that many large cities now have two or more major terminals and perhaps several smaller aerodromes, many of them built, at least in part, on reclaimed land.

Not so far considered in the reclamation model proposed here is the role of solid waste disposal, one of the most important factors contributing to the infilling of water bodies adjoining cities. Urban waste disposal often begins by dumping in or on the banks of the nearest river, lake, swamp or, in coastal areas, on the nearby seashore. As cities grow and quantities of refuse increase, disposal areas are usually found further away from the expanding built up area, but still commonly on the shore. These dumps are usually later incorporated in urban developments on reclaimed land as city expansion absorbs land further and further out from the original core. As the old dumps are developed, often for open space uses, new ones are created on the urban fringe, including the shore, and, in some cases, on specially created artificial offshore island sites which eventually become absorbed into the fabric of the city proper. Industrial waste dumps are likely to be found well outside the city proper, near the plants which produce the waste material. This is commonly used as fill for reclamation, often creating valuable waterfront sites for industrial expansion. As we have seen (Chapter 4), the combination of economical waste disposal with other objectives of reclamation often helps to make feasible landfill projects which create valuable land for urban development at an acceptable cost. Hence, while playing an important role in the reclamation process, waste disposal is not a factor which requires significant adjustment of the model as represented in Figures 10.1(c) to (f).

By definition, the model greatly simplifies the urban development and reclamation process and, of course, in the real world, the form, direction and sequence of expansion varies from place to place, influenced largely by local circumstances including the physical characteristics of the site. While the model represents widespread trends, the importance of the various factors involved varies considerably from city to city. This influences development in different ways, including the order in which different types of development occurs. For example, reclamation to provide a by-pass transport route as discussed in relation to Figure 10.1(f) is undertaken at a late stage, Phase 4, but reclaiming littoral strips to accommodate roads and railways has a long history (Chapter 4). Many of these reclaimed transport corridors, which date back to the nineteenth century or the early part of the twentieth, acted for a long time as barriers separating the city proper from its waterfront. Only recently, mainly from the 1960s onwards, has urban waterfront redevelopment in many cities improved public access to former harbour front and dockside areas. Now the urban waterfront, so long isolated from the rest of the city by railway lines and trunk roads as well as by dock perimeter walls, is again becoming accessible to the public.

One special but very important case which is not well represented by the model depicted in Figures 10.1(a) to (f), is the estuary. Typically, an estuary widens gradually towards the sea forming a funnel-shaped inlet. Commonly, a port city develops at the head of the estuary perhaps at or near the limit of tidal influence, often at the lowest bridging point on the river. Ships may be assisted into port by the incoming tide and out on the ebb, but before harbour improvements, navigating the shallow meandering channel with its hazardous shifting mud and sand banks, barely submerged at high tide, can be difficult.

Figure 10.2 is a representation of a typical estuary with a city established at the head of the tidal inlet. Downstream the river mouth widens into a characteristic funnel shape, but at low tide the river meanders between exposed inter-tidal flats, dividing into several channels as it enters the sea between sand- or mud-banks that are submerged at high water. The High

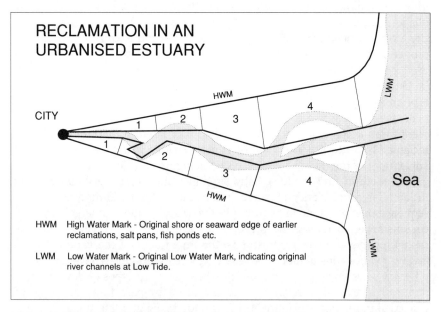

Figure 10.2 Stages of reclamation in an urbanized estuary. The seaward progression of development is not usually as orderly as shown here and, in some cases, later reclamations may occur upstream. In general, however, reclamation tends to progress downstream towards deeper water, later stages commonly being larger in area than earlier ones.

Water Mark (HWM) may be the natural shoreline of the estuary or it may be wholly or partly an artificial creation defined by a bund, dike or sea-wall of some kind built to protect the enclosed area from tidal influence. Such non-urban reclamations might have been for pasture or agriculture or, in some cases, these areas may be enclosed for artificial wetland uses such as aqua-culture or salt making.

Bird (1971) chose to use a typical estuarine site to illustrate his 'Anyport' model which describes how technological advances have influenced the growth and form of the port. The reader with an interest in port development may find it useful to compare Anyport with the reclamation model described here. The earliest reclamations for urban uses in the river port are likely to be in the form of marginal quays created by infilling a foreshore strip behind a revetment but, with the increasing size of ships, the port moves downstream to deeper water. In Figure 10.2 the areas marked '1' and '2' on both sides of the river represent the first reclamations associated with this downstream movement. Here fill, which is likely to comprise harbour dredgings, industrial waste, and probably domestic and other urban refuse, is deposited on the foreshore behind retaining walls, which confine the naturally winding river to a straighter, narrower course. The channel is deepened by dredging oper-ations which also provide fill for nearby reclamation areas, and the artificial straightening and confinement of the river increases the tidal scour which helps to maintain the depth of water. Apart from the construction of marginal quays with deep water berths created by dredge and fill, dock basins may be developed along the river by excavation into the foreshore and banks, sometimes making use of parts of the old channel as in the example shown in Figure 10.2.

The downstream trend in port development continues with the increase in size of ships and demands for more space for cargo-handling. Reclamation Stages 3 and 4 provide more deep water frontage allowing ships to lie alongside the quay or wharf. Though not shown in the diagram, these reclamation areas might also contain dock basins branching from the river as well as marginal quays parallel to it. The straightening and deepening of the channel has now continued to the mouth of the river and beyond into the open sea where the river mouth is protected by artificial breakwaters. Two of the three original channels by which at low tide the river entered the sea have now been closed, confining the flow to a single improved navigable chan-nel.

The size of the reclamation areas generally increases seawards. This is partly because, over time, technological advances facilitate increasingly large-scale harbour and coastal engineering work, but it also reflects the larger expanses of readily reclaimable inter-tidal flats which normally occur nearer the sea at the mouths of rivers. In addition, there is the growing demand for increasingly large level areas for industrial uses including many for which a waterfront site is important – power stations, oil refineries and ore-processing plants for example. Many of these find it convenient to make use of foreshore areas for waste disposal, thus reclaiming more land for possible future development. For different reasons, a waterfront site is often appropriate for airports where an unobstructed approach over the sea is generally advanta-geous; but, as with large-scale industry, the availability of extensive and relatively cheap flat land readily reclaimable from foreshore areas and ad-jacent shallows commonly encourages airport development on sites won from the sea and littoral wetlands.

While the general trend of port and industrial development in the estuary is for growth to occur in a downstream, seaward direction, it is not likely to take place in as orderly a sequence as that indicated in Figure 10.2. For various reasons, including chance availability of land, local topographic conditions or significant leaps in technological progress, development of areas near the river mouth may occur which plentiful vacant sites remain further upstream. Nevertheless, the general trend of sectoral expansion indicated in Figure 10.2 can be recognized in many parts of the industrialized world, and as the development on earlier reclamations becomes increasingly obsolete and decayed, opportunities for urban renewal arise similar to those previously mentioned in the discussion of Figures 10.1(c) to (f).

Reclamation need not stop when all reclaimable areas within the estuary have been developed for, with improved technology, it is now often possible to make considerable extensions into the open sea beyond the original river mouth. While technology may permit further reclamation and economic forces may encourage it, environmental considerations can impose limits on this form of development. Indeed, as we have seen (Chapter 9), the new environmental awareness of the last few decades has considerably slowed the rate of reclamation in several coastal areas, even starting a reversal in some places where fill is being removed from water margins and enclosed fore-shores are being reopened to tidal influence. Hence in Figure 10.2 the Stage 4 reclamations may not be proceeded with, or, more likely, their design might be modified to reduce adverse environmental impact, possibly preserving some of the mud-flats and sand banks near the mouth of the estuary as nature reserves or creating artificial habitats. Apart from their ecological value, inter-tidal areas of this kind often perform a useful function as spending beaches which dissipate wave energy.

Alternatives to reclamation

As the twentieth century comes to a close and world urbanization trends make the prospect of littoral ecumenopolis more likely, there will be increas-ing pressure to create additional space for urban development by making extensions into the sea (Stewart, 1970). At the same time, rising concern for the environment, including growing awareness of the value of wetlands and the fragility of the oceans, will strengthen the forces opposed to further diminution of the hydrosphere by reclamation. In some coastal urban areas, most of the tracts of readily reclaimable wetlands and shallows have been developed, and any future expansion seawards will require either the use of landfill in water of much greater depth than was hitherto regarded as suitable for reclamation, or alternative methods of building human settlements at sea. Some of these alternatives, such as floating cities or cities on piles, may be less damaging to the marine ecosystem but, as explained in Chapter 9, floating fill and pile-supported fill are also detrimental to the natural environment. So, too, is submerged fill which would be necessary for the construction of submarine settlements.

While human colonization of the sea-bed is still at the exploratory stage, settlements on or just above the surface of the sea are now found in many parts of the world, particularly where submarine oil and natural gas deposits are being exploited. Some of these settlements are in many ways similar to mining towns which have developed in hostile environments on land, typically small and characterized by an abnormal population profile domi-nated by transient males in the working age group. Some, however, have developed into substantial settlements on stilts. One, which began in 1945 as an oil rig platform in the Caspian Sea off Azerbaijan, had a quarter of a century later grown into a sizeable community with 240 kilometres of steel trussed roadways and platforms resting on stilts which supported shops, a school, and a hospital as well as the oil derricks (Guardian, 1969). Not all offshore settlements on stilts are associated with the oil industry, however, and 'Stiltsville' off the Florida coast near Miami is an example where buildings were erected on pile-supported platforms out at sea to cater for leisure pursuits not legally permitted within the boundaries of the city proper. Subsequently, a seaward extension of the local authority's area of jurisdiction brought this offshore satellite development within the embrace of mainland laws (Chardon, 1974). It is likely that more urban developments on pile-supported platforms will be built, and a 200,000 square metre extension of Fontvieille, Monaco, is now under consideration, a scheme which envisages the use of offshore oil industry technology (Lloyd's List, 1994).

Modern settlements on piles have their floating equivalents including permanently or semi-permanently moored houseboats and floating restau-rants which can be seen in and near cities in many parts of the world. Perhaps the best known of these floating settlements are the sampan dwellings which are still found in Hong Kong's Aberdeen Harbour with its even more famous floating restaurants. More luxurious floating homes include houseboats moored in the hearts of great cities such as those on the Thames beside London's Chelsea Embankment.

In addition to individual floating dwellings which may be grouped together as settlements on the water, there are floating structures which contain dwellings or apartments together with service facilities. Large ships fit this description, but here we are concerned with dwelling places which remain at least semi-permanently in one spot. An interesting example is provided by the floating living quarters for expatriate oil workers constructed in Singapore, towed to the Persian Gulf, and anchored off the oil export terminal of Ras Tanurah. Among the amenities provided in this offshore residential unit were laundries, dining rooms and recreation facilities together with access to liquor, something forbidden on the nearby Arabian coast (*Economist*, 1976).

Thus updated, the ancient traditions of pile dwellings and homes afloat have continued into the twentieth century, and many of the futuristic aquatic urban development proposals put forward since the end of the 1950s are but technologically advanced versions of the traditional littoral settlement. This can certainly be said of the proposals by Thai architect Sumet Jumsai (1992) for floating houses, restaurants, shops, markets, hotels and even public parks in Bangkok. The city's famous floating market, so popular with today's tourists, is a survival of the time when most of the population lived in floating houses, some three-quarters of the 400,000 residents in mid-nineteenth-century Bangkok dwelling afloat. Jumsai (1992) believes that Bangkok has much to gain from returning to its traditional urban life style of living literally on the water, not least in the minimization of flood problems.

Not surprisingly, many of the futuristic urban development proposals emanate from Japan where cities on pile-supported platforms, floating structures, solid fill or on combinations of these forms have been suggested. Most of these projects relate to the Tokyo region where both Lake Kasumi-ga-uri and Tokyo Bay have been considered for urban expansion (Stewart, 1970). Tange's (1987) Tokyo Bay City plan is the recent successor to his famous Tokyo Bay Plan of 1960 which envisaged development on reclaimed land and pile-supported platforms extending from the inner city to the opposite shore of the bay. The Tokyo Bay City proposal requires the creation of a complex of artificial islands stretching from central Tokyo to Kisarazu, covering some 7,000–8,750 hectares, supporting a resident population of 2.7–3.9 million, and providing jobs for 1.5–2.3 million people. Even more ambitious are the Ministry of International Trade and Industry's Tokyo Bay Cosmopolis and architect Kurokawa's (1987) New Tokyo Plan, 2025, both proposed in the late 1980s. The former would require the creation of four new artificial islands totalling 10,000 hectares in area and supporting a gigantic city of indeterminate population, while the latter would involve the infilling of almost all the upper bay with a 30,000 hectare island which together with much of the adjacent land in Chiba Prefecture would be developed as a huge addition to Tokyo with several million residents.

While throughout the world, buildings constructed over water on piles are not uncommon, apart from the proposed Monaco expansion, I am aware of no large-scale modern urban development which takes this form, even less floating cities of the kind which were spawned in the minds of some imaginative thinkers and designers during the 1960s. Among the proposed floating cities noted by Stewart (1970) were the Japanese Unabara Ocean City (1960), Paul Maymont's city of floating towers suggested for Tokyo Bay (1961), the Houseboat Villages (1962) which Richard Meier envisaged for densely populated coastal areas beside the China Sea and the Indian and Pacific Oceans, and Buckminster Fuller's Supernatant City (1968) which would utilize current ship-building technology to prefabricate floating neighbourhoods to be moored off existing cities which front deep water. There were also proposals for floating airports, including one considered by the Roskill Commission for London's third airport. This design was initiated by the Shell Company which hoped to find a large new market for expanded polystyrene with which the proposed floating concrete caissons were to be filled (Architectural Design, 1970). Unfortunately for Shell, the idea of the floating airport failed to take off.

Another projected urban form which was capable of application to marine and other aquatic areas was Yona Friedman's Spatial Town in which human habitations and other urban activity spaces are inserted into a many-layered space frame supported on pilotis. Applied to existing cities, this type of development could triple current densities. A similar approach was adopted by Eckhard Schulze-Fielitz who evolved his own Spatial City concept and collaborated with Friedman in the design of an elevated linear city in the form of a huge bridge spanning the English Channel (*Progressive Architecture*, 1964).

Particularly since the development of the North Sea oil and gas fields, the seas off the English coast inspired other marine city ideas, including Sea City (1968) to be located in ten metres of water 40 kilometres from Yarmouth. Within an encircling 16 storey pre-cast concrete megastructure supported on piles resting on the sea-bed were proposed three-storey fibre-glass reinforced plastic buildings on floating pontoons. Although conceived for a possible North Sea location, Sea City was considered by its designers as a suitable form of development in other marine areas including parts of the North and South American coast and the Yellow and China Seas (Stewart, 1970). Another type of urban development proposed for the North Sea was the submarine city visualized by a design team led by Roy Gazzard. Floating like icebergs with the main structure submerged, these mainly underwater settlements would comprise huge interlocking concrete caissons with 'conning towers' projecting above the sea surface to give access and provide living quarters and recreation for workers and their families. Gazzard foresaw the eventual development of marine communities on the sea-bed, itself (Observer Staff Reporter, 1966).

The technology is already available for the realization of futuristic marine city projects of the kind just mentioned and, for some, these innovative living environments may be preferable to the alternative of more intensive development on land. Higher densities and the use of areas previously regarded as unsuitable for development, steeply sloping sites, for example, are two possible means of providing for future urban growth on existing land. Alternatively, it is possible to expand cities in a vertical rather than a horizontal direction. Inspired by advances in architectural technology, Le Corbusier pioneered the vertical city concept, and visions of future cities in the sky include Frank Lloyd Wright's sketch design for a mile-high building, and Yona Friedman's Spatial Town mentioned earlier. Today city buildings commonly rise one hundred to four hundred metres into the air, some even further, and the vertical extent of human settlements is also being increased by ever deeper excavation for the creation of usable underground space. In some suitable areas with appropriate geological and seismological conditions, cavern engineering can be used to create large underground spaces, a technology based on the principle of using the strength of the rock itself to support the roof and walls. Among the appropriate uses for such underground areas are storage facilities of various types and waste treatment, but many other urban uses are accommodated below ground level, including a variety of commercial activities. A proposed artificial cavern in Hong Kong has been designed to accommodate 200,000 square metres of mixed retail, restaurant and recreational floorspace (Arup *et al.*, 1989). Even in Tokyo, with its less favourable geological conditions, serious consideration is being given to the 'Geofront', the use of deeper underground space as an alternative or additional means of urban expansion (Cybriwsky, 1991).

Ideas for alternative forms of urban development abound, and the technology already exists for the implementation of many of them. Indeed, the human colonization of Space has begun and pioneer space stations with human occupants now orbit our planet. Nevertheless, despite enormous technical advances in recent decades, floating, submarine and space-frame cities of the kinds proposed since 1960 have yet to be built. The latest plans for Tokyo Bay, ambitious though they are, involve development on extensive landfill rather than the futuristic structures envisaged by Kikutake, Kurokawa and their ilk over thirty years ago. Similarly, the new airport for Osaka, planned in the 1960s as a huge floating structure, has recently come into being on an artificial island made of solid fill.

All this may be a disappointment to any who share the view which Kikutake (quoted in Stewart, 1970:410) expressed:

> History has shown that the human being carries his inner and outer confusion with him onto reclaimed land. The sea will go on refusing such intrusions. New

human communities have never been created by the human beings who escaped onto newly gained land, because the relationship of the human being to the land and to the organization of his activities stayed the same

Marine civilizations are seen by Kikutake as a means of reforming this relationship, but the psychological and social implications of transplanting people from a familiar land-based environment to a totally new type of settlement in an alien aquatic setting have yet to be ascertained. To date, offshore settlements have generally been for atypical temporary communities such as those associated with the exploitation of submarine mineral resources. Despite the advantages claimed by visionary architects and planners, serious problems can be expected when trying to adapt human life to a marine environment. The familiar 'new town blues' and stress associated with high-rise living could seem trivial matters when compared with problems which might be generated by life in an alien 'hi-tech' environment on, above, or below, the sea. Meier (1966) acknowledged that there would be serious problems and opposition even when proposing his floating settlements for Hong Kong, a place where some ethnic groups have a long-established tradition of living afloat.

Nitschke (1965:219) roundly condemned the kind of technological solution proposed by Kikutake and others as a disintegration of the relationship between human beings and nature.

> Living in mechanized towers is not a solution to the chaos of contemporary existence. Behind this vision lies modern man's desire to be free from an earth which represents to him bondage and restraint in his quest for external freedom. True freedom is found within and needs no towers in the air or plunges into the sea. Only the lopsided development of his intellectual powers can have made man conceive of so miserable an answer to human existence.

Present trends and future prospects

At the approach of the twenty-first century, despite enormous technological advances including the emergence of the 'intelligent' building, the prospect of technopolis as envisioned in the 1960s seems further away than ever. Whatever form the future city may take, it is probable that, in the immediate future, it will remain firmly founded on solid ground. In 'cities on the shore' we can expect that landfill reclamation will continue to be a favoured method of urban expansion because this requires no radical changes or innovations in city-building and yet does not preclude them. Moreover, it allows growth by incremental extension of the existing urban infrastructure instead of having to provide a complete new infrastructural system from scratch, as would be necessary in the case of many of the proposed types of offshore marine development. In terms of living environment, there is usually little to distinguish parts of a city which are built on reclaimed sites from those districts which developed on 'natural' dry land. Except, possibly, where the original shore was backed by hilly terrain, most residents and visitors move between reclaimed areas and other parts of the city without being aware of any significant change in their urban environment.

Problems such as structural damage due to fill subsidence or, more dramatically, that caused by earthquakes which are often most destructive to buildings on landfill and recent alluvial and marine deposits, might alert citizens to possible disadvantages of urban development on reclaimed land. So, too, might serious flooding, a common hazard in low-lying reclaimed areas. The latter problem is one which might become increasingly serious as sea-levels continue to rise, a trend which many believe could accelerate as global temperatures rise under the influence of the so-called 'greenhouse effect' (Frassetto, 1991).

Localized ground subsidence of up to ten millimetres a year is common in large cities which have developed on coastal lowlands such as Venice, London, Bangkok, New Orleans and Houston – Galveston, the principal causes being groundwater withdrawal, hydrocarbon extraction, and wetland drainage and development (Belperio, 1993; Carbognin, 1985). In places such as these, where much development is on reclaimed land, even a slight rise in sea-level poses a serious threat.

In his study of the effects of a rising sea-level on coastal environments, Bird (1993) discusses many different types of coast, including artificial and developed coasts. Accepting the likelihood of a global sea-level rise in the order of about one metre in the next 150 years, Bird (1993:125) describes three probable human response scenarios:

1. evacuation, abandoning the land as it is submerged and eroded, and where possible adapting to the effects of the rising sea;
2. attempts to maintain the existing coastline and coastal margin by engineering works; and
3. counter-attack, notably by building walls to enclose and reclaim intertidal and nearshore areas.

Where societies have the organization, technology and resources to do so, they are likely to counter the effects of a sea-level rise by coastal protection works, following the Dutch example, but elsewhere evacuation on a large scale is probable. Abandonment of submerging areas may occur on some developed coasts in countries which have the means to build structures capable of holding back the sea and preventing erosion and flooding. As Bird (1993: 125) points out: 'Few buildings, roads and bridges have been designed to last more than 50 years without substantial renovation, and the cost of maintaining them has to be considered in relation to the expense of maintaining the land they stand upon.'

Conversely, a possible response to rising sea-levels might be more extensive coastal land reclamation, a strategy which Bird (1993:141) terms 'counter-attack'. Because it will require enormous expenditure just to maintain the coastline in the face of a rise in sea-level, it may be found more economical to construct sea-walls offshore and reclaim the enclosed shallow areas for productive use. Where this is possible, the economic returns from the land thus gained could offset the costs of building sea-walls and associated structures.

Among the places where this kind of strategy has been suggested are the coast near Bangkok at the head of the Gulf of Thailand, and Australia's Port Phillip Bay on which stands Melbourne. Port Phillip Bay has a shoreline 260 kilometres long but its mouth is only 3 kilometres wide, and it would be less expensive to defend this narrow marine entrance than to maintain the existing lengthy coastline. Ship access to the ports of Melbourne and Geelong could be maintained by the construction of canals which would also act as drainage channels. Another Australian city where a similar counter-attack strategy might be implemented is Cairns, but recent controversy over proposed limited reclamation work there is a reminder of the serious environmental and other objections which can be made against schemes of this kind (Hudson, 1989a).

MIT's Tunney Lee believes that in order to deal with the threat of rising sea-level 'it is necessary to rethink our present methods of planning, management and governance of urban areas'. He observes that 'traditional master plans which direct the physical growth of the city are no longer sufficient', and warns that the construction of dikes, sea-walls and barriers of various kinds will not be effective by themselves (Lee, 1991:35). Lee classifies the necessary countermeasures into three categories: construction, prevention and adaptation. Of these, construction, including the use of traditional dikes, sea-walls and movable barriers, is the most visible and the most costly. Because constructions of this type are visible evidence that 'something is being done', such measures are often politically favoured despite their enormous expense, but they can have harmful environmental effects which may not always be foreseen. Prevention, in many ways the most important approach and less costly from a total point of view, is often politically unpopular because it involves controversial measures such as the prohibition of building and the gradual removal of existing uses from vulnerable areas. Another part of prevention is the promulgation of strict standards for buildings, roads and infrastructure, thus incurring additional costs of development. This may be difficult to accept when scientists are uncertain about the future world climate and consequent sea-level change, unlike earthquakes whose terrifying reality has been demonstrated in several major cities in recent years, encouraging authorities to take appropriate measures. A traditional way for littoral cities to deal with problems of fluctuating water levels is adaptation, 'a much neglected area of planning' (Lee, 1991:36). Adaptations are both physical and behavioural, examples of the former including the floating and stilt supported dwellings of Thailand and the ground floors of the Venetian palazzi which are used for storage not habitation. Lee (1991:37) advises that we have to learn new versions of the traditional wisdom which can be found in

cities and cultures that deal with water on a seasonal and daily basis ... We must develop designs of buildings that recognize the variability of water levels and preserve natural areas that absorb tides and storms. Very importantly new institutions and rituals need to be invented to prepare for periodic and unexpected changes and to provide for public safety.

Appropriate planning policies might include land use restrictions in vulnerable areas, zoning them for open space use rather than for building, for example. Alternatively, ground levels might be raised to compensate for rising sea-levels, a response which would also require improved defence against marine erosion as storm waves become potentially more destructive. Galveston has already demonstrated how even an existing city can be raised by jacking up buildings and placing fill beneath them (see Chapter 7). Looking further into the future, van Veen suggested a drastic solution to the marine threat to The Netherlands, proposing to raise the country above sea-level by pumping ashore a layer of sand nearly thirty metres thick. The example of Galveston shows that this need not involve 'burying all its history' as the Dutch engineer suggested (van Veen, 1962:195). Though technically not very difficult, such a task would require exceptional vision and commitment on the part of the nation, but we have come to expect this of the Dutch for whom the struggle against the sea is a way of life.

Around the world, sea defence, flood control and flood mitigation are matters of growing concern in several major urban areas on the coast (Frasseto, 1991; O'Neill, 1990). London is now protected by the Thames Barrier, designed to be effective until the middle of the twenty-first century, and more recently a 25-kilometre barrier was constructed across the Neva estuary to protect St Petersburg. Political wranglings have delayed completion of the proposed barriers across the entrances to the Venetian Lagoon, but this has the benefit of ensuring that the designs can be based on data which incorporate the latest estimates on the consequences of global warming. In Japan, coastal protection and flood control planning for urban areas includes proposals for improved earthquake resistant dikes and the construction of artificial underground rivers (Bureau of City Planning, 1992; Morioka, 1991).

In 1987 the Dutch – past masters in the field of coastal engineering – completed a massive 3.2 kilometre storm-surge barrier across the East Scheldt estuary, a project which was the focus of environmental protest. More recent coastal engineering work in The Netherlands reflects an environmentally sensitive soft engineering approach. One of the leading proponents of soft engineering solutions is Ronald Waterman, an environmental adviser to the Dutch Public Works Department and the city of Rotterdam. He has adopted the approach of hydraulic engineer, J.N. Svasek who, in 1979, launched a new concept for coastal extension, basing his method on morpho-logical theories and practice aptly described as 'building with Nature'. 'Solid stone or concrete bulwarks against the sea are no longer considered of prime importance, but instead use is made of various forces acting on the mobile loose sand material while creating a flexible new dynamic equilibrium coast' (Waterman, 1991:67). Based on Svasek's concept, there are now plans for remodelling parts of The Netherlands coast including the stretch from Sche-veningen south to the Hook of Holland and across the New Waterway entrance to Europoort, together with other coastal areas to the north. Among the planned developments are a 3,000-hectare wedge-shaped addition of new land between Scheveningen and Hook of Holland designed to improve flood protection, including provision for possible sea-level rise, and providing space for a variety of urban and rural uses including housing, industry, port, recreation, tourism, horticulture, aquaculture and nature conservation. South of the New Waterway, an artificial peninsula will be used for 'environmentally friendly storage and processing of all types of wastes', as well as industrial and port development, a recreation area and a nature reserve (Waterman, 1991:68).

Others promoting a soft engineering approach to coastal protection in-clude the University of Western Australia's Richard Silvester and John Hsu (1991; 1993) who also have sought to emulate the example of nature in the design of artificial coasts which maintain stability under the influence of marine processes. They seek to achieve this by creating crenulate-shaped bays separated by artificial headlands designed to encourage accretion and minimize scour. An example of the successful application of this approach is found on a 30 kilometre stretch of coast on the south side of Singapore where land reclaimed for high-rise residential and commercial development was originally to be protected by a revetment wall. The failure of the short length of sea wall which was actually built suggested a search for alternative solutions and, after pilot constructions proved the viability of the new approach, 48 artificial headlands were created forming between them bays, most of which were in a static equilibrium (Silvester and Hsu, 1991).

Henceforth, anthropogenic coasts, hitherto normally readily distinguish-able by their straight margins and geometric shapes, are more likely to resemble natural forms, a development which, one hopes, will bring aesthetic and environmental benefits as well as technical advantages in coastal protec-tion. Ideas such as these are being adopted in other parts of the world, signifying, perhaps, that the history of land reclamation may be entering a new phase. While, in places, heightened environmental awareness and concern is slowing the rate of reclamation, even reversing the process in a few localities, elsewhere coastal protection and massive reclamation schemes, many on an unprecedented scale, are in progress or are planned. Today,

however, engineering methods and coastal management practices are beginning to reflect greater environmental knowledge and sensitivity. It is within
this context that, in the face of rising sea-levels, 'cities on the shore' continue
to advance their urban littoral frontier.

Glossary

Anthropogenic coast: a coast shaped by human action; one where anthropogene landforms dominate. Anthropogenic coasts include those modified by excavation and dredging and, more commonly, those where reclamation by landfill or by enclosure and drainage, has extended the land area into the sea. Many anthropogenic coasts are the product of dredge and *fill* operations.

Ashlar: (1) squared stone; (2) masonry constructed of squared stones. *Seawalls* and river embankments are often faced with ashlar which provides protection against erosion and is of attractive appearance.

Breakwater: a wall built out into the sea to protect a harbour from the waves; sometimes called a *mole*.

Bulkhead: a term commonly applied to an upright partition dividing watertight compartments of a ship; in coastal engineering, it refers to a vertical structure, often of sheet piling, which retains landfill and protects it from the erosive action of waves and currents. Bulkhead development is a term sometimes applied to landfill schemes which involve the use of this type of structure.

Bund: an embankment or causeway, sometimes applied to a *quay*. The Bund on the Shanghai waterfront is a well-known example.

Fill: artificially deposited solid material which raises land levels or which creates dry land in place of water areas including coastal shallows, margins of lakes and rivers, and *wetlands*. Sometimes the term 'fill' is also applied to pile-supported and floating structures which provide solid surfaces on top of, or above, the water.

Groins or groynes: coastal structures built more or less at right angles to the shoreline to trap sand, gravel, etc. and to stabilize beaches by decreasing littoral drift.

Jetty: sometimes applied to a *breakwater* or *mole*, this term normally refers to a landing stage which projects into the water, generally in the form of a deck supported on piles.

Marsh: a *wetland* where the dominant vegetation is non–woody plants such as grasses and sedges.

Mole: a massive structure serving as a *breakwater* or *pier*.

Pier: a *breakwater* or *mole*; or commonly, a large *jetty* in the form of a deck supported on piles, used as a landing stage and sometimes as a promenade.

Praya: an anglicized version of the Portuguese 'praia' which means beach or strand. This word was formerly commonly applied in Hong Kong to waterfront structures such as embankments, esplanades and marine roads.

Quay: an artificial landing place of solid construction built along the bank of a river or the harbourfront for the purpose of loading and unloading vessels.

Revetment: a structure designed to give protection to fill materials, preventing *scour*. Sometimes in the form of a wall, but often of timber construction, it protects the banks or shore of the water body, but is not designed to withstand the thrust of landfill deposits.

Rip-rap: loosely deposited stones placed on the sea-shore or bed and banks of a river to give protection from *scour*.

Scour: erosion of the river bed, river banks or sea-bed by the action of flowing water or waves.

Sea-wall: a coastal wall, often of massive construction, built to provide protection against flooding or erosion.

Shore: 'The strip of ground bordering any body of water which is alternately exposed, or covered by tides and/or waves. A shore of unconsolidated material is usually called a beach. Sometimes used synonymously with bank of a stream but such use is, in a strict sense, incorrect' (Volmer, 1967). *The New Collins Dictionary and Thesaurus* (1987) defines 'shore' as 'the land along the edge of a sea, lake, or wide river', and it is in this broader sense that the word is used in *Cities on the Shore*.

Slurry: a suspension of solid particles, such as sand or silt, in a liquid, usually water. Commonly, dredged material is conveyed along a pipe-line in a slurry and pumped ashore, usually behind a *bund* which is designed to allow the water to drain away leaving behind the solids as *fill*.

Swamp: a *wetland* where the dominant vegetation is woody plants such as trees and shrubs. Mangroves are typical plants of many tropical and sub-tropical swamps.

Tetrapod: a very stable four-legged equiangular figure, often made of re-inforced concrete and commonly used in large numbers in sea defence and reclamation works as protection for *breakwaters* and *sea-walls*. Piled along the shore, tetrapods are effective in breaking the force of the waves and reducing *scour*.

Tidal prism: the total amount of water that flows into, and then out of, a coastal inlet such as an estuary with the movement of the tide, excluding any fresh water flow.

Wetlands: a general term for areas which are waterlogged or permanently or intermittently inundated by shallow fresh or salt water, often occurring as transitional zones between terrestrial and aquatic environments. Definitions vary according to their purpose, but tidal flats, coastal and lacustrine shallows, *swamps*, *marshes*, bogs and similar areas are all normally regarded as wet-lands.

Wharf: a substantial platform of stone, concrete, timber, etc. at the water's edge for loading and unloading ships lying alongside. Normally built parallel to the waterfront, it may be of solid or open construction. In the latter case, the wharf takes the form of a large deck supported on piles driven into the bed of the harbour.

References

Abercrombie, P. (1948) *Hong Kong Preliminary Planning Report*. Hong Kong: Hong Kong Government

Abercrombie, P. (Sir) (1959) *Town and Country Planning*. 3rd edn, revised by D. Rigby Childs, London: Oxford University Press

Adejumo, A. (1964) *Reclamation of Victoria Island*. Mimeographed report by the Resident Engineer, Lagos, Nigeria.

Alabaster, E. (1899) *Notes and Commentaries on Chinese Criminal Law and cognate topics ... together with a brief Excursus on the Law of Property*. London: Luzac.

Amphoux, M. (1949) Les functions portuaires *Revue de la Porte Oceane*, **10**:19–22.

Anderson, A. (1931) (Introduction by H.T. Creasy) Hong Kong Praya East Reclamation Scheme. Final Report. *Hong Kong Sessional Papers* no. 1.

Andersons, A. (1980) Circular quay: the image of the city, in P. Weber (ed.) *The Design of Sydney: Three Decades of Change in The City Centre*, Sydney: Law Book Co. (158–76).

Arai, Y., Oikawa, K., Suzuki, S. and Hayashi, K. (1992) Construction of an artificial island for Kansai International Airport, in Institution of Civil Engineers (eds), *Coastal Structures and Breakwaters*, London, Thomas Telford (499–512).

Architectural Design (1970) Floating airport, *Architectural Design*, **40**, (3):125.

Arup, O. and Partners (1989) *Space Underground. The Potential in Hong Kong for Development in Man–made Caverns* (fold-out brochure). Hong Kong: Hong Kong Government.

Ault, W. (1992) *Cleveland Structure Plan. Explanatory Memorandum*, Middlesbrough: Cleveland County Council.

Auly, J. (1993) Personal communication. Letter from the Estates Officer, Tees and Hartlepool Port Authority.

Barker, J. (1991) Ports in the 1990s and beyond'. *Dock and Harbour Authority*, **71**: 227–30.

Belperio, A.P. (1993) Land subsidence and sea level rise in the Port Adelaide estuary: implications for monitoring the greenhouse effect'. *Australian Journal of Earth Sciences*, **40**:359–68.

Bennett, A. (1924) The place you live in. *Royal Magazine*, **51**:446–52.

Bird, E.C.F. (1993) *Submerging Coasts: The Effects of a Rising Sea Level on Coastal Environments*. Chichester: Wiley.

Bird, J. (1971) *Seaports and Seaport Terminals*. London: Hutchinson.

Bourassa, S.C. (1991) *The Aesthetics of Landscape*. London: Belhaven.

Bowring Praya Commission (1856) Report of the Bowring Praya Commission, in *Supplement to the Hong Kong Government Gazette*, New Series, **1**(43).

Brand, E.W. and Whiteside, P.G.D. (1990) Hong Kong's fill resources for the 1990s, in P. Fowler and Q. Earle (eds) *The Hong Kong Quarrying Industry 1990–2000. A Decade of Change*, Hong Kong: Institute of Quarrying, Hong Kong Branch (101–12).

Briscoe, J. (1979) Legal problems of tidal marshes, in T.J. Conomos (ed.), *San Francisco Bay. The Urbanized Estuary. Investigations into the Natural History of San Francisco Bay and Delta with Reference to the Influence of Man*, San Francisco: Pacific Division/American Association for the Advancement of Science (387–400).

Bunting, B. (1967) *The Houses of Boston's Back Bay: An Architectural History 1840–1917*, Cambridge: Belknap Press of the Harvard University Press.

Bureau of City Planning (1992) *Planning of Tokyo 1992*. Tokyo: Tokyo Metropolitan Government.

Burgess, E.W. (1925) The growth of the city, in R.E. Park, E.W. Burgess and R.D. McKenzie (eds) *The City*, Chicago: University of Chicago Press (47–62).

Burke, G.L. (1956) *The Making of Dutch Towns*. London. Cleaver–Hume Press.

Buttenwieser, A.L. (1987) *Manhattan Water–bound: Planning and Developing Manhattan's Waterfront from the Seventeenth Century to the Present*. New York: New York University Press.

Canton Register (1841) **14** (49), 7 December.

Canton Register (1842) **15** (1), 4 January.

Carbognin, L. (1985) Land subsidence: a worldwide environmental hazard, *Nature and Resources*, **21**, 2–12.

Chardon, R.E. (1974) Personal communication, Miami, 14 Oct. 1974. The late Professor Roland Chardon was a member of the faculty of the Department of Geography and Anthropology, Louisiana State University, Baton Rouge.

China Mail (1852) 15 January.

China Mail (1921) 29 April:9.

Chiu, T.N. (1973) *The Port of Hong Kong. A Survey of its Development.* Hong Kong: Hong Kong University Press.

Clark, G. (1967) *The Stone Age Hunters.* New York: McGraw Hill.

Clayton, I. and Peppin, T. (1990) *The Single European Market. Industry and European Environmental Legislation. A Summary for Companies in Cleveland.* A report by the Research and Intelligence Unit for the Department of Economic Development and Planning no. 1., Middlesbrough: Cleveland County Council.

Clearwater, J.L. (1985) Port Construction since 1885: evolving to meet a changing world. *Dock and Harbour Authority,* **66**: 1–3.

Cleveland County Council and Nature Conservancy Council [n.d.] *Cleveland Wildlife Strategy.* Middlesbrough: Cleveland County Council.

Cleveland INCA [1990?] *INCA in Cleveland. The First Year,* Billingham: INCA.

Coles, B. (1990) Wetland archaeology: A wealth of evidence, in M. Williams (ed.) *Wetlands. A Threatened Landscape.* Oxford: Blackwell (234–66).

Coles, B. and Coles, J. (1989) *People of the Wetlands: Bogs, Bodies and Lake–Dwellers,* London: Thames and Hudson.

Colonial Office (1852) Despatches; Bonham, No. 5, 23 January 1852. Colonial Office Records Series 129/39, Public Record Office, London.

Conzen, M.P. and Lewis, G.K. (1976) Boston: a geographical portrait, in J.S. Adams (ed.) *Contemporary Metropolitan America, vol. 1. Cities of The Nation's Historic Metropolitan Core.* Cambridge, MA: Ballinger (51–138).

Cosgrove, D. (1990) An elemental division: water control and engineered landscape, in Cosgrove and G. Petts (eds) *Water, Engineering and Landscape: Water Control and Landscape Transformation in the Modern Period.* London: Belhaven Press: (1–11).

Coughlan, J. (1979) Aspects of reclamation in Southampton Water, in B. Knights and A.J. Phillips (eds) *Estuarine and Coastal Land Reclamation and Water Storage.* Farnborough: Saxon House (99–124).

Couper, A.D. (1972) *The Geography of Sea Transport.* London: Hutchinson.

Craig–Smith, S.J. and Fagence, M. (eds) (1995) *Recreation and Tourism as a Catalyst for Urban Waterfront Development.* New York: Praeger.

Crawford, R. (1993) Personal communication. Geography Department, San Francisco State University.

Cressey, G.B. (1955) *Land of 500 Million: A Geography of China.* New York: McGraw Hill.

Crooke, P. (1971) The community in Latin America, *Report of Proceedings. Town and Country Planning Summer School, Southampton University, 1–12 September 1971.* London: Royal Town Planning Institute (68–70).

Cybriwsky, R. (1991) *Tokyo. The Changing Profile of an Urban Giant.* London: Belhaven Press.

Daly, T.V. (1975) *A Short History of the Guyanese People,* London: Macmillan.

Davenport, J. (1990) *The Street Names of Auckland: Their Story.* Auckland: Hodder and Stoughton.

Davidson, N.C. (1980) *Seal Sands Feasibility Study.* A Report to Cleveland County Council and the Nature Conservancy Council. Department of Zoology, University of Durham (mimeo).

Davis, D.W., McCloy, J.M. and Craig, A.K. (1988) Man's response to coastal change in the northern Gulf of Mexico, in K. Ruddle, W.B. Morgan and J.R. Pfafflin (eds), *The Coastal Zone: Man's Response to Change.* Chur, Switzerland: Harwood Academic (257–97).

Des Voeux, G.W. (1903) *My Colonial Service,* vol. 2, London: John Murray.

Downs, A. (1970) *Urban Problems and Prospects.* Chicago: Markham.

Drake, S.A. (1971) *Old Landmarks and Historic Personages of Boston* (revised edn), Rutland, Vermont: Charles E. Tuttle. First edition published in 1872; revised edition first published in 1906 by Little, Brown, and Co., Boston. Re–published by Charles E. Tuttle in 1971.

Dreisbach, R.H. (1969) *Handbook of the San Francisco Region.* Palo Alto: Environmental Studies.

Du–Plat–Taylor, F.M. (1931) *The Reclamation of Land from the Sea.* London: Constable.

Economist (1976) Work onshore, live offshore. *The Economist,* 7 August: 63.

Eitel, E.J. (1895) *Europe in China: The History of Hongkong from the Beginning to the Year 1882.* London: Luzac; Hong Kong: Kelly and Walsh.

Elliot, C. (1841) Public Notice and Declaration, *Canton Register,* **14**, (18), 4 May: 105; *Canton Press,* **6**, (32), 8 May.

Endacott, G.B. (1962) *A Biographical Sketch–book of Early Hong Kong.* Singapore: Donald Moore for Eastern Universities Press.

Endacott, G.B. (1964) *A History of Hong Kong.* London: Oxford University Press.

Environmental Protection Department (1992) *Environment Hong Kong 1992: A Review of 1991.* Hong Kong: Hong Kong Government.

Evans, E. and Jones, E. (1955) The growth of Belfast. *Town Planning Review,* **26**(2): 92–111.

Evans, P.R. (1990a) Cleaning up the Tees – Progress and prospects, in *Cleaning Up the Tees. Progress and Prospects,* Proceedings of the conference held at the Forum Theatre, Billingham, Cleveland on 15th September 1990, under the auspices of the Cleveland INCA and the University of Durham. Two pages of a mimeographed report.

Evans, P.R. (1990b) The ornithological importance of Teesmouth, in *Cleaning Up the Tees*. (see Evans (1990a).

Eyre, J.D. (1956) Japanese land development in Kojima Bay. *Economic Geography*, **32**: 58–74.

Fairbank, W. (1970) Planning in Teesside County Borough, in J.C. Dewdney (ed.), *Durham County and City with Teesside*, Durham: Local Executive Committee for the British Association (443–51).

Fallows, W. (1878) *Fragments of the Early History of the Tees*. Middlesbrough: Middlesbrough Printery and Publishing.

Far East Engineer (1960) H.K. Electric Co's new power station. *Far East Engineer*, **1**:31–2.

Fleming, W.B. (1915) *The History of Tyre*. Columbia University Oriental Studies Vol. 10. New York: Columbia University Press.

Frassetto, R. (1991) *Impact of Sea Level Rise on Cities and Regions*. Venice: Marsilio Editore.

Friend of China and Hong Kong Gazette (1843) Letter to the Editor, signed A.X., **2**(89), 30 Nov.:174.

Friend of China and Hong Kong Gazette (1856), **15**(38), 10th May.

Gilliam, H. (1969) *Between the Devil and the Deep Blue Bay*. San Francisco: Chronicle Books.

Gillis, J. (1990) *Cleveland Structure Plan* Middlesbrough: Cleveland County Council.

Guardian (1969) 25th February: 3 (air photograph with caption).

Hall, P. (1991) *Waterfronts: A New Urban Frontier*. (Working Paper 538), Berkeley: Institute of Urban and Regional Development, University of California.

Harden, D. (1962) *The Phoenicians*. London: Thames and Hudson.

Hardoy, J. (1968) *Urban Planning in Pre–Columbian America*. New York: Braziller.

Harris, D.D. and Stephens, I.R. (1981) *Settlement Patterns and Processes*. Melbourne: Longman Cheshire.

Hawkes, J. and Hawkes, C. (1958) *Prehistoric Britain*. (revised edn) Harmondsworth: Penguin.

Hazlitt, W.C. (1900) *The Venetian Republic: Its Rise, Its Growth, and Its Fall. 421–1797* (2 vols). London: Adam and Charles Black.

Henry, J.K.M., Villiers, A.W.C. and Gandy, J.J. (1961) The construction of the new Hong Kong Airport. *Proceedings of the Institution of Civil Engineers*, **19**:157–84.

Herm, G. (1975) (translated by Caroline Hillier) *The Phoenicians: The Purple Empire of the Ancient World*. London: Gollancz Ltd.

Herodotus (1882) A new literal version from the text of Baehr, with a Geographical and General Index by Henry Carey. London: Routledge.

Hiroshima Prefectural Government [n.d.] *The Itsukaichi District Port Improvement Project* (pamphlet) produced by Hiroshima Prefectural Hiroshima Port and Harbour Promotion Bureau.

Hobley, B. (1981) The London waterfront: the exception or the rule?, in G. Milne and B. Hobley (eds), *Waterfront Archaeology in Britain and Northern Europe*, Research Report No. 41. The Council for British Archaeology. London: The Council (1–9).

Hong Kong Government (1888) Praya Reclamation Scheme, *Hong Kong Sessional Papers, 1888*. Also published separately as Chater, P.C. (1888) *The Praya Reclamation Scheme*. Hong Kong: Noronha.

Hong Kong Government (1922) Report of the Director of Public Works for the Year 1992, Appendix Q. *Hong Kong Administrative Reports, 1922*: Q82.

Hong Kong Government (1923) Report of the Director of Public Works for the Year 1923, Appendix Q. *Hong Kong Administrative Reports, 1923*:Q100.

Hong Kong Government (1964) *Hong Kong Report for 1963*. Hong Kong: Government Press.

Hong Kong Land Investment and Agency Co. Ltd. [n.d.] *The Hong Kong Land Investment and Agency Company Ltd. A Short History, 1889–1964*. Hong Kong. (This history was written by B.C. Field, who had a long association with the Agency but he is not named as the author.)

Hong Kong Planning Department (1991) *Metroplan. The Selected Strategy Executive Summary*. Hong Kong: Hong Kong Government.

Hori, N. (1984) A history of the expansion of the reclaimed areas and some environmental problems in Hiroshima, western Japan. *Geographical Reports of Tokyo Metropolitan University*, no. 19, the Memorial Volume to Professor Takamasa Nakano, Department of Geography, Tokyo Metropolitan University (149–61).

Hosomi, A. (1982) *Environmental Issues in Japan's Seto Inland Sea*. Akashi: People's Alliance to Protect the Environment of the Seto Inland Sea, Special Publication, no. 1.

House, J.W. and Fullerton, B. (1960) *Teesside at Midcentury*. London: Macmillan.

Hoyle, B.S., Pinder, D.A. and Husain, M.S. (eds) (1988) *Revitalising the Waterfront: International Dimensions of Dockland Redevelopment*, London: Belhaven Press.

Hudson, B.J. (1962) Land reclamation in the Tees Estuary. Unpublished MCD. Special Study, Department of Civic Design, University of Liverpool.

Hudson, B.J. (1970) Land reclamation in Hong Kong. Unpublished PhD thesis, Department of Architecture, University of Hong Kong.

Hudson, B.J. [1974] Coastal land reclamation in Jamaica, in B. Hudson (ed.) *Conservation in Jamaica*, Kingston: Jamaican Geographical Society.

Hudson, B.J. (1978) Paul Chater and the Praya Reclamations: wetland development in Hong Kong 1887–1930. *Journal of Oriental Studies,* **16** (1/2): 79–86.

Hudson, B.J. (1979) Coastal land reclamation with special reference to Hong Kong, *Reclamation Review,* **2**:3–16.

Hudson, B.J. (1980) Anthropogenic coasts, *Geography,* **65** (3):194–202.

Hudson, B.J. (1983) Wetland reclamation in Jamaica. *Caribbean Geography,* **1**(2):75–88.

Hudson, B.J. (1989a) Coastal land reclamation and urban expansion: littoral thinking for Queensland planners', *Queensland Planner,* **29** (2):6–10.

Hudson, B.J. (1989b) Waterfront development and redevelopment in the West Indies *Caribbean Geography,* **2** (4):229–40.

Hudson, B.J. (1995) Technology, tourism and heritage: waterfront redevelopment in the Caribbean, in S.J. Craig–Smith and M. Fagence (eds) *Recreation and Tourism as a Catalyst for Urban Waterfront Development,* New York: Praeger.

Jamieson, G. (1921) *Chinese Family and Commercial Law,* Shanghai: Kelly and Walsh.

Jarrett, H.R. (1951) Bathurst: Port of the Gambia River, *Geography,* **36**:98–107.

Jellicoe, G. and Jellicoe, S. (1987) *The Landscape of Man* (revised and enlarged edn), London: Thames and Hudson.

Jernigan, T.R. (1905) *China in Law and Commerce.* New York: Macmillan.

Johnson, D. (1988) *Auckland by the Sea. 100 Years of Work and Play.* Auckland: David Bateman.

Jones, E. (1960) *A Social Geography of Belfast.* London: Oxford University Press.

Josselyn, M.N. and Atwater, B.F. (1982), Physical and biological constraints on Man's use of the shore zone of the San Francisco Estuary, in W.J. Kockelman, T.J. Conomos, and A.E. Leviton (eds), *San Francisco Bay. Use and Protection,* San Francisco: Pacific Division of the American Association for the Advancement of Science, 57–84.

Jumsai, S. (1992) Aquatic Bangkok from the [sic] 1550 to the year 2000 and beyond. *Aquapolis* **1** (2):6–13.

Kay, J.H. (1980) *Lost Boston.* Boston: Houghton Mifflin.

Kennedy, L.W. (1992) *Planning the City upon a Hill: Boston Since 1630.* Amherst: University of Massachusetts Press.

Kihara, K. (1978) Coastline conservation. Establishing common tideland use rights. *Japan Quarterly* **25**:47–8.

Kramer, S.N. (1956) *From the Tablets of Sumer.* Indiana Hills, Colorado: Falcon Wings.

Lane, F.C. (1973) *Venice: A Maritime Republic.* Baltimore: Johns Hopkins University Press.

Leakey, R. and Lewin, R. (1979) *People of the Lake. Man; His Origins, Nature and Future.* London: Collins.

Lee, T. (1991) Cities: crisis or planning, in R. Frassetto (ed.) *Impact of Sea Level Rise on Cities and Regions.*Venice: Marsilio Editore (33–8).

Le Guillou, M. (1978) *A History of the River Tees 1000–1975.* Middlesbrough: Cleveland County Libraries.

Lewis, P.F. (1976) *New Orleans: the making of an urban landscape,* in J.S. Adams (ed.) *Association of American Geographers Comparative Metropolitan Analysis Project. Contemporary Metropolitan America Vol. 2 Nineteenth Century Ports,* Cambridge, MA: Ballinger Publishing (97–216).

Lockhart, J.H.S. (1900) *Extracts from a Report by Mr Stewart Lockhart on the Extension of the Colony of Hong Kong.* Hong Kong: Hong Kong Government.

Lloyd's List (1994) *France & Monaco* (special supplement), April, 1994.

Lumb, P. (1966) Personal communication, Department of Civil Engineering, University of Hong Kong.

McCord, D. (1973) *About Boston. Sight, Sound, Flavor and Inflection.* Boston: Little, Brown and Co.

McDonald (1988) *Gladstone: City that Waited.* Brisbane: Boolarong Publications.

McGloin, J.B. (1978) *San Francisco. The Story of a City.* San Rafael, CA: Presidio Press.

Martin, R.M. (1847) *China; Political, Commercial and Social; an Official Report to Her Majesty's Government.* (2 vols). London: James Madden.

Matsutaro, N., Nobuo, M., Kazutaka, U. (eds) and Murray, P. (translator) (1973) *Old Maps in Japan* (Translated by P. Murray). Osaka: Sogensha.

Mayers, W.F., Dennys, N.B. and King, C. (1867) *The Treaty Ports of China and Japan.* London:Trubner; Hong Kong: A. Shortrede.

Meier, R.L. (1966) *Studies on the Future of Cities in Asia.* Berkeley: Center for Planning and Development Research: Institute of Urban and Regional Development, University of California.

Meli, R. (1988) Effects of the September 19, 1985 Earthquake on the buildings of Mexico City, in Council on Tall Buildings and Urban Habitat, Lynn S. Beadle (Ed. in Chief), *Second Century of the Skyscraper,* New York: Van Nostrand Reinhold (667–78).

Melville, H. (1988) *Moby Dick or The Whale, The Writings of Herman Melville,* vol. 6, Evanston: Northwestern University Press and The Newberry Library.

Miles, B.R. (ed.) (1947) *Gibraltar Directory and Guide Book* Gibraltar: Benedict R. Miles.

Milne, G. (1981) Medieval riverfront reclamation in London, in G. Milne and B. Hobley (eds) *Waterfront Archaeology in Britain and Northern Europe* (32–6).

Milne, G. and Hobley, B. (1981) *Waterfront Archaeology in Britain and Northern Europe*. Research Report No.41. The Council for British Archaeology, London: The Council for British Archaeology.

Milne, G. and Milne, C. (1982) *Medieval Waterfront Development at Trig Lane, London*. Special Paper No. 5, London and Middlesex Archaeological Society, London: The Society.

Mitsch, W.J. and Gosselink, J.G. (1986) *Wetlands*. New York: Van Nostrand Reinhold.

Mogi, H. (1966) A Historical Study of the Development of Edo 1600–1860. Master of Regional Planning Thesis, Cornell University. Tokyo: City and Town Planners Inc.

Morgan, F.W. (1958) *Ports and Harbours* (2nd edn, revised by J. Bird). London: Hutchinson.

Morioka, T. (1991) Effective adaptation strategy to sea level rise risk: Forecasted impacts and strategies learned from experience of flood and land subsidence in Japan, in R. Frassetto (ed.) *Impact of Sea Level Rise on Cities and Regions*, Venice: Marsilio Editore (117–24).

Morrison, J.R. (1841) Terms of Sale. *Canton Press*, **6** (40), 3rd July; *Canton Register*, **14** (26), 29th June:163–4.

Mumford, L. (1966) *The City in History*. Harmondsworth: Penguin.

Muth, R.F. (1969) *Cities and Housing: The Spatial Pattern of Urban Residential Land Use*, Chicago: University of Chicago Press.

Navarette, G.B., Canales, M.D., Vera, A.V., Maldonado, A.A., Gonzalez, G.M. and Calderon, E.D. (1988) Damage statistics of the September 19, 1985 Earthquake in Mexico City, in Council on Tall Buildings and Urban Habitat, Lynn S. Beadle, Editor in Chief, *Second Century of the Skyscraper*, New York: Van Nostrand Reinhold: (657–66).

Needham, J. (1964) Science and China's Influence on the World in R. Dawson (ed.) *The Legacy of China*, Oxford: Clarendon Press (234–308).

Needham, J. with collaboration of Wang Ling and Lu Gwei–Djen (1971) *Science and Civilisation in China. Vol.4 Physics and Physical Technology. Part III Civil Engineering and Nautics*, Cambridge University Press.

Nelson, H.J. (1983) *The Los Angeles Metropolis*. Dubuque, Iowa: Kendall/Hunt.

Nitschke, G. (1965) Japan's second heroic age: the age of barbarism. *Architectural Design*, **35** (5):218–21.

Ng, H.Y. (1991) Case histories of reclamation techniques, in P. Blacker (ed.) *Reclamation: Important Current Issues*, Hong Kong: Hong Kong Institution of Engineers, Geotechnical Division (57–74).

Norman, R. [1990?] Chairman's review, in Cleveland INCA, *INCA in Cleveland: The First Year*, Billingham: INCA.

Norwich, J.J. (1982) *A History of Venice*, London: Allen Lane.

Observer Staff Reporter (1966) Submarine cities in North Sea?, *Observer*, 10 April.

Odell, R. (1972) *The Saving of San Francisco Bay. A Report on Citizen Action and Regional Planning*. Washington Conservation Foundation.

Office of Tokyo Frontier Promotion [n.d.] *Creating a New Character for Seaside Tokyo. Metropolitan Waterfront Subcenter. Tokyo Teleport Town*. Tokyo:Tokyo Metropolitan Government.

Olson, S. (1976) Baltimore, in J.S. Adams (ed.) *Association of American Geographers Comparative Metropolitan Analysis Project. Contemporary Metropolitan America* Vol. 2. *Nineteenth Century Ports*. Cambridge, MA: Ballinger.

O'Neill, B. (1990) Cities against the seas. *New Scientist*, 3 Feb.:26–9.

Palermo, M.R. (1992) Dredged material disposal, in J.B. Herbich (ed.), *Handbook of Coastal and Ocean Engineering Vol. 3, Harbors, Navigational Channels, Estuaries, Environmental Effects*, Houston: Gulf (393–464).

Palmer, D. (1993) Personal communication. Tees and Hartlepool Port Authority Limited.

Parsonson, G.S. (1966) Artificial islands in Melanesia: the role of malaria in the settlement of the Southwest Pacific. *New Zealand Geographer*, **22**(1):1–21

Pattenden, D.W. (1990) *The History of the River Tees in Maps*. Middlesbrough: Cleveland and Teesside Local History Society in conjunction with the Tees and Hartlepool Port Authority.

Patterson, O. (1982) *The Children of Sisyphus*, Harlow: Longman.

Pawson, M. and Buisseret, D. (1975) *Port Royal, Jamaica*. Oxford: Clarendon.

Peil, M. (1991) *Lagos: The City Is the People*. Boston: Hall.

Petts, G. (1990) Forested river corridors: a lost resource, in D. Cosgrove and G. Petts (eds) *Water, Engineering and Landscape: Water Control and Landscape Transformation in the Modern Period*, London Belhaven (12–34).

Phillips Petroleum Company [n.d.] *Oilport Teesside*. Middlesbrough: Phillips Petroleum.

Pinder, D.A. and Witherick, M.E. (1990) Port Industrialisation, urbanisation and wetland loss, in Williams, M. (ed.) *Wetlands. A Threatened Landscape*. Oxford: Blackwell (234–66).

PLA Monthly (1960) Disposal of dredgings ashore *PLA Monthly* 421:285.

Porter, E. (1973) *Pollution in Four Industrialised Estuaries, Four case studies undertaken for the Royal Commission on Environmental Pollution*. London: Her Majesty's Stationery Office.

Potter, R.B. (1985) *Urbanisation and Planning in the Third World*. London Croom Helm.

Pottinger, H. (1842) Government Notification. *Canton Press*, **7**(26), 26th March; *Canton Register*, **15** (13), 29th March: 62.

Powell, T. (1992) The MFP as an urban development project. *Australian Planner*, **30**(1) 51–3.

Progressive Architecture (1964) Aesthetics and technology of preassembly. *Progressive Architecture*, **45**(10):162–83.

Quayle, B. and Bellamy, D. (1988) *The Tees: The Living River*. Durham: David Bellamy.

Reed, A.W. (1955) *Auckland: City of the Seas*. Wellington: A.H. and A.W. Reed.

Relph, E. (1976) *Place and Placelessness*. London: Pion.

Rhodes, M. (1982) The Finds: introduction: a discussion of the significance of waterfront dumps and their contents, in G. Milne and C. Milne, (eds) *Medieval Waterfront Development at Trig Lane, London*.

Rodney, W. (1981) *A History of the Guyanese Working People, 1881–1905*. London: Heinemann.

Rushdie, S. (1982) *Midnight's Children*. London: Pan.

San Francisco Bay Conservation and Development Commission (1969) *San Francisco Bay Plan*. San Francisco: The Commission.

San Francisco Bay Conservation and Development Commission (1987) *Mitigation Practices Guidebook*. San Francisco: The Commission.

San Francisco Bay Conservation and Development Commission (1988) *Mitigation: An analysis of Tideland Restoration Projects in San Francisco Bay*. San Francisco: The Commission.

San Francisco Bay Conservation and Development Commission [1992?] *San Francisco Bay Conservation and Development Commission* (4-page information pamphlet).

San Francisco Bay Conservation and Development Commission (1993) *1992 Annual Report*. San Francisco: The Commission.

San Francisco Estuary Project (1992a) *State of the Estuary: A Report on Conditions and Problems in the San Francisco Bay/Sacramento – San Jaoquin Delta Estuary*. Prepared in cooperation with the US Environment Protection Agency by the Association of Bay Area Governments, Oakland.

San Francisco Estuary Project (1992b) *Comprehensive Conservation and Management Plan for the Bay and Delta: A Summary for Public Review*. Oakland: San Francisco Estuary Project.

Sauer, C.O. (1963) Seashore: primitive home for man? *Proceedings of the American Philosophical Society*, **106** (1962): 41–7. Reprinted in John Leighly (ed.) *Land and Life. A Selection from the Writings of Carl Otwin Sauer*, Berkeley: University of California Press (300-312).

Scott, M. (1963) *The Future of San Francisco Bay*, Berkeley: Institute of Governmental Studies, University of California.

Scott, M. (1985) *The San Francisco Bay Area: A Metropolis in Perspective*, 2nd ed, Berkeley: University of California Press.

Shapiro, H.A. (1988) Japan's coastal environment and responses to its recent changes, in K. Ruddle, W.B. Morgan and J.R. Pfafflin (eds) *The Coastal Zone: Man's Response to Change*, Chur, Switzerland: Harwood.

Silvester, R. and Hsu, J.R.C. (1991) New and old ideas in coastal sedimenta tion. *Reviews in Aquatic Sciences*, 4 (4). 375 110.

Silvester, R. and Hsu, J.R.C. (1993) *Coastal Stabilisation. Innovative Concepts*, Englewood Cliffs. Prentice Hall.

Slater, D., Summers, L. and Gamon, L.R. (1987) Direct labour sea defenses in the West Indies, in Nanjing Hydraulic Research Institute (eds) *1987 Proceedings of Coastal and Port Engineering in Developing Countries*, vol. 1, China Ocean Press (303–17).

Sokolov, R. (1995) Personal communication. San Francisco Estuary Project.

Soustelle, J. (1964) *The Daily Life of the Aztecs on the Eve of the Spanish Conquest*, (translated by Patrick O'Brian). Harmondsworth: Penguin.

Stamp, L.D. (1957) Brazil; a geographer's view. *Geographical Journal*, **123**(3):335–40.

Stephensen, P.R. (1966) *The History and Description of Sydney Harbour*. Adelaide: Rigby.

Stewart, J.R. (1970) Marine ecumenopolis, *Ekistics*, **29**(175):399–418.

Styles, K.A. and Hansen, A. (1989) *Geotechnical Area Studies Programme: Territory of Hong Kong. GASP Report 12*. Hong Kong: Geotechnical Control Office, Civil Engineering Department.

Szczepanik, E. (1960) *The Economic Growth of Hong Kong.*, London: Oxford University Press.

Takasaki, H. (1977) An introduction to the movement of the right of common shore, Irihama–ken, *Kogai: The Newsletter from Polluted Japan*, Series 13, **5**(2):5–11.

Tange, K. (1987) A plan for Tokyo: 1986–. *Japan Architect*, 367–8:8–45.

Te Brake, W.H. (1985) *Medieval Frontier. Culture and Ecology in Rijnland*. College Station: Texas A and M University Press.

Tees Conservancy Commissioners (1952) *The River Tees. 1852–1952: The Development of a Modern River*. Middlesbrough: The Commissioners.

Tees Conservancy Commissioners [1954?] *The River Tees. Official Handbook*. Cheltenham Ed. J. Burrow.

Teesside Development Corporation [n.d.] *The European Chemical Centre on Teesside* Middlesbrough: Teesside Development Corporation; London.

Thomas, G. and Witts, M.M. (1971) *The San Francisco Earthquake*. New York: Stein and Day.

Time International (1993) Megacities. *Time*, 11 Jan.: 32–42.

Titus, J.G. (1986) Greenhouse effect, sea level rise, and coastal zone management. *Coastal Zone Management Journal*, **14**(3):147–71.

Tomlinson, K.W. (1993) Personal communication. The Joint University College on Teesside, Stockton–on–Tees.

Towle, E.L. (1985) St. Lucia: Rodney Bay/Gros Islet, in T. Geoghegan (ed.) *Proceedings of the Caribbean Seminar on Environmental Impact Assessment*. Halifax: NS: Institute for Resource and Environmental Studies, Dalhousie University; St. Michael, Barbados: Caribbean Conservation Association.

Tregear, T.R. and Berry, L. (1959) *The Development of Hong Kong and Kowloon as Told in Maps*. Hong Kong: Hong Kong University Press.

Urry, J. (1990) *The Tourist Gaze: Leisure and Travel in Contemporary Societies*, London: Sage.

Vaillant, G.G. (1950) *The Aztecs of Mexico*. Harmondsworth: Penguin.

Vance, J.E. (1964) *Geography and Urban Evolution in the San Francisco Bay Area*. Berkeley: Institute of Governmental Studies, University of California.

Vance, J. (1976) The Cities by San Francisco Bay, in J.S. Adams (ed.) Association of American Geographers Comparative Metropolitan Analysis Project. *Contemporary Metropolitan America. Vol.2 Nineteenth Century Ports*, Cambridge, MA.: Ballinger (217–307).

van Veen, J. (1962) *Dredge, Drain, Reclaim. The Art of a Nation*. 5th Edn, The Hague: Martinus Nijhoff.

Volmer, E. (1967) *Encyclopaedia of Hydraulics, Soil and Foundation Engineering* Amsterdam: Elsevier.

Wagret, P. (1968) *Polderlands*. London: Methuen.

Waley, P. (1991) *Tokyo: City of Stories*. New York.

Waterman, R.E. (1991) Integrated coastal policy via building with nature, in R. Frassetto (ed.) *Impact of Sea Level Rise on Cities and Regions*, Venice: Marsilio Editore (64–74.)

Webb, R.J. and van Gulik, B. (1979) Dredging and land reclamation, in B. Knights and A.J. Phillips (eds) *Estuarine and Coastal Reclamation and Water Storage*. Farnborough, Hants: Saxon House: 125–31.

Whitehill, W.M. (1975) *Boston. A Topographical History*. 2nd ed. with 1975 postscript. Cambridge, MA: The Belknap Press of Harvard University Press.

Wilmar, M.B. (1982) Bay Conservation and Development Commission's experience in shoreline management: problems and opportunities, in J. Kockelman, T.J. Conomos and A.E. Leviton (eds) *San Francisco Bay Use and Protection*, San Francisco: Pacific Division of the American Association for the Advancement of Science (99–108).

Wilson, G. (1967) Personal communication, Scott and Wilson, Kirkpatrick and Partners, Hong Kong.

Wilson, S. and Jackson, D.B. (1990) The Tees seals programme, in *Cleaning up the Tees, Progress and Prospects*, Proceedings of the conference held at the Forum Theatre, Billingham, Cleveland on 15 September 1990, under the auspices of the Cleveland INCA and the University of Durham.

Wittfogel, K.A. (1956) The Hydraulic Civilizations, in William L. Thomas (ed.) *Man's Role in Changing the Face of the Earth*, Chicago: The University of Chicago Press (152–64).

Wittfogel, K.A. (1957) *Oriental Despotism: Comparative Study of Total Power*. Newhaven: Yale University Press.

Wong, K., Au, C., Cheung, K. and Tan, W. (1987) Reclamations in Hong Kong: design considerations, in Nanjing Hydraulic Research Institute (eds), 1987 *Proceedings of Coastal and Port Engineering in Developing Countries Vol. 1*, China Ocean Press: 385–96.

Wong, P.P. (1985) Artificial coastlines: the example of Singapore. *Zeitschrift für Geomorphologie*, N.F. Suppl. – Bd **57**:175–92.

Woolley, L. (1954) *Excavations at Ur*, London: Ernest Benn.

Wright, R.M. (1976) Earthquake risk and hazard. *Jamaica Journal,* **10**, (2–4): 52–60.

Yim, W.W.S. (1991) Future sea level rise and coastal land reclamations for urbanisation in Hong Kong, in R. Frassetto (ed.) *The Impact of Sea Level Rise on Cities and Regions*, Venice: Marsilio Editore: (136–42).

Zusho, H. (1707) *Sesshū Osaka Zukan Kōmoku (Map of Osaka, Settsu Province)*. Osaka: Yorozuya Hikotarō, reproduced in Nanba Matsutaro, Muroga Nobuo and Unno Kazutaka (eds), Patricia Murray (translator), *Old Maps in Japan*, Osaka: Sogensha. 1973.

Index